NEW National Mathema... im 5

K. M. Vickers
M. J. Tipler
H. L. van Hiele

© K. M. Vickers, M. J. Tipler and H. L. van Hiele 1991, 1995

First published in 1991 by Canterbury Educational Ltd
Revised edition published in 1995 by:
Stanley Thornes (Publishers) Ltd
Ellenborough House, Wellington Street
CHELTENHAM, Glos. GL50 1YW
England

98 99 00 / 10 9 8 7 6 5 4

A catalogue record for this book is available from the British Library

ISBN 0 7487 2812 0
ISBN 0 7487 2813 9 (with answers)

Printed and bound in Italy by
STIGE, TURIN

PREFACE

"National Curriculum Mathematics" by K.M. Vickers and M.J. Tipler is a complete course carefully designed and now updated to ensure full coverage of the revised National Curriculum.

In the 1995 revised National Curriculum, the Level Descriptions describe the performance that pupils working at a particular level should demonstrate. This book covers all the material in **Level 5** of the National Curriculum in four separate sections: Number; Algebra; Shape, Space and Measures; and Handling Data. Using and Applying Mathematics is integrated throughout the book. The material is presented in this order to enable pupils, or a group of pupils, to work across the different areas of mathematics at different levels.

Each section begins with revision from previous levels, printed on pink paper for ease of identification. Each section ends with a review chapter which contains revision questions on the material developed in this book. In each of the other chapters, every skill developing exercise finishes with review questions.

With the exception of the Review chapters, all chapters begin with "Around and About" which encourages the pupils to relate the topic to their everyday experiences; and finish with "What? When? Where? Who? How? Why?" which encourages the pupils to relate the topic to other areas of the school curriculum and to people and careers which use the mathematics. Throughout each topic, relevance to everyday life is emphasised. The acquisition of knowledge and skills is integrated with the use and application of these skills and this knowledge.

This book does not replace the teacher. Rather, it is a resource for both the pupil and the teacher. The teacher can be flexible about what is taught and when.

Throughout the book there is a variety of activities: skill developing exercises, investigations, practical work, problem solving activities, discussion exercises, puzzles and games. All the activities are related to the topic being studied. Whenever possible, activities and exercises have been written as open rather than closed tasks.

There is a good balance between tasks which develop knowledge, skills and understanding, and those which develop the ability to tackle and solve problems. Many activities do both. There is a thorough and careful development of each topic. Questions within each exercise or activity are carefully graded to build pupil confidence.

This book takes into consideration:
> pupils' needs
> pupils' interests
> pupils' experiences
> the need for pupils to explore mathematics
> the use of technology
> both independent and co-operative work habits

2

This book encourages pupils to:
    use a wide range of mathematics
    discuss mathematical ideas
    undertake investigations
    participate in practical activities
    use reference material
    relate mathematics to everyday life
    select appropriate methods for a task
    analyse and communicate information
    discuss difficulties
    ask questions

It is hoped that the pupil who uses this book will:
    develop a real interest in mathematics
    become well motivated
    gain much enjoyment from mathematics
    develop a fascination with mathematics
    develop an ability to use mathematics in other subjects
    become confident in the use of the calculator and computer
    gain a firm foundation for further study
    become proficient at applying mathematics to everyday life
    develop both independent and co-operative work habits
    become aware of the power and purpose of mathematics
    develop an ability to communicate mathematics
    develop an appreciation of the relevance of mathematics
    develop an ability to think precisely, logically and creatively
    become confident at mathematics
    gain a sense of satisfaction

Calculator keying sequences are for the Casio *fx–82LB*. Some slight variation may be needed for other models and makes.

The version of LOGO used is LOGOTRON—standard LOGO for the BBC. The version of BASIC used is BBC BASIC.

K.M. Vickers
1995

Acknowledgements

The author wishes to thank all those firms and enterprises who have so kindly given permission to reproduce tables and other material. A special thanks to S.M. Bennett, S. P. R. Coxon, J.A. Ogilvie and S. Napier for their valuable contributions; to F. Tunnicliffe for the illustrations and J. McClelland for the photographs.

Every effort has been made to trace all the copyright holders. If any have been inadvertently overlooked the publishers will be pleased to make the necessary arrangement at the first opportunity.

Contents

ALGEBRA

SHAPE, SPACE and MEASURES

HANDLING DATA

Level Descriptions for Level 5

Attainment Target 1: Using and Applying Mathematics

■ Level 5

In order to carry through tasks and solve mathematical problems, pupils identify and obtain necessary information; they check their results, considering whether these are sensible. Pupils show understanding of situations by describing them mathematically using symbols, words and diagrams. They make general statements of their own, based on evidence they have produced, and give an explanation of their reasoning.

Attainment Target 2: Number and Algebra

■ Level 5

Pupils use their understanding of place value to multiply and divide whole numbers and decimals by 10, 100 and 1000. They order, add and subtract negative numbers in context. They use all four operations with decimals to two places. They calculate fractional or percentage parts of quantities and measurements, using a calculator where appropriate. Pupils understand and use an appropriate non-calculator method for solving problems that involve multiplying and dividing any three-digit by any two-digit number. They check their solutions by applying inverse operations or estimating using approximations. They construct, express in symbolic form, and use simple formulae involving one or two operations.

Attainment Target 3: Shape, Space and Measures

■ Level 5

When constructing models and when drawing or using shapes, pupils measure and draw angles to the nearest degree, and use language associated with angle. They identify all the symmetries of 2-D shapes. They know the rough metric equivalents of Imperial units still in daily use and convert one metric unit to another. They make sensible estimates of a range of measures in relation to everyday situations.

Attainment Target 4: Handling Data

■ Level 5

Pupils understand and use the mean of discrete data. They compare two simple distributions, using the range and one of the measures of average. They interpret graphs and diagrams, including pie charts, and draw conclusions. They understand and use the probability scale from 0 to 1. Pupils find and justify probabilities, and approximations to these, by selecting and using methods based on equally likely outcomes and experimental evidence, as appropriate. They understand that different outcomes may result from repeating an experiment.

NUMBER

Number from Previous Levels

ADDITION and SUBTRACTION

Addition and **subtraction**, using numbers as large as 20, should be done mentally.

For instance, $14 + 9 = 23$
$$19 - 7 = 12$$
$$18 + 0 = 18$$

Mental calculations can sometimes be made easier by rewriting the numbers.

For instance, $23 + 34 = 20 + 3 + 30 + 4$
$$= 20 + 30 + 3 + 4$$
$$= 50 + 7$$
$$= 57$$

MULTIPLICATION and DIVISION

The **multiplication facts** given in this table should be known.

×	1	2	3	4	5	6	7	8	9	10
1	1	2	3	4	5	6	7	8	9	10
2	2	4	6	8	10	12	14	16	18	20
3	3	6	9	12	15	18	21	24	27	30
4	4	8	12	16	20	24	28	32	36	40
5	5	10	15	20	25	30	35	40	45	50
6	6	12	18	24	30	36	42	48	54	60
7	7	14	21	28	35	42	49	56	63	70
8	8	16	24	32	40	48	56	64	72	80
9	9	18	27	36	45	54	63	72	81	90
10	10	20	30	40	50	60	70	80	90	100

continued . . .

. . . *from previous page*

PLACE VALUE

Place value is given by this chart.

thousands	hundreds	tens	units (ones)
2	3	4	7

For instance; in the number 2347, the digit 2 means 2 thousands
the digit 3 means 3 hundreds
the digit 4 means 4 tens
the digit 7 means 7 ones.

ROUNDING

27 is closer to 30 than to 20.
27 rounded to the nearest 10 is 30.

327 is closer to 300 than to 400.
327 rounded to the nearest 100 is 300.

45 is halfway between 40 and 50.
45 rounded to the nearest 10 is 50.

CALCULATION

If 11 is divided by 5, the answer is 2 with remainder 1.

If we do the multiplication £1·35 × 4 on the calculator, the display is 5·4.
The answer to the multiplication £1·35 × 4 is not
written as £5·4; it is written as £5·40.

$$5.4$$

To find the answer to 17 ÷ 6 we key

| 17 | ÷ | 6 | = | to get

$$2.8333333$$

To the nearest whole number the answer is 3.

continued . . .

. . . *from previous page*

NEGATIVE NUMBERS

Numbers less than zero are called **negative numbers.**
The number -4 is a negative number. -4 means 4 less than zero.

For instance, if a temperature is given as $-4°C$, the temperature is $4°$ below zero.

FRACTIONS and PERCENTAGES

$\frac{2}{5}$ is read as "two-fifths" and means 2 parts out of every 5.

For instance, $\frac{3}{7}$ of these horses are red.

7% is read as "seven percent" and means 7 out of every 100.

For instance, if Rachel got 69 out of 100 in her maths. test this is 69%.

DECIMALS

In 0·25, the digit 2 means 2 tenths
the digit 5 means 5 hundredths.

To add and subtract decimals we line up the units.

For instance, $14·87 - 3·6$ is written as

$$\begin{array}{r} 14·87 \\ -3·6 \\ \hline 11·27 \end{array}$$

PATTERNS

The **even** numbers are 2, 4, 6, 8, . . .
The **odd** numbers are 1, 3, 5, 7, . . .

The . . . shows that the pattern continues.

continued . . .

. . . from previous page

SYMBOLS

Symbols may be used to stand for a number.

For instance, in $3 + \star = 7$ the $\star$ stands for 4
           in $5 - 2 = \square$ the $\square$ stands for 3.

$<$ means "is less than". For instance, $24 < 33$.
$>$ means "is greater than". For instance, $16 > 12$.

REVISION EXERCISE

1. Four hundred and two =

   A. 42   **B.** 420   **C.** 402   **D.** 4002

2. Write these in order, from the smallest to the largest.

   4210   4102   4201   4120   4021

3. 20 eggs are to be put into cartons which each hold 6 eggs.

   (a) How many cartons will be completely filled?

   (b) How many eggs will be in the carton that is partly filled?

4. Write these as figures.

   (a) four hundred and eighty four thousand, five hundred and six

   (b) zero point eight one five

5. What fraction of these clocks is reading 8 o'clock?

6. What is the place value of 9 in these?

   (a) 54962   (b) 8390543   (c) 6804329   (d) 900327   (e) 9050

7. Out of every 100 students, 19 have a Saturday job.
    What percentage of students is this?

8. Rebecca has ten coins; three £1 coins and seven 1p coins.
    What total amount of money does she have?

9. (a) How many diaries can be bought with £20?
         How much change will there be?

    (b) How much change is there from £20 if two
         calculators and three diaries are bought?

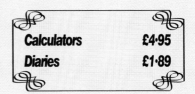

| Calculators | £4·95 |
| Diaries | £1·89 |

10. Copy and fill in these addition and multiplication squares.

+	17		83
	41	67	
19			
			121

(a)

×	5		
	40		
6		18	
9			36

(b)

+	472		891
	549		
234			
104		683	

(c)

11. Which of these statements are true?

    (a) 596 > 634   (b) 407032 < 407049   (c) 10000 > 9999

12. Find the answer to these.

    (a) $4·8 + 4·06$ (b) $1·04 - 0·9$ (c) $18·6 - 3$ (d) $15 - 3·68$ (e) £51·32 + £4·90

13. What is the next line in this number pattern?

$$5 + 17 = 22$$
$$15 + 17 = 32$$
$$25 + 17 = 42$$

14.   5   7   4   3   6   9

    (a) What is the smallest even number that can be made using these digits?

    (b) What is the largest odd number that can be made?

15. In which of the following would the answer be rounded down and in which would it be rounded up?
    Find the answers.

    (a) 100 supporters of a football team hired mini-coaches.
    Each mini-coach could hold 16 people.

    How many mini-coaches did these 100 supporters hire?

    (b) Cliff packs 100 tennis balls into tubes. Each tube holds 6 balls.
    How many full tubes does Cliff pack?

16. What is the reading on this thermometer?

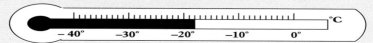

17. Sheena used the calculator for a calculation.
    Give the answer to

    (a) the nearest 100   (b) the nearest 10   (c) the nearest whole number.

18. Patricia bought 20 cans of drink for her party. Half were Coca Cola and one quarter were Fanta.

    (a) How many cans were Coca Cola?

    (b) How many were Fanta?

    (c) What fraction were not Fanta?

19. What is the next number in these patterns?

    (a) 3, 7, 11, 15, ...   (b) 12, 23, 34, 45, ...

20. Which number is one hundred times smaller than 7000?

21. A parking building charges 80p for the first hour and 50p for each half hour, or part of a half hour, after that. Rob parked there from 11·15am until 2·55pm. How much did he pay?

22. Use all the digits 2, 3, 4, 7, 8 and 9 to make two 3-digit numbers so that

    (a) the difference between these numbers is as small as possible

    (b) the sum of these numbers is 1032.

    Is there more than one answer to each of these?

23. Use place value to find the answer to these.

    (a) 35×10 (b) 70×10 (c) $700 \div 10$

    (d) 35×100 (e) $83000 \div 100$ (f) $270 \div 10$

24. Courtney bought 13·5m of ribbon. She used 12·75m.
    How much did she have left?

25. How many times larger is the 4 in 354231 than in 356241?

26. Alexandra had 39cm of plastic to cover her book.
    She needed 44cm. She did the calculation 39 − 44 on her calculator.

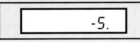

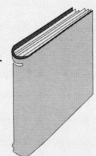

    Explain what this −5 means.

27. Find the missing number.

    (a) 1, 8, 11, 18, . . . , 28, 31, 38   (b) 21, 25, 29, . . . , 37

28. Casey got these marks in his music tests.

    practical — 42 out of 50
    scales — 18 out of 25
    theory — 8 out of 10

    Which test did Casey do best in? What percentage did he get in this test?

AROUND and ABOUT

DISCUSSION EXERCISE 1:1

- We often need to solve problems. Think of ways you know to solve problems. **Discuss.**
  Why do we not solve all problems the same way? **Discuss.**

- The sum of two numbers is 24 and the product is 108. Find the two numbers.

  How many different two-digit numbers can you make from these numbers?

  4 5 7 8 3

  What is the least number of coins needed to be able to pay the exact price of any item costing from 1p to £1?

Think of ways you could solve these problems. **Discuss.**
Think of other problems you know. Give them to your group to solve.

MAKING a LIST

Worked Example

Simon chooses three of these numbers and adds them together. How many different totals could Simon get?

Answer

Numbers Chosen			Total
7	6	4	17
7	6	2	15
7	6	0	13
7	4	2	13
7	4	0	11
7	2	0	9
6	4	2	12
6	4	0	10
6	2	0	8
4	2	0	6

The different totals are 17, 15, 13, 12, 11, 10, 9, 8, 6. That is Simon could get 9 different totals.

Note The list was organised, firstly by taking all the possibilities that included both 7 and 6, then the others that included 7 and 4, then the others that included 7 and 2. Once all the possibilities with 7 had been listed, the remaining possibilities with 6 were listed. Once these had been listed, the remaining possibility with 4 was listed.

EXERCISE 1:2

1. A group of friends bought 9 items from Eddies Eater. The total cost was £10. What did they buy?

EDDIES EATER

HAMBURGER	£1·20
FISH (PER PIECE)	£1·80
CHIPS (PER SCOOP)	55P

2. How many different three-digit numbers can be found using three of the digits 6, 7, 8, 9 only once in each number?

3. The Blue Boys scored 13 points in a rugby league match. In how many ways could they get this score?

   Note A conversion can only be attempted after each try is scored.

   Try — 4 points
   Goal (conversion) — 2 points
   Field Goal — 1 point

4.

   Each domino is divided into two parts as shown above.
   The number of dots on each part can be anything from 0 to 6.
   How many different dominoes are possible?

5. A dart thrown at this board scores either 3 or 7. Adrienne throws as many darts as she wishes and adds together all her scores. No matter how many darts she throws, there are some totals she will never be able to get.

   Which totals are not possible?

   7
   3

6. The digit sum of the number 124 is 1 + 2 + 4 = 7.

   How many numbers between 1 and 200 have a digit sum of 7?

7. Andrew's mother gave Andrew a problem to solve that she had been given when she was at school. It was: "In how many ways can you have coins that total exactly 18 pence? You may use just 1p, 2p, 5p and 10p coins but you may use as many of each as you like". Andrew worked out that there were 31 ways. Was he right?

8. There is a song which begins like this:

"On the first day of Christmas my true love sent to me
A partridge in a pear tree.
On the second day of Christmas my true love sent to me
Two turtle doves and a partridge in a pear tree.
On the third day of Christmas my true love sent to me
Three french hens, two turtle doves and a partridge in a pear tree.
On the fourth . . ."

And finishes like this:

"On the twelfth day of Christmas my true love sent to me
12 drummers drumming, 11 pipers piping, 10 lords a-leaping, 9 ladies dancing,
8 maids a-milking, 7 swans a-swimming, 6 geese a-laying, 5 gold rings,
4 calling birds, 3 french hens, 2 turtle doves and a partridge in a pear tree".

After the twelve days, how many turtle doves had been sent?

9. Kashyapa throws a die 10 times and adds together all 10 scores. The total is 34. If he throws each possible score (1, 2, 3, 4, 5 or 6) at least once, what numbers came up on his die?

Is there more than one answer?

Review   Three darts are thrown at this unusual dart board.

What total scores are possible if all three darts hit the board?

What if one or more darts miss the board?

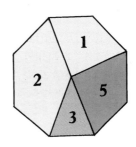

WHAT   WHEN   WHERE   WHO   HOW   WHY

What problems might a sports club need to solve?

When do you need to problem solve in your everyday life?

Where, in your other subjects, do you need to problem solve?

Who, in their job, needs to solve problems?

How would an understanding of problem solving help a doctor or nurse?

Why is it important for a school teacher to be able to problem solve?

AROUND and ABOUT

DISCUSSION EXERCISE 2:1

•

In the photos the snooker balls are arranged in the shape of a triangle. The squares on the chessboard are arranged in the shape of a square.

Think of some more examples of objects which are in triangular or square patterns or in the shape of a cube.
Discuss with your neighbour or group or class.

• Frederick said "Once you've done something you can't undo it."

Amy said "You can always undo any calculation in maths."

Discuss these statements. Find examples of things that can never be undone. Find other examples of things that can be undone.

Make up some calculations such as 79 − 32 or 5 × 9.
Discuss how these could be undone.

INVERSE OPERATIONS. Using these to CHECK ANSWERS

DISCUSSION EXERCISE 2:2

×	1	2	3	4	5	6	7	8	9	10
1	1	2	3	4	5	6	7	8	9	10
2	2	4	6	8	10	12	14	16	18	20
3	3	6	9	12	15	18	21	24	27	30
4	4	8	12	16	20	24	28	32	36	40
5	5	10	15	20	25	30	35	40	45	50
6	6	12	18	24	30	36	42	48	54	60
7	7	14	21	28	35	42	49	56	63	70
8	8	16	24	32	40	48	56	64	72	80
9	9	18	27	36	45	54	63	72	81	90
10	10	20	30	40	50	60	70	80	90	100

We can use this table to find the answer to multiplications such as 8×4.
Discuss how to use this table to find the answer to divisions such as $32 \div 4$.
As part of your discussion, use the following pairs of calculations.

since $6 \times 2 = 12$ then $12 \div 2 = 6$
since $5 \times 7 = 35$ then $35 \div 7 = 5$
since $4 \times 6 = 24$ then $24 \div 4 = 6$
since $8 \times 3 = 24$ then $24 \div 8 = 3$

$96 \div 6 = 16$ What multiplication could you do to check that this calculation was correct? **Discuss.**

Write down some more divisions. **Discuss** how you could check the answers.

Discuss how to complete these statements.
$7 \times 8 \div \ldots = 7$ $19 \div 5 \times \ldots = 19$

- **Discuss** how to complete these statements.
$19 + 2 - \ldots = 19$ $26 - 5 + \ldots = 26$
Since $32 - 2 = 30$ then $30 \ldots = 32$.
Since $48 + 8 = 56$ then $56 \ldots = 48$.

What additions could you do to check the answers to these?
$11 - 4 = 7$ $42 - 9 = 33$ $150 - 20 = 130$
Write down some more subtractions. **Discuss** how you could check your answers.

Write down some additions such as $101 + 30 = 131$. **Discuss** how you could check your answers.

Inverse operations "undo" each other.

Adding and subtracting are inverse operations as are multiplying and dividing.

EXERCISE 2:3

1. Write down a multiplication you could do to check the answer to these.

    (a) $63 \div 7 = 9$ (b) $54 \div 6 = 9$ (c) $78 \div 3 = 26$

    (d) $96 \div 8 = 12$ (e) $95 \div 5 = 19$ (f) $72 \div 4 = 18$

2. Find the missing number.

    (a) Since $9 \times 4 = 36$ then $36 \div 4 = \square$.   (b) Since $9 \times 4 = 36$ then $36 \div 9 = \square$.

    (c) Since $9 \times 4 = 36$ then $\square \div 4 = 9$.   (d) Since $9 \times 4 = 36$ then $\square \div 9 = 4$.

    (e) Since $81 \div 3 = 27$ then $27 \times \square = 81$.   (f) Since $28 \div 7 = 4$ then $\square \times 7 = 28$.

3. What is the missing number in these?

    (a) $7 + 3 - \ldots = 7$ (b) $8 \times 6 \div \ldots = 8$ (c) $27 - 5 + \ldots = 27$

    (d) Since $14 - 9 = 5$ then $5 + \ldots = 14$.

    (e) Since $59 + 6 = 65$ then $65 - \ldots = 59$.

4. What addition could you do to check these answers?

    (a) $24 - 8 = 16$ (b) $17 - 9 = 8$ (c) $55 - 7 = 48$

5. Neroli wanted to know how many 6p
    lollies she could buy for 96p. She did
    the calculation $96 \div 6 = 16$.
    What calculation could she do to
    check her answer?

Review 1   (a)   What multiplication could you do to check the answer to
                 $92 \div 4 = 23$?

           (b)   What addition could you do to check the answer to $37 - 8 = 29$?

Review 2   What is the missing number in these?

           (a) $31 - 8 + \square = 31$

           (b)   Since $6 \times 9 = 54$ then $54 \div \square = 6$.

           (c)   Since $78 + 11 = 89$ then $89 - \square = 78$.

DISCUSSION EXERCISE 2:4

●

$$8 \times 6 = 48$$
$$4 \times 12 = 48$$

$$8 \times 6 \qquad = 48$$
halved $\downarrow$ $\quad$ $\downarrow$ doubled
$$4 \times 12 \qquad = 48$$

In the second calculation the 6 has been doubled to 12.
We need to halve the 8 to 4 to get the same answer of 48.

Does this work for just this calculation or does it work for others as well?
Discuss.

Use calculations such as the following in your discussion.

$10 \times 4 = 40$ $\quad$ $12 \times 8 = 96$ $\quad$ $22 \times 2 = 44$ $\quad$ $14 \times 6 = 84$ $\quad$ $2 \times 12 = 24$ $\quad$ $4 \times 6 = 24$

●

$$12 \times 6 = 72$$
$$4 \times 18 = 72$$

$$12 \times 6 \qquad = 72$$
divide $\downarrow$ $\quad$ $\downarrow$ multiply
by 3 $\qquad$ by 3
$$4 \times 18 \qquad = 72$$

In the second calculation the 6 has been multiplied by 3.
We need to divide the 12 by 3 to get the same answer of 72.

Does this work for just this calculation or does it work for others as well?
Discuss.

Use calculations such as the following in your discussion.

$9 \times 6 = 54$ $\quad$ $12 \times 3 = 36$ $\quad$ $15 \times 9 = 135$ $\quad$ $6 \times 18 = 108$ $\quad$ $18 \times 30 = 540$

●

23×8 may be rewritten as $23 \times 8 = 46 \times 4 = 92 \times 2 = 184 \times 1 = 184$
19×6 may be rewritten as $19 \times 6 = 38 \times 3 = 114 \times 1 = 114$

Discuss this method of multiplying a two-digit number by a one-digit number.

Use multiplications such as the following in your discussion.

19×8 $\qquad$ 28×9 $\qquad$ 78×4 $\qquad$ 69×6 $\qquad$ 29×8 $\qquad$ 47×6

You may like to extend this discussion to include multiplications such as
17×16, 23×24, 41×27.

●

How can inverse operations be used to explain each of the above? **Discuss.**

PUZZLE 2:5

16	8	2	2	8	6
5	6	18	16	4	40
6	18	2	6	10	32
32	2	24	3	3	4
8	4	6	8	24	8
18	32	5	8	2	3
12	18	40	6	10	24
12	24	2	9	6	12

Using the numbers in the squares write

4 divisions such as $16 \div 2 = 8$

4 multiplications such as $8 \times 3 = 24$

4 additions such as $16 + 2 = 18$

and 4 subtractions such as $12 - 2 = 10$.

Each square must be used only once.
The 16 calculations will use all of the numbers.
(***Hint:*** $16 \div 8 = 2$ uses the same three numbers as $8 \times 2 = 16$.)

INDEX NOTATION

$4^2 = 4 \times 4$
$4^3 = 4 \times 4 \times 4$
$4^4 = 4 \times 4 \times 4 \times 4$
$4^5 = 4 \times 4 \times 4 \times 4 \times 4$

We read 4^2 as "4 squared" or "4 to the power of 2".
We read 4^3 as "4 cubed" or "4 to the power of 3".
We read 4^4 as "4 to the power of 4".
We read 4^5 as "4 to the power of 5".

4^2, 4^3, 4^4, 4^5 are written in **index notation**.

Worked Example   Write $7 \times 7 \times 7$ in index notation.

Answer $7 \times 7 \times 7 = 7^3$

Worked Example   Find the value of 3^4.

Answer $3^4 = 3 \times 3 \times 3 \times 3$
$= 81$

EXERCISE 2:6

1. Write these in index notation.

    (a) $2 \times 2 \times 2$ (b) 3×3 (c) $5 \times 5 \times 5 \times 5$

    (d) $3 \times 3 \times 3 \times 3$ (e) $9 \times 9 \times 9$ (f) $2 \times 2 \times 2 \times 2 \times 2$

    (g) $7 \times 7 \times 7$ (h) 8×8

2. Find the value of these.

    (a) 2^4 (b) 3^3 (c) 2^6 (d) 4^2 (e) 5^3

    (f) 2^5 (g) 2^3

Review   (a) Write $6 \times 6 \times 6$ in index notation.

(b) Find the value of 3^2 and 2^7.

SQUARES and CUBES

INVESTIGATION 2:7

SQUARE NUMBERS

This is a square of side 1 cm.

This is a square of side 2 cm.
How many squares of side 1 cm are there in this diagram?

How many squares of side 1 cm would there be in a square of side 3 cm?

What if the square was of side 4 cm?
What if the square was of side 5 cm?
What if . . .

1 dot   4 dots   9 dots

How many dots would there be in a square pattern which had 4 dots along each side?

What if the square pattern had 5 dots along each side?
What if the square pattern had 6 dots along each side?
What if . . .

```
10   FOR NUMBER = 1 TO 5
20   PRINT NUMBER * NUMBER
30   NEXT NUMBER
40   END
```

What does this program do? **Investigate.**

INVESTIGATION 2:8

CUBE NUMBERS

fig 1 represents a cube of side 1cm.
fig 2 represents a cube of side 2cm.

fig 1   fig 2

How many cubes of side 1cm are there in the cube of side 2cm?

What if the cube was of side 3cm?

What if the cube was of side 4cm?

What if . . .

fig 1   *fig 2*

These diagrams show dots arranged in the shape of cubes.
How many dots are hidden from view in *fig 1*?
How many dots are hidden from view in *fig 2*?
How many dots are there altogether in *fig 1*?
How many dots are there altogether in *fig 2*?

What if the dot pattern was 4 wide and 4 deep and 4 high?

What if the dot pattern was 5 wide and 5 deep and 5 high?

What if the dot pattern was 1 wide and 1 deep and 1 high?

What if . . .

Investigate ways to write a program that would have 1, 2, 3, 4, 5 as INPUT and 1, 8, 27, 64, 125 as OUTPUT.

In index notation, the **square numbers** are 1^2, 2^2, 3^2, 4^2 etc.

1^2 is read as "one squared", 2^2 is read as "two squared" etc.

The square numbers can be found on the calculator by using the $\boxed{x^2}$ key.

Example   To use the calculator to find 4^2, key as follows:

Key $\boxed{4}\boxed{\text{SHIFT}}\boxed{x^2}$ to get answer of 16.

We can use the calculator to find the square of any number. For instance, to find $7 \cdot 3^2$ we key as in the example above replacing 4 with $7 \cdot 3$.

In index notation, the **cube numbers** are 1^3, 2^3, 3^3, 4^3 etc.

1^3 is read as "one cubed", 2^3 is read as "two cubed" etc.

Most calculators do not have an $\boxed{x^3}$ key. On most calculators, to find a cube we must multiply the number by itself three times.

EXERCISE 2:9

1. Copy and complete the tables.

(a)

1^2	2^2	3^2	4^2	5^2	6^2	7^2	8^2
1	4						

(b)

1^3	2^3	3^3	4^3	5^3
1	8			

(c)

Number	1	2	3	4	5
Square	1	4			
Cube	1	8			

2. Find the missing numbers.

   (a) 16 is the square of . . .   (b) . . . is the square of 6.

   (c) 5 squared equals . . .   (d) 3 cubed equals . . .

   (e) 64 is the cube of . . .   (f) . . . is the cube of 3.

3. Write programs to print these.

   (a) The first 100 square numbers.

   (b) The first 20 cube numbers.

4. Use the calculator to find these.

   (a) 15^2 (b) 9^2 (c) 17^2 (d) 12^2 (e) $2 \cdot 5^2$ (f) $4 \cdot 8^2$

   (g) 12^3 (h) 20^3 (i) $9 \cdot 2^3$ (j) $4 \cdot 8^3$.

5. Find (a) the sum of the cubes of 3 and 5

   (b) the cube of the sum of 3 and 5.

6. Which is the larger: the sum of the cubes of 1, 2, 3, 4, 5 and 6 or the cube of the sum of 1, 2, 3, 4, 5 and 6?

Review 1   Find the missing numbers.

   (a) 8 squared equals . . .   (b) 8 is the cube of . . .

   (c) 8 cubed equals . . .   (d) 81 is the square of . . .

Review 2   Calculate   (a) 13^2 (b) 13^3 (c) $1 \cdot 3^2$ (d) $1 \cdot 3^3$

Review 3   Which is the smaller: the sum of the squares of 5 and 6 or the square of the sum of 5 and 6?

INVESTIGATION 2:10

HAPPY NUMBERS

A **happy number** is one for which the sum of the squares of its digits ends in 1 after repeated squaring and adding as shown below.

Is 13 a happy number?
$1^2 + 3^2 = 10$ and then $1^2 + 0^2 = 1$. Yes 13 is a happy number.

Sometimes many repetitions are necessary.
Is 44 a happy number?
$4^2 + 4^2 = 32$ and $3^2 + 2^2 = 13$ and $1^2 + 3^2 = 10$ and $1^2 + 0^2 = 1$. Yes.

Is your house number a happy number?
Is your telephone number a happy number?
Is your birthdate a happy number?
Is today's date a happy number?

A **happy number name,** or word, is found by giving each letter of the alphabet a number i.e. A B C D ... Z
               1 2 3 4 ... 26

Is MATHS a happy number word?
MATHS is 13 1 20 8 19.
$13^2 + 1^2 + 20^2 + 8^2 + 19^2 = 995$ and $9^2 + 9^2 + 5^2 = 187$ etc.
Continue, to find if MATHS is a happy number word.

Which days of the week are happy number days?
Which months of the year are happy number months?
Is your name a happy number word?
Is the name of your city or town or district a happy number name?

PUZZLES 2:11

? ?

1. I have two digits.
   I am a square.
   I am also a cube.
   What number am I?

2. I am a two-digit number.
   I am the square of the sum of my digits.
   What number am I?

3. The sum of the squares of six consecutive whole numbers is 1111.
   Find the six whole numbers.

4. Great Grandmother wouldn't tell when she was born.
   She did say that she was A years old in the year A^2.
   What year was she born? (**Hint:** A is between 40 and 50.)

5. The difference of the squares of two consecutive even numbers is 20.
   What are these even numbers?

? ?

INVESTIGATION 2:12

SQUARES and CUBES

1. $1^2 = 1$ $1^3 = 1$
   $2^2 = 1 + 3$ $2^3 = 3 + 5$
   $3^2 = 1 + 3 + 5$ $3^3 = 7 + 9 + 11$
   Investigate these number patterns.

2. **Investigate** square numbers or cube numbers.

   You could test one of the following statements (which may be true or false), or you could make and test a statement of your own.

   Statement 1   No square number can end with a 2 or 3 or 7 or 8.

   Statement 2   No square number has just odd digits.

   Statement 3   The largest number, the square of which can be found on a calculator with an 8-digit display is 4275.

SQUARE ROOTS and CUBE ROOTS

SQUARE ROOTS and CUBE ROOTS

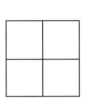

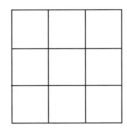

4 squares   **9 squares**

How many squares are there along each side of these diagrams?

What if the diagram had 25 squares?

What if the diagram had 36 squares?

What if the diagram had just 1 square?

What if . . .

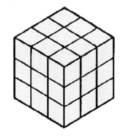

8 cubes   **27 cubes**

How many cubes are there along each edge of these diagrams?

What if the diagram had just 1 cube?

What if the diagram had 64 cubes?

What if . . .

The answer to "what number squared gives 4" is 2. 2 is called the "square root of 4".

The sign for a square root is $\sqrt{}$.

For instance, $\sqrt{4}$ means "the square root of 4".

Squaring and finding the square root are inverse operations. One "undoes" the other.

For instance, $2^2 = 4$ and $\sqrt{4} = 2$.

Square roots are found on the calculator by using the ⌐√⌐ key.

Example To find $\sqrt{4}$ using the calculator,

Key ⌐4⌐ ⌐√⌐ to get answer of 2.

The answer to "what number cubed gives 64" is 4. 4 is called the "cube root of 64".

The sign for a cube root is $\sqrt[3]{}$.

For instance, $\sqrt[3]{64}$ means "the cube root of 64".

Cubing and finding the cube root are inverse operations. One "undoes" the other.

For instance, $4^3 = 64$ and $\sqrt[3]{64} = 4$.

Cube roots are found on the calculator by using the ⌐$\sqrt[3]{}$⌐ key.

Example To find $\sqrt[3]{64}$ using the calculator, **Key** ⌐64⌐ ⌐SHIFT⌐ ⌐$\sqrt[3]{}$⌐ to get answer of 4.

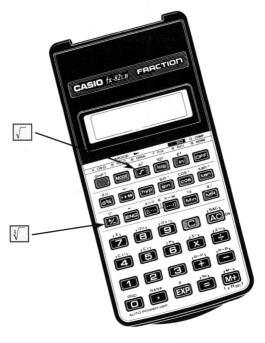

EXERCISE 2:14

1. Find the missing numbers.
   (a) the square root of 36 is . . .   (b) 4 is the square root of . . .
   (c) 4 is the cube root of . . .   (d) the cube root of 8 is . . .
   (e) the square root of . . . is 4

2. Find (a) $\sqrt{81}$ (b) $\sqrt{100}$ (c) $\sqrt{49}$ (d) $\sqrt{1}$ (e) $\sqrt[3]{8}$
   (f) $\sqrt[3]{125}$ (g) $\sqrt[3]{1}$.

Review 1   Find the missing numbers.
   (a) the cube root of . . . is 3   (b) 2 is the square root of . . .

Review 2   Find (a) $\sqrt{9}$ (b) $\sqrt[3]{27}$ (c) $\sqrt[3]{216}$ (d) $\sqrt{16}$

SPATIAL ARRANGEMENTS of NUMBERS

When we talk about the **spatial arrangement** of a number we mean that the number is shown by a pattern of dots.

EXERCISE 2:15

1.

$$1 \qquad\qquad 3 \qquad\qquad 6$$

These diagrams show the first three triangular numbers; 1, 3 and 6.

Draw diagrams to show the next two triangular numbers. What are the first five triangular numbers?

2. The first five square numbers are 1, 4, 9, 16, 25.
   Draw diagrams to show these.

3.

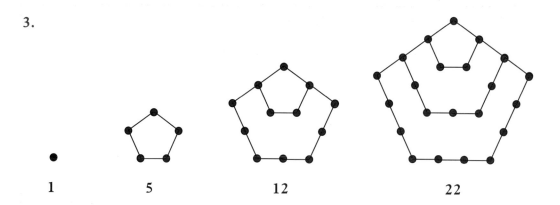

These diagrams show the first four pentagonal numbers.
Why are 1, 5, 12, 22 called pentagonal numbers?

Draw a diagram to find the fifth pentagonal number.
What is this fifth pentagonal number?

Review

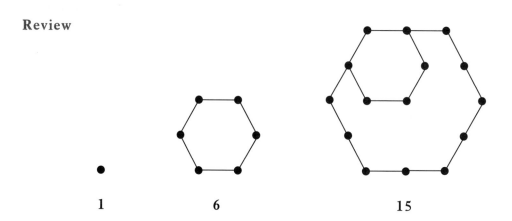

These diagrams show the first three hexagonal numbers.
Why are 1, 6, 15 called hexagonal numbers?

Draw a diagram to show the fourth hexagonal number.
Write down the first four hexagonal numbers.

INVESTIGATION 2:16

SPATIAL NUMBER RELATIONSHIPS

The triangular numbers can be shown in one of these ways:

Is there more than one way to show the square, pentagonal and hexagonal numbers?
Investigate.

There is a relationship between the pentagonal numbers and the square and triangular numbers. **Investigate.**

There is a relationship between the hexagonal numbers and the square and triangular numbers. **Investigate.**

Investigate either triangular, square, pentagonal or hexagonal numbers more fully. As part of your investigation you could investigate sums and differences and products.

WHAT   WHEN   WHERE   WHO   HOW   WHY

What examples of spatial arrangements can you find in games that you know?

When might an engineer or builder use squares and cubes?

Where, in your other subjects, might you use squares, cubes, square roots and cube roots?

Who, in their job, might need to check calculations?

How might a scientist use index notation?

Why would an understanding of spatial arrangements be of use to an architect?

AROUND and ABOUT

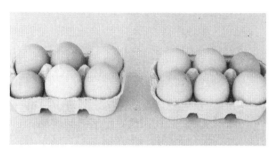

DISCUSSION EXERCISE 3:1

- We often need to put things, or people, into equal sized groups. Think of many examples.
  What has this got to do with division?
  Discuss with your neighbour or group or class.

  We often need to put groups of things, or people, together into one large group. Think of many examples.
  What has this got to do with multiplication?
  Discuss.

- The Mayans lived in Central America. They were one of the first people to use place value. They used sticks and stones to show numbers.

0   1   2   3   4   5

6 was written as (one and five)

7 was written as (two and five)

We count in lots of 10. The Mayans counted in lots of 20. Place value was shown by putting one place above the other.

52 was written as 2 lots of 20 (40)
and
2 lots of 5 and 2 ones (12)

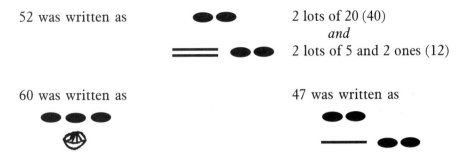

60 was written as   47 was written as

How might the Mayans multiply and divide? **Discuss.**

- The people who live on Mars only have five symbols for numbers.

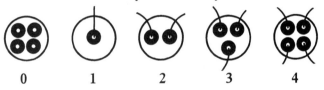

0   1   2   3   4

When *we* get to 10 in our counting we have no more digits so we have 1 in the tens column and 0 in the ones column.
On Mars when they get to 5 they have no more symbols so they have to write it as 1 lot of 5 and 0 ones.

5 is written as 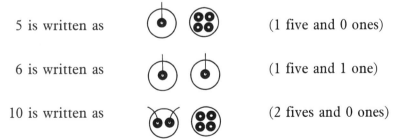 (1 five and 0 ones)

6 is written as (1 five and 1 one)

10 is written as (2 fives and 0 ones)

How easy is it to +, −, ×, ÷ in this system? **Discuss.**
As part of your discussion, do many calculations.

- Make up a number system. **Discuss** how to add, subtract, multiply and divide in your system.

Using PLACE VALUE to MULTIPLY and DIVIDE

Using **place value** $23 \times 10 = 230$
    $23 \times 100 = 2300$

Also $23 \times 1000 = 23000$
    $23 \times 10000 = 230000$
        etc.

We can often use multiplication by 10 or 100 or 1000 etc. to help us when we are multiplying by 80 or 800 or 8000 etc.

We can often use division by 10 or 100 or 1000 etc. to help us when we are dividing by 40 or 400 or 4000 etc.

Worked Example   Find 40×70.

Answer 70 may be written as 10×7.

To find 40×70, first multiply 40 by 10 and then multiply the answer by 7. This is shown below.

$40 \times 10 = 400$; $400 \times 7 = 2800$ Then $40 \times 70 = 2800$.

Worked Example   Find $8000 \div 200$.

Answer 200 may be written as 100×2.

To find $8000 \div 200$, first divide 8000 by 100 and then divide the answer by 2. This is shown below.

$8000 \div 100 = 80$; $80 \div 2 = 40$

Then $8000 \div 200 = 40$.

EXERCISE 3:2

Do not use the calculator for this exercise.

1. Copy this table.

							E							E			E									E		
5	14	4	9	14	12	11	1	3	14	9	13	10	8	1	12	14	3	1	10	9	7	10	6	9	2	1	3	9

Do the calculations in **Box A.**
As soon as you have done each calculation, find the answer in **Box B.**
Fill in the table.

For instance, the answer to **question 1.** has the letter **E** beside it so **E** is filled in above **1** on the table.

<table>
<tr><td colspan="2" align="center">**Box A**</td><td colspan="2" align="center">**Box B**</td></tr>
</table>

Box A		Box B	
1. 80 × 20	8. 9000 ÷ 300	A. 10	O. 6300
2. 30 × 40	9. 800 × 500	E. 1600	R. 20000
3. 400 × 50	10. 5000 ÷ 500	F. 300	S. 400000
4. 700 × 300	11. 80 × 900	K. 30	T. 210000
5. 600 ÷ 30	12. 6000 ÷ 20	L. 20	W. 1200
6. 8000 ÷ 20	13. 6000 ÷ 30	M. 200	Y. 280000
7. 4000 × 70	14. 90 × 70	N. 400	Z. 72000

2. Jamie taught himself to type using a keyboard skills program on a computer. He can now type 20 words in one minute.
   How many words can Jamie type in 30 minutes?

3. Angela trained on a 200m track. Each week she ran a total of 6000m.
   How many laps of the track did Angela run each week?

4. Which two numbers could you multiply together to get an answer of 80000?

5. Make up some divisions that have an answer of 20.

Review 1   Find   (a) 200 × 300

(b) 900 ÷ 30

(c) 80000 ÷ 400.

Review 2   At a supermarket, a lorry unloaded 80 boxes. Each of these had 40 tins of soup.
How many tins of soup were there altogether?

CALCULATOR ERRORS

When using the calculator, it is a good idea to have a rough idea of the answer.
It is easy to key a calculation into the calculator incorrectly.
If the answer given by the calculator is very different from the rough estimate, the calculation should be keyed in again.

When using the calculator, common mistakes are:

Pressing a wrong operation key e.g. + instead of ×.

Reversing digits when keying in e.g. keying 6387 instead of 6378.

Repeating the wrong digit e.g. 556 instead of 566.

Reversing digits when copying from the calculator screen.

Forgetting to press the = key.

EXERCISE 3:3

1. Copy this chart.

6	3	2	8	4	7	2	6		1	8	5	3	2
									F				

The calculation 56×31 was done on the calculator.
Match each wrong answer from **Box A** with a mistake from **Box B.**
Fill in the chart.
For instance, **F** is placed under **1** since mistake **F** gives wrong answer **1.**

Box A

1. 56 × 31 = 1·8064516
2. 56 × 31 = 2015
3. 56 × 31 = 1763
4. 56 × 31 = 31
5. 56 × 31 = 1376
6. 56 × 31 = 25
7. 56 × 31 = 728
8. 56 × 31 = 87

Box B

E. Pressed − instead of ×
T. Pressed 65 instead of 56
M. Forgot to press =
I. Pressed + instead of ×
S. Reversed last 2 digits of answer
A. Pressed 13 instead of 31
R. Reversed middle 2 digits of answer
F. Pressed ÷ instead of ×

Review When the calculator was used to do the calculation 42 × 14 the following **wrong** answers were given.

(a) 42 × 14 = 3   (b) 42 × 14 = 56   (c) 42 × 14 = 28

(d) 42 × 14 = 14   (e) 42 × 14 = 1722   (f) 42 × 14 = 336

(g) 42 × 14 = 885

For each wrong answer, state which of the following mistakes was made.

1. Forgot to press =
2. Pressed + instead of ×
3. Pressed 24 instead of 42
4. Reversed the digits on the calculator screen
5. Pressed ÷ instead of ×
6. Pressed − instead of ×
7. Pressed 41 instead of 14

ESTIMATING ANSWERS using APPROXIMATION

We can check that the answer to a calculation such as 423 × 76 is about the right size by **approximating.**

We can approximate 423 as 400.
We can approximate 76 as 80.

$$400 \times 80 = 400 \times 10 \times 8$$
$$= 4000 \times 8$$
$$= 32000$$

So we estimate 423 × 76 to be about 32000.

Always estimate answers when using the calculator.

Worked Example　　630 books are to be put onto shelves in a library. Each shelf can hold 28 books.
How many shelves are needed?

Answer　　An estimate of the answer is 600 ÷ 30.
　　　　　600 ÷ 10 = 60　and　60 ÷ 3 = 20
The answer should be about 20.

Using the calculator, 630 ÷ 28 = 22·5.
23 shelves will be needed.

23 agrees with our estimate of about 20.

DISCUSSION EXERCISE 3:4

Sandhya worked out her own method for estimating answers for divisions. It is shown below.
Discuss Sandhya's method.

Division	Approximation	Simpler Approximation	Estimate
623 ÷ 87	600 ÷ 90	60 ÷ 9	7
678 ÷ 59	700 ÷ 60	70 ÷ 6	12

What other methods might be used to estimate answers to multiplications and divisions? **Discuss.**

EXERCISE 3:5

1. Choose the best estimate for the answer to each calculation.

   (a) 33×57 A. 180   B. 1500   C. 1800

   (b) 82×78 A. 5600   B. 640   C. 6400

   (c) 748×26 A. 21000   B. 24000   C. 16000

   (d) 2658×73 A. 140000   B. 210000   C. 240000

2. Estimate the answer to these calculations.

   (a) 58×23 (b) 67×27 (c) 42×36 (d) 323×59

   (e) 125×76 (f) 341×77 (g) 234×178

For questions 3, 4, and 5   **(a) Write down the calculation that is needed.**
                                (b) Estimate the answer to the calculation.
                                (c) Use your calculator to find the answer.

3. Each class in the middle school at Hendley had 32 students.
   How many students were in this school if there were 17 classes?

4. 46 students each made 23 masks to be sold at
   the school fête.
   How many masks did these students make
   altogether?

5. The school bought a box of counters for use in the mathematics classes. This
   box had 24 plastic bags, each of which had 96 counters. How many counters
   were there altogether in the box?

6. Choose the best estimate for the answer to each calculation.

    (a) $624 \div 28$ **A.** 20   **B.** 30   **C.** 2

    (b) $942 \div 32$ **A.** 3   **B.** 30   **C.** 300

    (c) $254 \div 53$ **A.** 50   **B.** 5   **C.** 6

    (d) $642 \div 43$ **A.** 24000   **B.** 160   **C.** 16

7. Estimate the answer to these calculations.

    (a) $234 \div 19$ (b) $527 \div 48$ (c) $871 \div 32$ (d) $583 \div 28$

    (e) $724 \div 31$ (f) $283 \div 42$ (g) $186 \div 19$

For questions 8, 9, 10   **(a) Write down the calculation that is needed.**
                               (b) Estimate the answer to the calculation.
                               (c) Use your calculator to find the answer.

8.

On an orchard, the pickers put their apples into a container which was taken to the packing shed. These apples were then packed into boxes which each held 42 apples.
How many complete boxes could be packed from a container which held 1874 apples?

9. For a fire drill, the students at a primary school lined up in rows of 38.
How many rows of students would there be if there were 798 students at school on the day of a fire drill?

10. Each row of seats in an assembly hall held 18 students.
How many rows of seats are needed for 834 students?

Review 1 Choose the best estimate for the answer to each calculation.

(a) 343×22 **A.** 60   **B.** 600   **C.** 6000

(b) $782 \div 38$ **A.** 2   **B.** 20   **C.** 200

(c) $128 \div 19$ **A.** 6   **B.** 2000   **C.** 60

(d) $343 \div 22$ **A.** 6000   **B.** 170   **C.** 17

Review 2 A British Rail one-day excursion train to Blackpool had 23 carriages. Each of these carriages could seat 88 people.

(a) Estimate the total number of passengers that could be seated in this train.

(b) Use your calculator to find the number of passengers.

Review 3 778 football fans travelled by coach from Derby to Liverpool. Estimate the number of coaches needed if each could carry 43 passengers.

LONG MULTIPLICATION without the calculator

There are many methods for finding the answer when two large numbers are multiplied together. Four of these are explained below.

Rectangle Method

Example

423×76 can be written as $(400 + 20 + 3) \times (70 + 6)$, since $423 = 400 + 20 + 3$ and $76 = 70 + 6$.
The numbers 400, 20, 3 that make up the 423 are written along the top of a rectangle.
The numbers 70, 6 that make up the 76 are written down the side of the rectangle.

	400	20	3
70	28000	1400	210
6	2400	120	18

Each pair of numbers is now multiplied to give six numbers in the rectangle.
We find the answer to 423×76 by adding these six numbers.
Add these. You should get 32148. Did you?

Grid Method

Example   We will do the same multiplication as before i.e. 423 × 76.
The steps taken are shown in the diagrams.

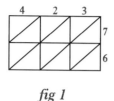

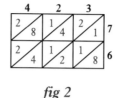

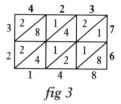

fig 1   *fig 2*   *fig 3*

Step 1.   Draw up a grid with diagonal lines, as shown in *fig 1*.
Place the numbers 4, 2, 3 along the top and the numbers 7, 6 down the side.

Step 2.   Multiply each number along the top with each number down the side. Put the answers in the squares with the first digit above the diagonal and the second digit below the diagonal. This is shown in *fig 2*.
For instance, 4 × 7 = 28; 2 is written above the diagonal, 8 is written below the diagonal.

Step 3.   Add the figures along each diagonal, beginning at the right and ending at the left. If the figures add to a two-digit number, the ten's digit is carried to the next diagonal. This is explained below.

There is only one figure (an 8) along the first diagonal. Put 8 at the bottom of this diagonal.
There are three figures along the next diagonal (2, 1, 1). These add to 4. Put 4 at the bottom of this diagonal.
There are four figures along the next diagonal (4, 1, 4, 2). These add to 11. Put 1 at the bottom of this diagonal. Carry the other 1 to the next diagonal. Adding this 1 in with 2, 8, 1 along the next diagonal we get 12. Put 2 at the bottom of this diagonal. Carry the 1 to the next diagonal.
Adding this 1 in with the 2 along the next diagonal we get 3. Put 3 at the bottom of this diagonal.

Step 4.   Write down the figures that are at the bottom of the diagonals. Write them as they appear from left to right.

In the example shown these are 32148.
This is the answer to the multiplication.

Russian Method

Example Again we will show this method with 423 × 76.

The steps taken are shown below.

423	×	76		423	×	76		423	×	76
211		152		211		152		211		152
105		304		105		304		105		304
52		608		~~52~~		~~608~~		~~52~~		~~608~~
26		1216		~~26~~		~~1216~~		~~26~~		~~1216~~
13		2432		13		2432		13		2432
6		4864		~~6~~		~~4864~~		~~6~~		~~4864~~
3		9728		3		9728		3		9728
1		19456		1		19456		1		19456
										32148

fig 1   *fig 2*   *fig 3*

Step 1. Write down 423 × 76.

Divide 423 by 2. Write down the answer, ignoring the remainder. Continue to divide by 2 until you get answer of 1.

Multiply 76 by 2. Write down the answer. Continue to multiply by 2 until you have a number beside each of the numbers in the first column.

This step is shown in *fig 1.*

Step 2. Cross out all pairs of numbers where there is an even number in the left-hand column.

This step is shown in *fig 2.*

Step 3. Add all the remaining numbers in the right-hand column.

This step is shown in *fig 3.*

This is the answer to the multiplication.

Concise Method

Example   Once again we will show this method with 423×76.

The steps taken are shown below.

423	423	423	423
× 76	× 76	× 76	× 76
	2538	2538	2538
		2961	2961
			32148
fig 1	*fig 2*	*fig 3*	*fig 4*

Step 1.   Set out the numbers as shown in *fig 1*.

Step 2.   Multiply 423×6. Notice that the first figure we get (the 8 from 18) is placed under the 6.
This step is shown in *fig 2*.

Step 3.   Multiply 423 by 7. Notice that the first figure we get (the 1 from 21) is placed under the 7.
This step is shown in *fig 3*.

Step 4.   Add the figures we get from multiplying firstly by the 6 and then by the 7. This step is shown in *fig 4*.

This is the answer to the multiplication.

DISCUSSION EXERCISE 3:6

What do you see as the advantages and disadvantages of each of the previous methods for long multiplication?
Discuss with your group or class.

Which method do you like best? Why?
Discuss.

EXERCISE 3:7

Choose the long multiplication method that you like best for the calculations in this exercise. *Do not use the calculator.*

Check your answer by estimation.

1. Copy the crossnumber.
   Use the clues to complete it.

1.	2.	3.	4.		■	5.	6.	7.	8.
9.				■	10.				
11.				■	12.				
13.				■	14.				
■		■			■		■		■

	Across		**Down**
1.	341 × 38	1.	59 × 19
5.	235 × 21	2.	321 × 76
9.	103 × 14	3.	211 × 45
10.	313 × 45	4.	131 × 40
11.	133 × 18	5.	128 × 35
12.	769 × 89	6.	266 × 34
13.	130 × 15	7.	447 × 86
14.	981 × 82	8.	104 × 53
		10.	99 × 17

2. There are 18 classrooms in a school. If each of these had 29 desks, how many desks would there be altogether?

3. Gina set herself a goal of doing 85 "push-ups" each day. She worked out how many "push-ups" she would do in a year by multiplying 365 and 85.
   What answer should Gina get?

Review   47 people work for the Daley clothing company.
Each is paid £334 a week.
How much does the Daley clothing company pay in wages each week?

INVESTIGATION 3:8

DIGIT REVERSALS

$$12 \times 42 = 504 \qquad\qquad 21 \times 24 = 504$$

When we reversed the digits of the numbers 12 and 42 to get 21 and 24, the product remained the same.
Notice that $12 \times 42 = 12 \times (2 \times 21)$.

$$39 \times 62 = 2418 \qquad\qquad 93 \times 26 = 2418$$
Notice that $39 \times 62 = (3 \times 13) \times (2 \times 31)$

Investigate to find other pairs of two-digit numbers that have the same product when the digits are reversed.

LONG DIVISION without the calculator

Most methods for long division are similar but the setting out is different.
Approximation can be used in the working.

Example   A 739cm length of wood is bought to make 23 shelf ends.
These shelf ends are to be as large as possible.
What length of wood will be used for each?
How much wood will be left over?

To find the length of wood used for each shelf end we need to divide 739 by 23. The answer we get will be the length of each; the remainder we get will be the length of wood left over.

The working could be set out in one of the following ways.

54

Method 1

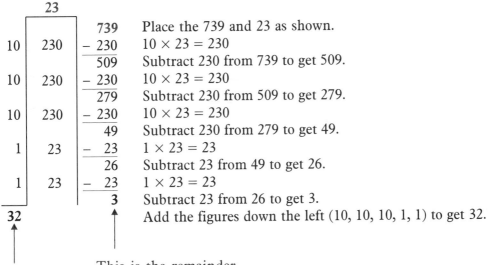

739   Place the 739 and 23 as shown.

10   230   − 230 $10 \times 23 = 230$

509   Subtract 230 from 739 to get 509.

10   230   − 230 $10 \times 23 = 230$

279   Subtract 230 from 509 to get 279.

10   230   − 230 $10 \times 23 = 230$

49   Subtract 230 from 279 to get 49.

1   23   − 23 $1 \times 23 = 23$

26   Subtract 23 from 49 to get 26.

1   23   − 23 $1 \times 23 = 23$

3   Subtract 23 from 26 to get 3.

32   Add the figures down the left (10, 10, 10, 1, 1) to get 32.

This is the remainder.

This is the answer.

By using approximation the working shown in Method 1 can be shortened. This is shown in Method 2.

Method 2

739 is about 700, 23 is about 20.
$20 \times 10 = 200$, $20 \times 20 = 400$, $20 \times 30 = 600$, $20 \times 40 = 800$. From this it seems that 23 will divide into 739 more than 30 times but less than 40 times. We would then begin with:

```
          23
    ┌──────────┐
    │          │   739
 30 │   690    │ − 690     23 × 30 is 690
    │          │    49
    └──────────┘
```

49 is about 50, 23 is about 20.
$20 \times 1 = 20$, $20 \times 2 = 40$, $20 \times 3 = 60$. From this it seems that 23 will divide into 49 more than 2 times but less than 3 times.

We would continue with:

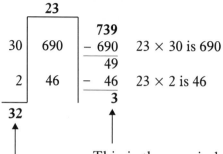

```
        23
              739
30   690   − 690    23 × 30 is 690
               49
 2    46   −  46    23 × 2 is 46
                3
32
```

↑   ↑
This is the answer.   This is the remainder.

We can use a combination of Method 1 and Method 2.

Suppose we began to use Method 2 and we decided that 23 divided into 739 about 20 times instead of 30 times. We would then have:

```
        23
              739
20   460   − 460
              279
```

Since $23 \times 10 = 230$, 23 will divide into 739 another 10 times.

We would then continue as follows:

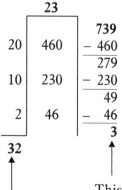

```
        23
              739
20   460   − 460
              279
10   230   − 230
               49
 2    46   −  46
                3
32
```

↑   ↑
This is the answer.   This is the remainder.

56

DISCUSSION EXERCISE 3:9

● Four other ways of setting out the division 739 ÷ 23 are shown below.
Discuss these with your group.

$$
\begin{array}{r}
32 \\
\hline
2 \\
30 \\
23\overline{)739} \\
-690 \\
\hline
49 \\
-46 \\
\hline
3
\end{array}
$$

$$
\begin{array}{r}
23\overline{)739} \\
-690 \quad 30 \\
\hline
49 \\
-46 \quad 2 \\
\hline
3 \quad 32
\end{array}
$$

$$
\begin{array}{r}
32 \\
23\overline{)739} \\
-690 \\
\hline
49 \\
-46 \\
\hline
3
\end{array}
$$

$$
\begin{array}{r}
32 \\
23\overline{)739} \\
-69 \\
\hline
49 \\
-46 \\
\hline
3
\end{array}
$$

● Suzanne checked the answer to 739 ÷ 23 using approximation. Her working is shown.

739 is about 700   23 is about 20
    700 ÷ 10 = 70   70 ÷ 2 = 35

Rochelle checked the answer to 739 ÷ 23 using inverse operations. Her working is shown.

32 is about 30   23 is about 20
        30 × 20 = 600

Discuss these methods of checking answers to divisions.

EXERCISE 3:10

Choose the method of setting out a division that you like best. Use this method for the following calculations. *Do not use a calculator.*

Check your answers using either inverse operations or approximation.

1. A group of 13 friends went on holiday together. They paid a total of £897 for their travel.
   How much did each of the friends pay?

2. The apples in a large box are packed into 35 bags. The same number of apples is packed into each bag.
   If there were 595 apples in the box, how many are in each bag?

3. The 912 students at YewHouse School are seated in 38 rows in the school hall. How many students are in each row? (There are the same number of students in each row.)

4. What is the remainder when 747 is divided by 27?

5. 680 eggs are packed into cartons which each hold 12 eggs.

    (a) How many cartons can be packed?

    (b) How many eggs are left over?

6. 784 boxes of tinned meat were to be given to 15 shops in a supermarket chain. Each shop was to get the same number of boxes.

    (a) Were there any boxes left over and if so how many?

    (b) How many boxes did each shop get?

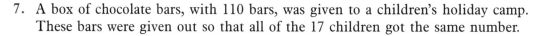

7. A box of chocolate bars, with 110 bars, was given to a children's holiday camp. These bars were given out so that all of the 17 children got the same number.

    (a) How many bars did each child get?

    (b) How many were left over?

Review 1   Yolande was knitting a scarf. One evening, she knitted 29 rows and a total of 435 stitches. How many stitches were there in each row?

Review 2   The 24 students in a maths. class were each making a "nail and thread" picture. They each took the same number of nails from a box which had 880 nails.

    (a) How many nails were left in this box if each student took as many as possible?

    (b) How many nails did each student take?

PUZZLES 3:11

? ?

1. A million (1,000,000) can be found by doing one of the following multiplications:

   $$10 \times 100000$$
   $$100 \times 10000$$
   $$1000 \times 1000$$

   It can also be found by multiplying two numbers, neither of which has the digit 0. What are these two numbers?

2. $\star \Delta$

   This is a two-digit number. The sum of the two digits is 7.

   i.e. $\star + \Delta = 7$

   When the number is multiplied by the number found by reversing the digits, the answer is 1462.

   i.e. $\star \Delta \times \Delta \star = 1462$

   What was the original number?

? ?

WHAT   WHEN   WHERE   WHO   HOW   WHY

What people in your local council will need to do calculations involving multiplication and division of large numbers?

When might you need to multiply and divide without using a calculator?

Where, might an understanding of long multiplication and long division be of use to someone whose job is to do with health?

Who, in their jobs, would need to do mental multiplication and division because they wouldn't always have a calculator with them?

How might knowing about long multiplication and division, using place value, be of use to a farmer?

Why is it important to always estimate an answer first when using the calculator?

AROUND and ABOUT

DISCUSSION EXERCISE 4:1

- Decimals are used in money and in measurement.
  Where else are decimals used? **Discuss.**

- **A Day in the City**   **A Day in the Country**

Imagine that you are to spend either a day in the city or a day in the country.
Discuss what you would do, and see, during this day.
Discuss where decimals would be involved in each of these.

- "Many sports involve decimals". **Discuss** this statement.
  Should this statement be "All sports involve decimals"? **Discuss.**

- Imagine a world without decimals.
  How would you cope?
  What might you use instead of decimals? **Discuss.**

DECIMAL PLACE VALUE

DISCUSSION EXERCISE 4:2

Allan said that £0·06 means 6 pence.   Meena said that £0·06 means $\frac{6}{100}$ of a £1.
Who is right? **Discuss.**

Remember $\frac{1}{10}$ can be written as 0·1

$\frac{2}{10}$ can be written as 0·2

$\frac{3}{10}$ can be written as 0·3

etc.

$\frac{1}{100}$ can be written as 0·01

$\frac{2}{100}$ can be written as 0·02

$\frac{41}{100}$ can be written as 0·41

$\frac{68}{100}$ can be written as 0·68

etc.

DISCUSSION EXERCISE 4:3

Each small square on these diagrams is 1 hundredth of a large square.

Which diagram shows 0·60?   Which shows 0·6?
Which diagram shows 0·90?   Which shows 0·9?

Is $\frac{20}{100}$ the same as $\frac{2}{10}$? **Discuss,** using the diagrams in your discussion.

Which decimal numbers could the first diagram show?
Which decimal numbers could the last diagram show?
Discuss.

● Draw diagrams to show 0·35, 0·71 and 0·59.

Draw a diagram to show the sum of $\frac{3}{10}$ and $\frac{5}{100}$.

Does one of the diagrams you have already drawn show the sum of $\frac{7}{10}$ and $\frac{1}{100}$?
Does one of them show the sum of $\frac{9}{10}$ and $\frac{5}{100}$? **Discuss.**

● How could you draw a diagram to show three thousandths? **Discuss.**

● How many times larger is the first 4 than the second 4 in the number 0·44?
Discuss using diagrams.

What if the number was 0·404?   What if the number was 4·34?
What if the number was 41·354?   What if the number was 24·054?

Place value is given by this chart.

100000	10000	1000	100	10	1	$\frac{1}{10}$	$\frac{1}{100}$	$\frac{1}{1000}$

For instance, in the number 305·724   the 3 means   three hundreds
the 5 means   five ones (or units)
the 7 means   seven tenths
the 2 means   two hundredths
the 4 means   four thousandths.

EXERCISE 4:4

1. (a) 0·34 = 3 tenths and 4 hundredths. What is the total number of hundredths in 0·34?

   (b) 0·204 = 2 tenths and 4 thousandths. What is the total number of thousandths in 0·204?

   (c) 0·348 = 3 tenths and 4 hundredths and 8 thousandths. How many thousandths are there altogether in 0·348?

   (d) How many thousandths are there altogether in 0·057?

2. Write these as decimals.

   (a) $\frac{7}{10}$ (b) $\frac{6}{10}$ (c) $\frac{31}{100}$ (d) $\frac{78}{100}$ (e) $\frac{251}{1000}$ (f) $\frac{25}{1000}$

   (g) $\frac{4}{100}$ (h) $\frac{7}{100}$ (i) $\frac{9}{1000}$

3. Write each of these as a single decimal number (e.g. $\frac{8}{10} + \frac{7}{100} = 0·87$).

   (a) $\frac{7}{10} + \frac{5}{100}$ (b) $\frac{4}{10} + \frac{8}{100}$ (c) $\frac{5}{10} + \frac{1}{100} + \frac{2}{1000}$

   (d) $\frac{3}{10} + \frac{4}{1000}$ (e) $\frac{1}{10} + \frac{1}{1000}$ (f) $\frac{6}{100} + \frac{7}{1000}$

4. Write as a decimal.

   (a) three hundred and five and four tenths

   (b) twenty five and six tenths

   (c) seventeen and three tenths

   (d) two thousand, five hundred and six and five hundredths

   (e) sixty five and two tenths and three hundredths

   (f) seven thousand and forty one and four hundredths and two thousandths

   (g) two tenths and five hundredths and six thousandths

   (h) seven hundredths

   (i) eight thousandths

5. Choose the correct answer for the meaning of the digit 4 in these.

   (a) 0·459   A. 4 tenths   B. 4 hundredths   C. 4 thousandths

   (b) 0·04   A. 4 tenths   B. 4 hundredths   C. 4 thousandths

   (c) 0·143   A. 4 tenths   B. 4 hundredths   C. 4 thousandths

   (d) 2·034   A. 4 tenths   B. 4 hundredths   C. 4 thousandths

   (e) 50·4   A. 4 tenths   B. 4 hundredths   C. 4 thousandths

6. What is the hundredths digit in these?

   (a) 4·0632   (b) 568·230   (c) 42·807   (d) 8930·049   (e) 4·50

7. How many times larger is the first 8 than the second 8 in these?

   (a) 818·3   (b) 188·05   (c) 18·83   (d) 0·88   (e) 0·838

Review 1   Write as a decimal   (a)   three tenths and five thousandths

                                     (b)   twenty and seven hundredths.

Review 2   What is the tenths digit in these?

                (a) 0·368   (b) 0·502   (c) 7·92   (d) 9·091   (e) 56·0

Review 3   Which of these is *not* the same as 0·34?

                A. 34 hundredths   **B.** 3 tenths and 4 hundredths

                C. $\frac{3}{100} + \frac{4}{100}$ **D.** $\frac{3}{10} + \frac{4}{100}$

PRACTICAL EXERCISE 4:5

Stevin, a Dutch mathematician, first used decimals in the late 16th century. From then, until Napier made the dot notation popular in the early 17th century, many different ways of showing a decimal number such as 3·654 were used.
Even today, methods other than the dot notation are used.

Find out all you can about these other methods.

Note A stamp collection could be a good source of information.

You could present your project as a small booklet or as a poster.
You could choose some other way to present it.

GAME 4:6

Decimal YES/NO

One student (the leader) writes down a decimal number.
This student does not show the number to anyone.

The rest of the students in the group have to find the number.
They do this by taking turns to ask the leader questions.
The leader may only answer Yes or No to each question.

The student who is able to correctly name the number becomes the leader for
the next round.

A sample round is shown below.

The leader writes down the number

Student	Question	Answer
Zara	Are there 2 digits after the point?	No
Max	Are there 3 digits after the point?	Yes
Shanna	Is the number less than 1?	No
Thomas	Is the number less than 100?	Yes
Irina	Is the first digit less than 5?	Yes
Justin	Is the number less than 20?	Yes
Zara	Are all the digits less than 5?	No
Max	Is the second digit less than 5?	Yes
Shanna	Is the second digit bigger than 2?	Yes
Thomas	Is the second digit 3?	Yes
Irina	Is there another digit 3?	Yes
Justin	Is the last digit 3?	Yes
Zara	Do the digits add up to more than 20?	No
Max	Is one of the digits 0?	Yes
Shanna	Is the hundredths digit 0?	No
Thomas	Is the hundredths digit less than 7?	Yes
Irina	Is one of the digits 6?	No
Justin	The number is 13·053.	Yes

Using PLACE VALUE to MULTIPLY and DIVIDE

DISCUSSION EXERCISE 4:7

- Simon said " to multiply 3 by 10 we put one zero after the 3,
  to multiply 3 by 100 we put two zeros after the 3,
  to multiply 3 by 1000 we put three zeros after the 3".

Ruth said "We can use place value charts to multiply 3 by 10, 100 and 1000".

1000	100	10	1
			3

1000	100	10	1
		3	0

3×10

1000	100	10	1
	3	0	0

3×100

1000	100	10	1
3	0	0	0

3×1000

She said "to multiply 3 by 10 move the 3 one place to the left,
to multiply 3 by 100 move the 3 two places to the left,
to multiply 3 by 1000 move the 3 three places to the left".

Are both Simon and Ruth right? **Discuss.**

- Use the calculator to find the answer to these.

0.3×10	0.3×100	0.3×1000
0.03×10	0.03×100	0.03×1000
0.003×10	0.003×100	0.003×1000

Ruth said that her method for multiplying 3 by 10, 100 and 1000 would also work
for multiplying 0.3, 0.03 and 0.003 by 10, 100 and 1000. She said that Simon's
method wouldn't work. Is Ruth right? **Discuss.**

- **Discuss** how to use place value to multiply decimals such as 1·2, 3·04, 25·6,
  1201·603 by 10, 100 and 1000.

- Ruth also used place value charts to divide 40000 by 10, 100 and 1000.

10000	1000	100	10	1
4	0	0	0	0

10000	1000	100	10	1
	4	0	0	0

$40000 \div 10$

10000	1000	100	10	1
		4	0	0

$40000 \div 100$

10000	1000	100	10	1
			4	0

$40000 \div 1000$

She also used place value charts to divide 17 by 10, 100 and 1000.

100	10	1	•	$\frac{1}{10}$	$\frac{1}{100}$	$\frac{1}{1000}$
	1	7				

100	10	1	•	$\frac{1}{10}$	$\frac{1}{100}$	$\frac{1}{1000}$
		1	•	7		

$17 \div 10$

100	10	1	•	$\frac{1}{10}$	$\frac{1}{100}$	$\frac{1}{1000}$
		0	•	1	7	

$17 \div 100$

100	10	1	•	$\frac{1}{10}$	$\frac{1}{100}$	$\frac{1}{1000}$
		0	•	0	1	7

$17 \div 1000$

How do you think Ruth explained her method? **Discuss.**

- **Discuss** how to use place value to divide numbers such as 264, 17·5, 1·3, 4·92, 25·607 by 10, 100 and 1000.

- Winstone worked out his own way for multiplying and dividing decimal numbers by 10, 100 and 1000.
  He said "to multiply 32·65 by 10, move the decimal point one place to the right to get 326·5".
  How would Winstone multiply 32·65 by 100 and 1000? **Discuss.**

  To divide 32·65 by 10, Winstone moved the decimal point one place to the left to get 3·265.
  How would Winstone divide 32·65 by 100 and 1000? **Discuss.**

  How would Winstone multiply 23 by 100? **Discuss.**

- Are Ruth's and Winstone's methods really the same? **Discuss.**

Worked Example Use place value to find the answers.

(a) $1·34 \times 10$ (b) $203·6 \times 100$ (c) $2·7 \times 1000$

(d) $1·34 \div 10$ (e) $58 \div 100$ (f) $2·7 \div 1000$

Answer (a) 13·4   (move each digit one place to the left)

(b) 20360   (move each digit two places to the left)

(c) 2700   (move each digit three places to the left)

(d) 0·134   (move each digit one place to the right)

(e) 0·58   (move each digit two places to the right)

(f) 0·0027   (move each digit three places to the right)

<u>or</u>

(a) 13·4   (move the decimal point one place to the right)

(b) 20360   (move the decimal point two places to the right to get
                 20360· which is usually written as 20360)

(c) 2700   (move the decimal point three places to the right to get
                 2700· or 2700)

(d) 0·134   (move the decimal point one place to the left to get ·134
                 which is usually written as 0·134)

(e) 0·58   (write 58 as 58·0, then move the decimal point two places
                 to the left)

(f) 0·0027   (move the decimal point three places to the left to get
                 ·0027 or 0·0027)

EXERCISE 4:8

Use place value to find the answers in this exercise.

1. Which of × or ÷ goes in the box?

    (a) 23·6 □ 100 = 0·236   (b) 1·054 □ 10 = 10·54

    (c) 0·59 □ 10 = 0·059   (d) 23·01 □ 100 = 2301

2. Which of 10, 100 or 1000 goes in the box?

    (a) 7·6 × □ = 7600   (b) 40·83 ÷ □ = 4·083

    (c) 0·31 × □ = 3·1   (d) 82·6 × □ = 8260

    (e) 894 ÷ □ = 89·4   (f) 6·05 ÷ □ = 0·0605

3. Find the answer to these.

    (a) 0·59 × 10   (b) 0·59 × 100   (c) 0·59 ÷ 10   (d) 0·59 ÷ 1000

    (e) 0·59 × 1000   (f) 0·59 ÷ 100   (g) 1·23 × 100   (h) 10·8 ÷ 10

    (i) 351 ÷ 1000   (j) 724·3 × 100   (k) 0·02 ÷ 100   (l) 3·04 × 10

    (m) 48·24 × 100   (n) 2 ÷ 100   (o) 67·9 × 1000   (p) 841·05 ÷ 100

4. Nick bought plastic to cover his books. He needed 41·5cm for each book.
    How much plastic did he need for 10 books?

5. How much does 1 chicken cost?

CHICKENS
10 for £26·80

6. Dianne measured the height of 1000 sheets of paper as 264mm.
   How thick was each of these sheets?

7. A builder bought 100 timber planks. Each was 2·6m long.
   What total length of timber did the builder buy?

8. Write some more problems in which a decimal is multiplied or divided by 10 or
   100 or 1000.

Review 1 Copy this diagram.
   Draw lines between the calculations on the left and their answers on the
   right.
   How many lines cross the shaded area?

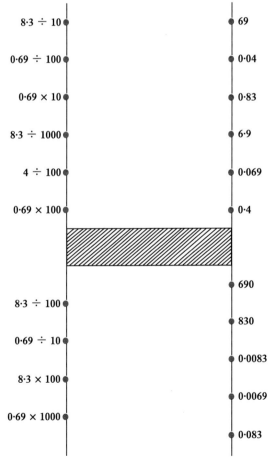

8·3 ÷ 10	69
0·69 ÷ 100	0·04
0·69 × 10	0·83
8·3 ÷ 1000	6·9
4 ÷ 100	0·069
0·69 × 100	0·4
	690
8·3 ÷ 100	830
0·69 ÷ 10	0·0083
8·3 × 100	0·0069
0·69 × 1000	0·083

Review 2 (a) A school bought 1000 tubs of ice-cream for
   £0·29 each. How much did they cost
   altogether?

   (b) The school sold these for a total of £360.
   How much was each sold for?

MULTIPLYING and DIVIDING DECIMALS by numbers other than 10, 100, 1000. CALCULATIONS with DECIMALS

DISCUSSION EXERCISE 4:9

- Atique's way of finding the answer to $4 \cdot 38 \times 3$ is shown.

$$4 \cdot 38 \times 3 \qquad \begin{array}{r} 438 \\ \times \ 3 \\ \hline 1314 \end{array}$$

Since $438 = 4 \cdot 38 \times 100$ then we must divide the answer to 438×3 by 100 to get the answer to $4 \cdot 38 \times 3$.

$$438 \times 3 = 1314 \qquad\qquad 4 \cdot 38 \times 3 = 13 \cdot 14$$

Discuss Atique's method. How else could you find the answer to $4 \cdot 38 \times 3$ without using the calculator? **Discuss.**

Atique's method for $23 \cdot 4 \times 0 \cdot 04$ is shown.

$$23 \cdot 4 \times 0 \cdot 04 \qquad \begin{array}{r} 234 \\ \times \ 4 \\ \hline 936 \end{array}$$

Since 234 is $23 \cdot 4 \times 10$ and $4 = 0 \cdot 04 \times 100$ we must divide the answer to 234×4 by 10 and then by 100 to get the answer to $23 \cdot 4 \times 0 \cdot 04$

$$936 \div 10 = 93 \cdot 6 \qquad\qquad 93 \cdot 6 \div 100 = 0 \cdot 936$$
$$\text{So } 23 \cdot 4 \times 0 \cdot 04 = 0 \cdot 936$$

Discuss Atique's method. How else could you calculate $23 \cdot 4 \times 0 \cdot 04$ without using the calculator? **Discuss.**

- Atique's way of finding the answer to $\dfrac{5 \cdot 58}{6}$ is shown.

$$\dfrac{5 \cdot 58}{6} \qquad\qquad \begin{array}{r} 093 \\ 6\overline{)5\,^5 5\,8} \end{array}$$

Since $558 = 5 \cdot 58 \times 100$ we must divide the answer to $558 \div 6$ by 100 to get the answer to $5 \cdot 58 \div 6$.

$$558 \div 6 = 93 \qquad\qquad 5 \cdot 58 \div 6 = 0 \cdot 93$$

Discuss Atique's method. How else could you calculate $\dfrac{5 \cdot 58}{6}$ without using the calculator? **Discuss.**

Worked Example   Calculate   (a) $16 \cdot 7 \times 0 \cdot 8$

(b) $30 \cdot 59 \div 7$

Answer   (a) $167 \times 8 = 1336$

$$\begin{array}{r} 167 \\ \times\ 8 \\ \hline 1336 \end{array}$$

So $16 \cdot 7 \times 0 \cdot 8 = 13 \cdot 36$

(b) $3059 \div 7 = 437$

$$7 \overline{)30^2 5^4 9} \quad \begin{array}{c} 4\ 3\ 7 \end{array}$$

So $30 \cdot 59 \div 7 = 4 \cdot 37$

EXERCISE 4:10

1. Choose the correct answer.

   (a) $60 \times 0 \cdot 4 =$ A. 2400   B.   240   C.   24   D.   2·4

   (b) $3 \cdot 6 \times 8 =$ A. 2·88   B.   28·8   C.   288   D.   2880

   (c) $7 \cdot 61 \times 0 \cdot 2 =$ A. 15·22   B.   1522   C.   1·522   D.   152·2

   (d) $34 \cdot 64 \div 8 =$ A. 433   B.   4·33   C.   43·3   D.   43300

   (e) $0 \cdot 18 \div 3 =$ A. 0·006   B.   6   C.   0·6   D.   0·06

   (f) $18 \cdot 3 \times 0 \cdot 05 =$ A. 91500   B.   915   C.   9·15   D.   0·915

2. Calculate.

   (a) $25 \times 0 \cdot 4$ (b) $25 \times 0 \cdot 004$ (c) $35 \cdot 5 \div 5$ (d) $6 \cdot 78 \div 2$

   (e) $8 \cdot 21 \times 8$ (f) $268 \cdot 2 \times 0 \cdot 9$ (g) $0 \cdot 51 \div 3$ (h) $2 \cdot 6 \times 0 \cdot 7$

   (i) $0 \cdot 96 \div 6$ (j) $34 \cdot 5 \div 5$ (k) $13 \cdot 61 \times 0 \cdot 6$ (l) $9 \cdot 38 \div 7$

   (m) $124 \cdot 8 \div 4$ (n) $0 \cdot 2 \times 0 \cdot 3$ (o) $0 \cdot 25 \div 5$ (p) $0 \cdot 08 \div 4$

3. What do you notice about the answers to these?

   (a) $24 \times 0 \cdot 2$ $1 \cdot 6 \times 3$ $9 \cdot 6 \div 2$ $14 \cdot 4 \div 3$ $120 \times 0 \cdot 04$

   (b) $\dfrac{0 \cdot 64}{2}$ $1 \cdot 6 \times 0 \cdot 2$ $3 \cdot 2 \times 0 \cdot 1$ $\dfrac{1 \cdot 6}{5}$ $6 \cdot 4 \times 0 \cdot 05$

4. *The answer is 2·4. Write down many calculations which have answer of 2·4.*

5. Fancy soaps are priced at 6 for £1·26.
   How much does 1 cost?

6. At a book and magazine sale, Dianne
   bought   6 at £0·27 each
            4 at £1·19 each
            8 at £0·23 each
      and   2 at £0·59 each.
   How much change does Dianne get from £10?

7. 46·4cm of liquorice is cut into 8 equal pieces.
   How long is each piece?

BEST BEEF
£5.45kg

8. Chris bought 0·8kg of this beef.
   How much did this cost?

9. Make up some word problems. Use decimals in your problems.

10. (a) I am a decimal number.   (b) I am a decimal number.
        When multiplied by 6 I become 7·2.   When divided by 0·6 I become 0·4.
        What number am I?   What number am I?

Review 1   Copy this grid of numbers.

0·5	0·48	0·9	2·03	3·6
0·6	4	0·4	36	900
2·3	9	4·8	100	48
1·6	0·56	0·06	0·36	5
40	6	0·09	60	90

Find the answer to each calculation. Shade the square on the grid that
has this answer.   What pattern do your shaded squares make?

$8 \times 0\cdot6$ $1\cdot2 \times 3$ $0\cdot8 \div 2$ $30 \times 0\cdot03$ $\dfrac{3\cdot84}{8}$

$2\cdot5 \div 5$ $6\cdot09 \div 3$ $0\cdot45 \times 0\cdot2$ $1\cdot5 \times 0\cdot04$

Review 2   Brigette changed 480 Swiss Francs into pounds. For each franc, she got
£0·40.
How many pounds did Brigette get?

ORDER of OPERATIONS

We do multiplication and division before addition and subtraction.

Examples   1. $7 + 3 \times 2 = 7 + 6$ 2. $4 + 6 \times 5 - 3 = 4 + 30 - 3$
                         $= 13$ $= 31$

         3. $17 - 6 \div 2 = 17 - 3$
                        $= 14$

We work out the brackets before multiplying.
A number immediately before a bracket means we multiply what is inside the bracket by this number.

Examples 1. $5(2 + 7) = 5 \times 9$
$= 45$

2. $13 - 2(5 - 1) = 13 - 2 \times 4$
$= 13 - 8$
$= 5$

The scientific calculator does operations in the correct order. Just key in the calculation from left to right.

Example   Using the calculator to find $13 - 2(5 - 1)$,

Key $\boxed{13}\ \boxed{-}\ \boxed{2}\ \boxed{(}\ \boxed{5}\ \boxed{-}\ \boxed{1}\ \boxed{)}\ \boxed{=}$ to get answer of 5.

Note   Some calculators need the $\boxed{\times}$ pressed immediately before the brackets. In this case, the keying for the above example is

$\boxed{13}\ \boxed{-}\ \boxed{2}\ \boxed{\times}\ \boxed{(}\ \boxed{5}\ \boxed{-}\ \boxed{1}\ \boxed{)}\ \boxed{=}$

Worked Example   Calculate   (a) $2\cdot 1 + 120 \times 0\cdot 002$

(b) $3(2\cdot 1 + 15\cdot 48)$

Answer   (a) $120 \times 2 = 240$
So $120 \times 0\cdot 002 = 0\cdot 24$
Then $2\cdot 1 + 120 \times 0\cdot 002 = 2\cdot 1 + 0\cdot 24$
$= 2\cdot 34$

$$\begin{array}{r} 2\cdot 1 \\ + \ 0\cdot 24 \\ \hline 2\cdot 34 \end{array}$$

(b) $2\cdot 1 + 15\cdot 48 = 17\cdot 58$

$1758 \times 3 = 5274$
$17\cdot 58 \times 3 = 52\cdot 74$
So $3(2\cdot 1 + 15\cdot 48) = 3(17\cdot 58)$
$= 52\cdot 74$

$$\begin{array}{r} 2\cdot 1 \\ + \ 15\cdot 48 \\ \hline 17\cdot 58 \end{array} \qquad \begin{array}{r} 1758 \\ \times \ 3 \\ \hline 5274 \end{array}$$

EXERCISE 4:11

1. Calculate.

(a) $4 \times 2 - 3$ (b) $4 + 2 \times 3$ (c) $2 + 3 \times 2$

(d) $2 \times 3 + 5$ (e) $11 - 3 \times 2$ (f) $3 \times 5 + 2 \times 4$

(g) $12 \div 2 + 5$ (h) $12 + 8 \div 4$ (i) $5 + 2 \times 3 - 1$

2. Calculate.

(a) $3(7 + 2)$ (b) $5(6 - 4)$ (c) $2(10 - 2 \times 3)$

(d) $21 - 3(4 - 1)$ (e) $2(4 + 3) - 7$ (f) $3 \times 4 - 2(5 - 1)$

3. What numbers can you make from 2, 3 and 6? That is, combine 2, 3 and 6 with the operations $+, -, \times, \div$ to get as many different answers as possible. You may also use brackets.

4. Choose any four numbers.
Combine these four numbers with the operations $+, -, \times, \div$ to get as many different answers as possible. You may also use brackets.

5. Insert $+, -, \times, \div$ and brackets to make the following statements true. You may use any of the operations more than once or not at all.

(a) 3 4 6 2 = 28   (b) 3 4 6 2 = 32   (c) 3 4 6 2 = 35

(d) 3 4 6 2 = 29   (e) 3 4 6 2 = 25   (f) 3 4 6 2 = 24

(g) 3 4 6 2 = 15   (h) 3 4 6 2 = 0   (i) 3 4 6 2 = 3

(j) 3 4 6 2 = 11

Do these have more than one possible answer?

6. Calculate.

(a) $32 \times 0.1 + 6.25$ (b) $2.7 + 3.06 \times 3$ (c) $4.6 + 25.7 \times 0.2$

(d) $\dfrac{3.26}{2} + 16.7$ (e) $80.5 - \dfrac{6.84}{4}$ (f) $25.7 - 3.45 \div 5$

(g) $4(2.62 - 1.09)$ (h) $0.6(3.4 + 1.8)$ (i) $4.2 + 0.8(6.8 - 2.76)$

(j) $0.2(6 - 4.6) + 0.3$

7. Insert decimal points, $+$, $-$, $\times$, $\div$, brackets to make these true. Each number in the calculation is either a whole number or has one number after the decimal point.

(a) $19 \quad 36 \quad 2 = 2.62$ (b) $128 \quad 69 \quad 3 = 10.5$

(c) $124 \quad 4 \quad 18 = 1.3$ (d) $84 \quad 4 \quad 16 \quad 2 = 36.8$

(e) $4 \quad 116 \quad 5 \quad 22 = 14.4$ (f) $24 \quad 4 \quad 68 \quad 27 = 18.8$

(g) $69 \quad 24 \quad 3 \quad 18 = 9.5$ (h) $34 \quad 2 \quad 66 \quad 3 = 4.6$

(i) $27 \quad 11 \quad 5 \quad 7 = 0.7$

Review 1   Copy the two columns of letters.

Circle the letters which have a **correct** statement beside them and you will have a message.

I.	$5 + 3 \times 2 = 16$		T.	$5(8 + 2) = 15$
W.	$5 + 3 \times 2 = 11$		D.	$5(8 + 2) = 50$
O.	$3 \times 4 - 6 \times 2 = 12$		Q.	$7 - 2(8 - 6) = 10$
C.	$3 + 4 \times 6 - 2 = 40$		T.	$6 + 9(3 - 1) + 5 = 35$
E.	$3 \times 4 - 6 \times 2 = 0$		O.	$7 - 2(8 - 6) = 3$
N.	$7 - 2 \times 2 - 1 = 9$		W.	$16 - 12 \div 2 = 2$
L.	$7 - 2 \times 2 - 1 = 2$		N.	$16 - 12 \div 2 = 10$
T.	$12 - 4 \times 3 = 24$		A.	$8 - 2 \times 0 + 6 = 12$
L.	$12 - 4 \times 3 = 0$		E.	$8 - 2 \times 0 + 6 = 14$

Review 2   Calculate.

(a) $4.8 + 0.1 \times 16.8$ (b) $0.9(3 - 2.4)$

(c) $5 - 2(1.2 - 0.07)$

GAME 4:12

CALCULATION FULL HOUSE: a game for a group.

Preparation: On a piece of card (or a piece of paper), each student writes down the numbers 1 to 20.

Beside each number they write a calculation that has this number as the answer.

For instance:
1. $3 + 4 + 5 - 9 + 1 - 3$
2. $8 \times 3 - 22$
3. $21 - 18$
4. $14 - 2 \times 5$
   .
   .
   .

The Play: One student is chosen as the leader.

Each of the other students in the group chooses five numbers between 1 and 20 and writes these down.
For instance, one student may write down 2, 3, 8, 10, 18.

The leader now calls calculations from his or her card.
The other students cross out the numbers corresponding to these calculations.
For instance, if the calculation $7 + 9 - 6$ is called, the number 10 is crossed out. The student who wrote down 2, 3, 8, 10, 18 has only four numbers left to cross out.

The first student to cross out all five of their chosen numbers is the winner. This student becomes the leader for the next round.

Notes 1. The leader should tick each number as the calculation for this is called. This will stop the leader from calling any calculation twice.

2. For a shorter game, use the numbers 1 to 10 rather than 1 to 20.

INVESTIGATION 4:13

NUMBER CHAINS

Begin with any number.
Carry out the following instructions to get a number chain.

If the number is even, divide it by 2.
If the number is odd, multiply it by 3 and add 1.
Repeat with the new number until you get the digit 1.

For instance, beginning with the number 20, we get the following.

$$20 \div 2 = 10$$
$$10 \div 2 = 5$$
$$5 \times 3 + 1 = 16$$
$$16 \div 2 = 8$$
$$8 \div 2 = 4$$
$$4 \div 2 = 2$$
$$2 \div 2 = 1$$

The number chain is 10, 5, 16, 8, 4, 2, 1. There are 7 numbers in this chain.

Investigate the number chains for other numbers.

You may wish to use the following program to make number chains on the computer.

```
10   CLS
20   INPUT "NUMBER FOR CHAIN" N
30   REPEAT
40   IF N/2 – INT (N/2) > 0 THEN N = N * 3 + 1 ELSE N = N/2
50   PRINT N
60   UNTIL N = 1
70   END
```

PUZZLE 4:14

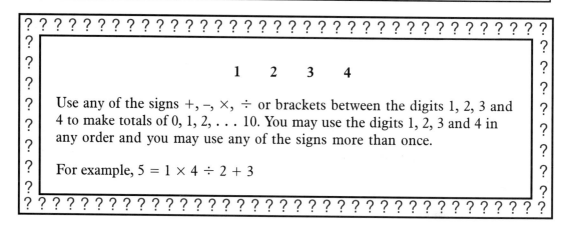

1   2   3   4

Use any of the signs +, −, ×, ÷ or brackets between the digits 1, 2, 3 and 4 to make totals of 0, 1, 2, . . . 10. You may use the digits 1, 2, 3 and 4 in any order and you may use any of the signs more than once.

For example, $5 = 1 \times 4 \div 2 + 3$

WHAT WHEN WHERE WHO HOW WHY

What might hotel staff, builders, pilots, teachers and mechanics need to know about decimals?

When, in your other subjects, might you need an understanding of decimals and order of operations?

Where might you need to calculate with decimals in your everyday life?

Who, in your school, needs to understand order of operations?

How might a knowledge of decimals help a farmer, accountant, manager or artist?

Why is it important to understand place value when multiplying and dividing with decimals?

AROUND and ABOUT

DISCUSSION EXERCISE 5:1

The advertisement in the centre is for loft conversions.

What might the other advertisements refer to?

Discuss with your neighbour or group or class.

FRACTIONS of QUANTITIES

The word "of" can be replaced by ×.

For instance, $\frac{1}{10}$ of 200 means $\frac{1}{10}$ × 200.

Worked Example   Find $\frac{3}{5}$ of £2·70.

Answer $\frac{3}{5}$ of £2·70 = $\frac{3}{5}$ × £2·70

On the calculator, **Key** 3 ÷ 5 × 2·7 = to get answer of 1·62.
Then, $\frac{3}{5}$ of £2·70 = £1·62.

EXERCISE 5:2

1. Find

    (a) $\frac{7}{10}$ of £5·40   (b) $\frac{1}{3}$ of £6·84   (c) $\frac{2}{5}$ of 6m

    (d) $\frac{3}{4}$ of 7·2m   (e) $\frac{4}{5}$ of 85cm

2. Give the answers to the nearest penny.

    (a) $\frac{2}{3}$ of £2·50   (b) $\frac{1}{4}$ of 89p   (c) $\frac{3}{5}$ of £1·99

3. Janice took home $\frac{1}{3}$ of her books. If she had 12 books altogether how many did she take home?

4. $\frac{3}{4}$ of Jeannie's darts scored bull's eyes. If she threw 20 darts, how many bull's eyes did she get?

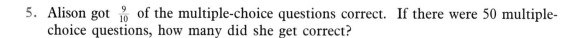

5. Alison got $\frac{9}{10}$ of the multiple-choice questions correct. If there were 50 multiple-choice questions, how many did she get correct?

6. In the story Peter Pan, the children spent $\frac{1}{8}$ of a day in NEVER-NEVER LAND. How many hours was this?

7. A Jupiter day is about $\frac{3}{8}$ of an Earth day. Approximately how many hours are there in a Jupiter day?

8. Gravity on the moon is about $\frac{1}{6}$ of the earth's gravity.
About how many kilograms would a person weigh on the moon if this person weighed 78kg on earth?

9. Brent always saved $\frac{1}{3}$ of his wages. Last week his wages were £220. How much of this did Brent save?

10. Sasha bought 35m of material. She used $\frac{4}{5}$ of it to make curtains and the rest to make two bedspreads.

    (a) How much did she use for curtains?

    (b) How much did she use for each bedspread?

Review 1 A basketball should bounce $\frac{2}{3}$ of the distance from which it was dropped. How high should a basketball bounce when it is dropped from a height of 1·8 metres?

Review 2 $\frac{1}{4}$ of the profit made at a gala day is to be given to charity. If the total profit was £213·17, how much is given to charity?

Review 3 600 people were surveyed about their television viewing habits. It was found that $\frac{7}{10}$ watched TV for more than 4 hours each day. Of these, $\frac{2}{3}$ watched for more than 6 hours.

    (a) How many of the people surveyed watched television for more than 4 hours a day?

    (b) Use your answer to (a) to find how many watched television for more than 6 hours each day.

PUZZLE 5:3

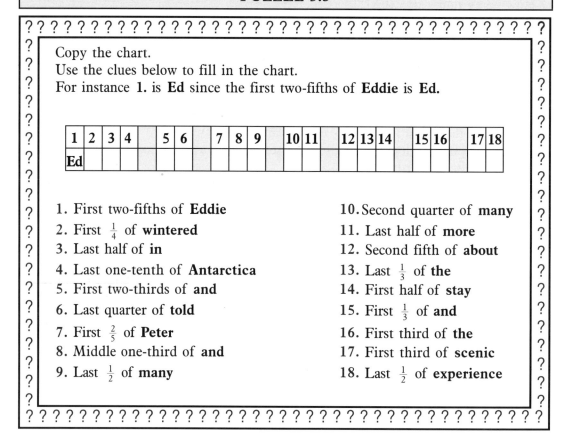

? ?

Copy the chart.
Use the clues below to fill in the chart.
For instance **1.** is **Ed** since the first two-fifths of **Eddie** is **Ed.**

1	2	3	4		5	6		7	8	9		10	11		12	13	14		15	16		17	18
Ed																							

1. First two-fifths of **Eddie**
2. First $\frac{1}{4}$ of **wintered**
3. Last half of **in**
4. Last one-tenth of **Antarctica**
5. First two-thirds of **and**
6. Last quarter of **told**
7. First $\frac{2}{5}$ of **Peter**
8. Middle one-third of **and**
9. Last $\frac{1}{2}$ of **many**

10. Second quarter of **many**
11. Last half of **more**
12. Second fifth of **about**
13. Last $\frac{1}{3}$ of **the**
14. First half of **stay**
15. First $\frac{1}{3}$ of **and**
16. First third of **the**
17. First third of **scenic**
18. Last $\frac{1}{2}$ of **experience**

? ?

PERCENTAGES of QUANTITIES

The word "of" can be replaced by ×.
For instance, 23% of 200 means 23% × 200.

Since 23% means 23 out of 100, 23% may be written as $\frac{23}{100}$.

Worked Example   Find 23% of 200cm.

Answer   23% of 200cm = 23% × 200cm

$$= \frac{23}{100} \times 200\text{cm}$$

On the calculator, **Key** $\boxed{23}\,\boxed{\div}\,\boxed{100}\,\boxed{\times}\,\boxed{200}\,\boxed{=}$ to get answer of 46.

Then 23% of 200cm = 46cm.

Sometimes we have to round our answer.

Worked Example   Find 37% of £5·15.

Answer   37% of £5·15 = 37% × £5·15

$$= \frac{37}{100} \times £5\!\cdot\!15$$

$$= £1\!\cdot\!91 \text{ rounded to the nearest penny.}$$

EXERCISE 5:4

1. Copy this table of numbers.

1	12	7	20	18	150	3	30	105	400	80	15	63	36	11	51	26
19	9	142	100	241	17	8	13	85	52	16	89	14	4·5	25	40	27
124	2	421	75	510	6	19·5	10	87	4	68	7·5	54	7·4	12·8	0·5	14·5

Do the following 24 calculations.
As soon as you do each one, shade the square on the table that has your answer.

The squares you have shaded should spell a word. What word?

Find 10% of   (a) 30   (b) 80   (c) 74.

Find 30% of   (a) 100   (b) 120   (c) 250.

Find 80% of   (a) 500   (b) 85   (c) 16.

Find 25% of   (a) 80   (b) 400   (c) 30.

Find 20% of   (a) 60   (b) 20   (c) 710.

Find 50% of   (a) 18   (b) 104   (c) 9.

Find 5% of   (a) 200   (b) 40   (c) 10.

Find 75% of   (a) 200   (b) 8   (c) 26.

2. An adult's brain weighs about 2% of a person's total weight. What is the approximate weight of Sandy's brain if Sandy weighs 56kg?

3. A computer salesperson got 5% commission on all sales. This person sold computers to Winstone School. How much commission did she get if the school paid £9000?

4. Jamie borrowed £160 from his aunt. She charged him 10% interest. How much interest did Jamie pay?

5. Calculate, rounding your answer to the nearest penny where necessary.

   (a) 25% of £8·40 (b) 20% of £3·15 (c) 50% of £210 (d) 30% of 75p

   (e) 15% of 99p (f) 95% of £314 (g) 5% of £1·07

6. David's family went out for dinner. The cost of the meal was £35. They gave a 10% tip. How much did they tip?

7.

Blood Type	% of population
O	42
A	44
B	10
AB	4

   (a) Out of 850 students at a school, how many would you expect to have type **O** blood?

   (b) Out of 26 students in a class, how many would you expect to have type **A** blood? (Round your answer sensibly.)

8. The femur (thighbone) is a long bone. Its length is about 25% of a person's height. Ann is 1·56m tall. About how long is her femur?

9. Jane said that 30% of £45 is the same as 45% of £30. Is Jane correct?

10. When Lucia's family visited England they bought clothing for the whole family. When they returned to Poland, they claimed back the VAT they had paid. The cost, without VAT was £458.

    How much VAT did they claim? (Take VAT to be 17·5%.)

Review 1   In an election only 55% of the people in a town voted. How many voted if there were 25,300 people in this town?

Review 2   About 70% of our body weight is water. Approximately how much water is in a person whose weight is 55kg?

Review 3   The same Adidas running shoes were usually £74·95 in two different shops. Both shops were offering "specials" on these shoes. J & C had them at "£15 off". B & M had them at "20% off". Which shop was cheaper?

DISCUSSION EXERCISE 5:5

Pupils in public sector secondary education
England, Wales, Scotland and Northern Ireland — Percentages and thousands

	1971	1981	1987		1971	1981	1987
England *(percentages)*				**Scotland** *(percentages)*			
Maintained secondary schools				Public sector secondary schools			
Middle deemed secondary	1.9	7.0	6.5	Selective	28.3	0.1	..
Modern	38.0	6.0	4.1	Comprehensive	58.7	96.0	..
Grammar	18.4	3.4	3.1	Part comprehensive/part selective	13.0	3.8	..
Technical	1.3	0.3	0.1				
Comprehensive	34.4	82.5	85.8	Total pupils (= 100%)			
Other	6.0	0.9	0.4	(thousands)	314	408	..
Total pupils (= 100%)							
(thousands)	2,953	3,840	3,240				
Wales *(percentages)*				**Northern Ireland** *(percentages)*			
Maintained secondary schools				Public sector secondary schools			
Middle deemed secondary	0.1	0.1	0.1	Secondary intermediate	87.7	88.6	88.5
Modern	22.3	1.8	0.6	Grammar	11.8	11.4	11.5
Grammar	15.4	1.3	0.5	Technical intermediate	0.5	—	—
Comprehensive	58.5	96.6	98.5				
Other	3.7	0.3	0.3	Total pupils (= 100%)			
Total pupils (= 100%)				(thousands)	96	119	109
(thousands)	191	240	210				

Source: Department of Education and Science

Source: Key Data 1989/90

Discuss the figures given on this table.

Calculate the actual numbers of pupils in each of the different types of secondary schools. **Discuss.**

PRACTICAL EXERCISE 5:6

1. Design a floor plan of a bungalow or house of total floor area 100 m². All 3 bedrooms are to take up a total of 40% of the space; the lounge and dining room are to take up another 40% and the kitchen, bathroom, stairs and hallway are to take up the remaining 20%.

2. Write a questionnaire on some topic that interests you. Write the questions so that they have Yes/No/Not Sure or Agree/Disagree/Not Sure responses. Have your class complete your questionnaire. For each question work out the % who answered Yes, the % who answered No and the % who answered Not Sure. Write a summary about your findings. You might like to ask questions about TV viewing habits, or leisure time activities or some part of school life or some part of mathematics.

3. Investigate the habit of tipping. You could include some of these: its origin, the countries where tipping is expected, the goods and services that a tip is expected for, the wages of people who get tips.

4. Investigate and make a report on the % "mark-up" that different types of shops make. Be sure to include greengrocers and a hardware shop. Try to justify the differences between the "mark-ups".

5. Do all makes and models of cars depreciate at the same rate? Does a car depreciate by the same percentage during the first and second years? Research these questions. Present your research as a wall chart.

WHAT   WHEN   WHERE   WHO   HOW   WHY

What percentage calculations might farmers make?

When do you use percentages or fractions in your other subjects?

Where, in business, are percentages and fractions used?

Who, in their job, would calculate fractions and percentages of quantities?

How can percentages be used to give false impressions of data?

Why are percentages quoted so often in the media?

AROUND and ABOUT

INTERNATIONAL TIME

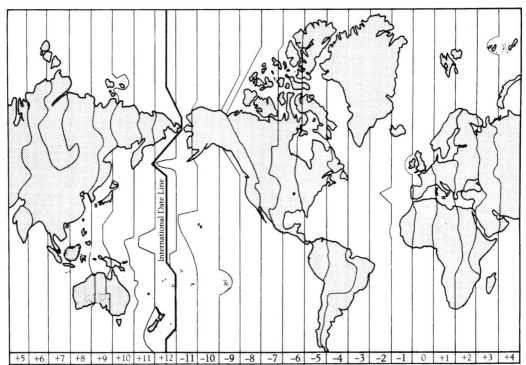

Hours ahead (+) or behind (-) Greenwich Mean Time (GMT)

DISCUSSION EXERCISE 6:1

The 10 groups in a class were asked to talk about negative numbers. Each group talked about different things.

Abbie's group talked about going up and down in a lift.
Robert's group talked about bank overdrafts.
Philippa's group talked about the "countdown" for launching a rocket. They talked about things such as "zero minus one".
Darren's group talked about cold temperatures such as –13°.

What might the other six groups have talked about?
Discuss.

SCALES and NUMBER LINES

Scales often have positive and negative numbers on them. For example, on a temperature scale 10° below 0° is shown as –10°.

Positive numbers, such as +4, are often written without the + sign. For instance, +4 is often written as 4.
Negative numbers, such as – 4, are always written with the – sign.

The positive and negative numbers are often called the **integers.** The integers include both the positive whole numbers and the negatives and also zero.
Zero is neither positive nor negative.

Worked Example

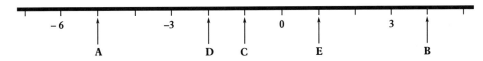

What number is at

        (a) A   (b) B   (c) C   (d) D   (e) E?

Answer (a) –5   (b) 4   (c) –1   (d) –2   (e) 1

EXERCISE 6:2

1. Copy these and fill in the missing numbers.

(a)

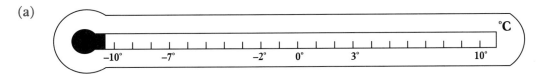

(b)

2.

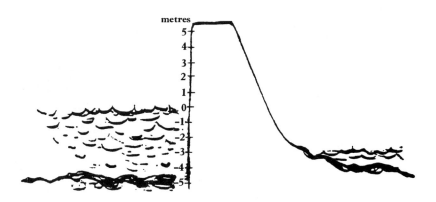

This shows a dam at normal water level.

Draw diagrams to show the level of the water in the dam if the water level

(a) rises 4 metres   **(b)** falls 4 metres.

3.

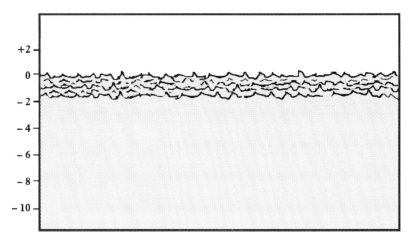

Copy the picture that is shown here.
The wavy line is the surface of the sea.
The scale is in metres.

On your picture draw in things such as a ship, a diver, fish, a submarine, swimmers, a bird.

4.

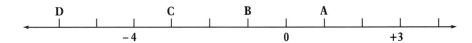

On this number line, which integer is at

(a) A   **(b)** B   **(c)** C   **(d)** D?

5.

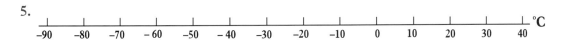

Copy this number line and mark these temperatures.

A. –89°. The coldest temperature ever measured (at a place in Antarctica).

B. –27°. The lowest temperature ever measured in Britain (on 11 February 1985 at Braemar).

C. 32°. 13 days in a row were hotter than this in the heatwave in 1976.

Review

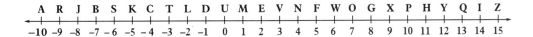

(a) Replace each of these integers with the letter that represents the integer.

+8, –3, –7, +6   –2, +5   +6, –3, –4   +6, –4, 0, +3, –4, +4, –7, +6, +7, +4, –4

(b) Find the answer to the question in (a) by replacing the integers with letters.

+1, +2, +6   +6, +2, +2   –6, +2, –1, –5   –7, +1, –5   +1, +2, +6   +6, +2, +2

–3, +2, +6

DISCUSSION and PRACTICAL EXERCISE 6:3

A R J B S K C T L D U M E V N F W O G X P H Y Q I Z
–10 –9 –8 –7 –6 –5 –4 –3 –2 –1 0 1 2 3 4 5 6 7 8 9 10 11 12 13 14 15

How has this code been made? **Discuss.**

Write a code of your own. Use this to code a question.
Give to your neighbour, or group, to decode and write a reply to your question. The reply should also be in code.

ORDERING NEGATIVE NUMBERS

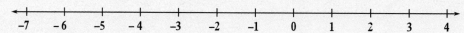

The further to the right a number is, the larger it is.
The further to the left a number is, the smaller it is.

Worked Example Insert < or > to make these statements true.

(a) 6   – 6   (b) –5   – 6   (c) – 4   –2   (d) –2   0

Answer (a) 6 > – 6   (Since 6 is greater than – 6.)

(b) – 5 > –6   (Since –5 is greater than – 6.)

(c) – 4 < –2   (Since – 4 is smaller than –2.)

(d) – 2 < 0   (Since –2 is smaller than 0.)

EXERCISE 6:4

1. Name the larger of these pairs of integers.

   (a) –3   1   (b) 2   –2   (c) – 4   3   (d) 0   –5

   (e) –2   –5   (f) – 4   –1   (g) – 3   –2   (h) –99   –100

   (i) – 68   –54   (j) –31   0

2.

   A   B   0

   One of the following pairs of numbers is at A and the other is at B. Which number is at A?

   (a) –7, –3   (b) –20, –50   (c) –1·5, –4   (d) –0·5, –0·2

3. Which of the three numbers would be furthest to the left if they were graphed on a number line?

   (a) – 4, –3, –5   (b) – 6, –8, – 4   (c) –2, –1, –1·5   (d) –2·5, –2·1, –2·6

4. Insert > or < to make these true.

   (a) –9   – 4   (b) – 6   –7   (c) –8   0   (d) 0   –15

   (e) –15   –14   (f) –25   –125   (g) –1·6   –1·7

92

5.

| 20° | –5° | 15° | 4° | –2° | –3° | –12° | 5° | 0° | –19° |
| –16° | – 4° | 21° | – 6° | –8° | –1° | 9° | –9° | 1° | –14° |

Write these temperatures from warmest to coldest.

6. Copy the pyramid of numbers.

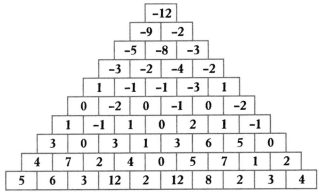

Find a path from the bottom of this pyramid to the top, always moving into a square which has a smaller number than the square you are moving from. You may go through only one square at each level i.e. you may **not** move sideways.

Is there more than one possible path?

Review 1 Are these statements true or false?

(a) 7 > –7   (b) 0 < –3   (c) 1 < –1   (d) –2 > –1

(e) –5 < –2   (f) –5 > – 6   (g) –52 > –32   (h) –2·5 < –2

(i) –3·6 > –3·9

Review 2 On February 12th, these minimum temperatures (in °C) were recorded.

Beijing	–5	Kiev	–2	New York	– 6
Calgary	–22	Montreal	–24	Warsaw	–2
Jerusalem	–1	Moscow	–8		

(a) Which city had the coldest night?

(b) Which city had the warmest night?

(c) Which was colder, Moscow or New York?

(d) Write the cities in order, from coldest to warmest.

PUZZLES 6:5

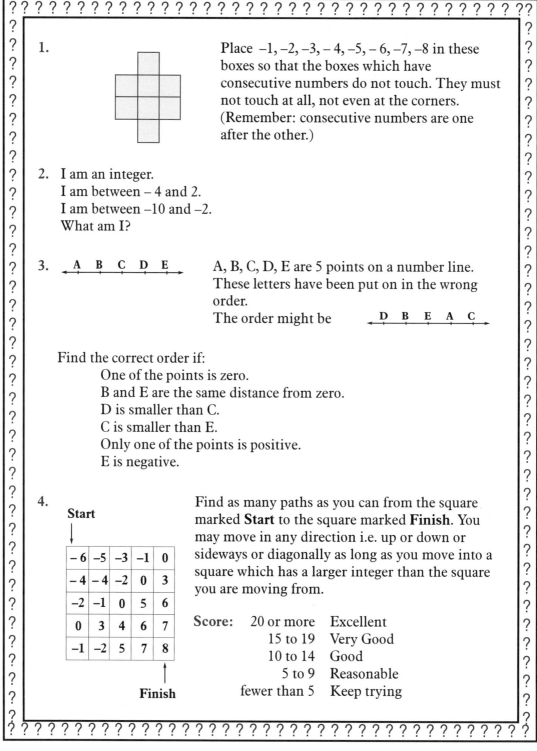

1. Place −1, −2, −3, − 4, −5, − 6, −7, −8 in these boxes so that the boxes which have consecutive numbers do not touch. They must not touch at all, not even at the corners. (Remember: consecutive numbers are one after the other.)

2. I am an integer.
   I am between − 4 and 2.
   I am between −10 and −2.
   What am I?

3. A B C D E

   A, B, C, D, E are 5 points on a number line.
   These letters have been put on in the wrong order.
   The order might be   D B E A C

   Find the correct order if:
        One of the points is zero.
        B and E are the same distance from zero.
        D is smaller than C.
        C is smaller than E.
        Only one of the points is positive.
        E is negative.

4. **Start**

− 6	−5	−3	−1	0
− 4	−4	−2	0	3
−2	−1	0	5	6
0	3	4	6	7
−1	−2	5	7	8

   Finish

   Find as many paths as you can from the square marked **Start** to the square marked **Finish**. You may move in any direction i.e. up or down or sideways or diagonally as long as you move into a square which has a larger integer than the square you are moving from.

   Score: 20 or more   Excellent
                 15 to 19   Very Good
                 10 to 14   Good
                   5 to 9   Reasonable
          fewer than 5   Keep trying

INTERPRETING NEGATIVE NUMBERS

Worked Example   Heights above sea level can be described with positive numbers and heights below sea level with negative numbers.
What do these heights mean?   (a) +260m   (b) – 6m

Answer   (a) 260m above sea level

(b) 6m below sea level

EXERCISE 6:6

1. The water level in a dam is described as +2 if it is 2 metres above normal and –2 if it is 2 metres below normal.
What do these mean?   (a) –3   (b) +1   (c) 0

2. In a dance movement –2 means move 2 steps back while +2 means move 2 steps forward.
What do these mean?   (a) –3   (b) +1   (c) 0

3. The students in a class were weighed during a P.E. lesson in September. In January they were weighed again.
A weight gain was given as a positive number. A weight loss was given as a negative number.
For example +3 means a student gained 3kg.

Student	A.C.	B.D.	X.S.	M.W.	K.C.	S.S.	D.F.	M.T.	K.V.	D.N.	D.A.	S.C.	R.I.	A.V.	E.B.	O.S.	J.H.	N.M.
Weight gain or loss (kg)	+1	+1	–1	0	+2	+1	–1	–2	+3	+2	–2	0	0	+1	–1	+1	0	–1

(a) How many students stayed the same weight?

(b) How many students lost weight?

(c) How many students gained weight?

(d) Which student (or students) gained the most weight?

(e) Who lost more than D.F.?

Review A factory makes bolts. A test run was made on 2cm bolts to find how accurately they were being made. If +1 means a bolt is 1mm too long and –1 means it is 1mm too short, explain what these mean.

(a) +3   (b) 0   (c) –2

WRITING NEGATIVE NUMBERS

Worked Example   Heights above sea level are to be described with positive numbers. Heights below sea level are to be described with negative numbers. Use positive or negative numbers to describe the height of a place which is

(a) 5m below sea level   (b) at sea level   (c) 5m above sea level.

Answer   (a) –5m   (b) 0m   (c) +5m

EXERCISE 6:7

1. In a dance, steps to the right are to be described with positive numbers and steps to the left are to be described with negative numbers.
   Use positive or negative numbers to tell a dancer to move

   (a) 3 steps to the right   (b) 5 steps to the left.

2. Use positive or negative numbers to describe how a lift moves if it goes

   (a) up 2 floors   (b) down 1 floor   (c) stays where it is.

3. Use positive or negative numbers to describe these amounts deposited or withdrawn from a bank account

   (a) £3 withdrawn   (b) £5 deposited.

4. The temperature of a hospital room must be kept as close as possible to 20°C.
    The temperature in the room is taken every hour.
    If the temperature is above 20° it is recorded as a positive integer.
    If the temperature is below 20° it is recorded as a negative integer.

    Copy and complete this table for a 12 hour period.

Actual Temperature	18°	21°	22°	19°	20°	18°	22°	19°	20°	20°	21°	18°
Recorded Temperature	−2	+1										

Review 1 Use positive or negative numbers to describe the change in a school roll if the roll

(a) rises by 12   (b) falls by 8.

Review 2 In a factory which makes biscuits, 20 packets are weighed each hour to check that they aren't too far over or too far under the weight of 250g.
A packet which weighed 260g was recorded as +10.
A packet which weighed 240g was recorded as –10.
How would the weights of the following packets be recorded?

(a) 270g   (b) 230g   (c) 235g   (d) 254g   (e) 244g

USING NEGATIVE NUMBERS

Worked Example   The temperature at 6 a.m. was –5°C. By 9 a.m. the temperature had risen by 7°. What was the temperature at 9 a.m.?

Answer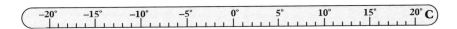

The temperature must rise 5° to be 0°. By the time the temperature had risen a further 2°, it would then be 2°C.

EXERCISE 6:8

1. (a) The temperature was 4°. It rises 6°. What is the temperature now?

   (b) The temperature was 4°. It drops 6°. What is the temperature now?

   (c) The temperature was – 4°. It rises 6°. What is the temperature now?

   (d) The temperature was – 4°. It drops 6°. What is the temperature now?

   (e) The temperature was – 6°. It rises 4°. What is the temperature now?

   (f) The temperature was – 6°. It falls 4°. What is the temperature now?

2. A diver is 20m below sea level.
   Her position is given as –20m.
   Give her new position as an integer if she

   (a) goes down a further 10m   (b) comes up 10m.

3. Andy has £25 in his bank account. Describe his new bank balance as a positive or negative number if

   (a) he withdraws £30   (b) he deposits £30.

4. In a maths. quiz, 1 mark is given for each correct answer and 1 mark is lost for each wrong answer. There are 20 questions. If all questions are answered correctly a student's score will be 20; if all questions are answered incorrectly a student's score will be –20.
   Part way through this quiz Karim has a score of 2.
   What will Karim's new score be if he

   (a) answers the next 5 questions correctly

   (b) answers the next 5 questions incorrectly

   (c) answers 2 of the next 5 questions correctly and 3 of them incorrectly

   (d) answers 4 of the next 5 questions incorrectly and 1 of them correctly?

5. In a board game Victoria has scored 5 points.
   What will Victoria's score be, if on her next
   turn she

   (a) gains 2 points

   (b) loses 3 points

   (c) loses 7 points?

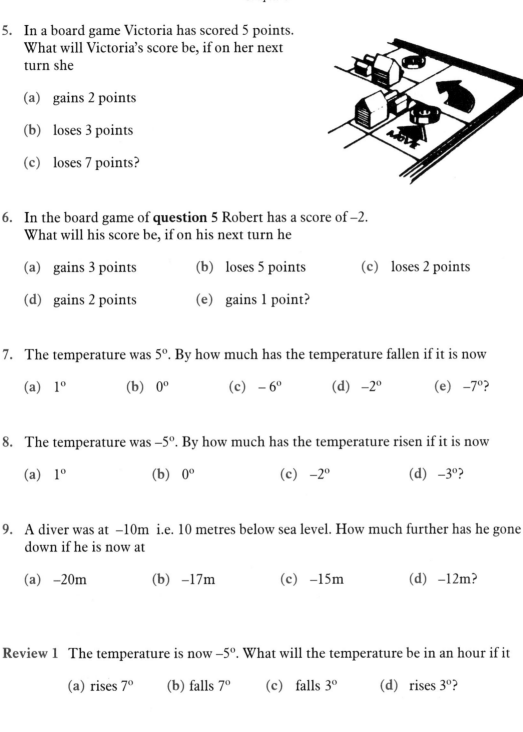

6. In the board game of **question 5** Robert has a score of –2.
   What will his score be, if on his next turn he

   (a) gains 3 points   (b) loses 5 points   (c) loses 2 points

   (d) gains 2 points   (e) gains 1 point?

7. The temperature was 5°. By how much has the temperature fallen if it is now

   (a) 1°   (b) 0°   (c) – 6°   (d) –2°   (e) –7°?

8. The temperature was –5°. By how much has the temperature risen if it is now

   (a) 1°   (b) 0°   (c) –2°   (d) –3°?

9. A diver was at –10m i.e. 10 metres below sea level. How much further has he gone
   down if he is now at

   (a) –20m   (b) –17m   (c) –15m   (d) –12m?

Review 1   The temperature is now –5°. What will the temperature be in an hour if it

   (a) rises 7°   (b) falls 7°   (c) falls 3°   (d) rises 3°?

Review 2   In a board game Sarah had –3 points. How many points did she gain if she
   now has

   (a) –2 points   (b) 0 points   (c) 2 points   (d) 10 points?

GAME 6:9

The GRID GAME: a game for 2 students.

Equipment: A grid, drawn up as shown.
2 dice (1 red, 1 white).
A blue and a red pen. One student has the blue pen, the other has the red pen.

10	3	8	3	6
5	2	2	11	6
11	4	5	7	10
4	12	12	5	7
7	9	9	8	6

The Play: The students take it in turn to throw the two dice together. The number on the red die is taken to be negative and the number on the white die is taken to be positive. The increase is taken as the score. For instance, if the number on the red die is four this is taken as -4, if the number on the white die is one this is taken as $+1$; the increase from -4 to $+1$ is 5 so the score would be 5. The student takes a square on the grid by colouring a square which has the score.

Rules: If all the squares with a student's score have already been coloured, no square can be taken at this turn.

The winner is the first student to have taken 13 of the squares.

NEGATIVE NUMBERS on the CALCULATOR

To get a negative number displayed on the calculator we use the ⊞⁄⁻ key.

Example   To get – 4 displayed: **Key** 4 +⁄-

Worked Example   Use the calculator to find the answers to these.

(a) $2 + (-6)$ (b) $2 - (-6)$ (c) $-2 - (-6)$ (d) $-2 + (-6)$

Answer   (a) **Key** 2 + 6 +⁄- = to get answer of – 4.

(b) **Key** 2 – 6 +⁄- = to get answer of 8.

(c) **Key** 2 +⁄- – 6 +⁄- = to get answer of 4.

(d) **Key** 2 +⁄- – 6 +⁄- = to get answer of –8.

EXERCISE 6:10

Use your calculator to find the answers to these.

1. (a) 3 + (−5)   (b) 3 − (−5)   (c) −3 + (−5)   (d) −3 + 5

   (e) 5 + (−3)   (f) 5 − (−3)   (g) −5 + (−3)   (h) −5 + 3

2. Find two numbers which add to − 4. How many can you find?

3. Find two numbers which subtract to − 4. How many can you find?

4. Think of a positive number. Write it down.
   Now make up some additions and subtractions which have this number as the answer.
   Use both positive and negative numbers in your additions and subtractions.

Review 1   Calculate   (a) 6 + (− 4)   (b) 4 − (− 6)   (c) −3 + (−7)

(d) −10 − 2   (e) − 4 + 3.

Review 2   Make up some additions and subtractions which have −3 as the answer.

ADDING and SUBTRACTING without the CALCULATOR

DISCUSSION EXERCISE 6:11

- On the calculator, 5 + (−2) is keyed as 5 + 2 +/- = .
  Use your calculator to find the answers to many additions.
  Look at additions in which both numbers are negative as well as those in which just one of the numbers is negative.

  Discuss your answers. As part of your discussion, make and test statements about adding without using the calculator.

  You may like to refer to movement along a number line.

  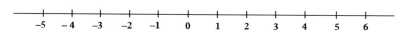

- Use your calculator to find the answers to many subtractions involving negative numbers. How could you subtract without using the calculator? **Discuss.**
  Make and test statements as part of your discussion.

We can use a number line to **add** or **subtract**.

To add a positive number, move to the right.
To add a negative number, move to the left.

Examples

$1 + 3$ Begin at 1, move 3 to the right. $1 + 3 = 4$

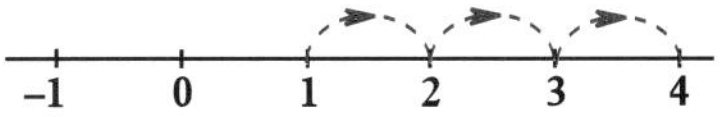

$2 + (-3)$ Begin at 2, move 3 to the left. $2 + (-3) = -1$

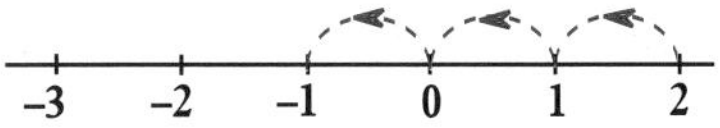

$-2 + 3$ Begin at -2, move 3 to the right. $-2 + 3 = 1$

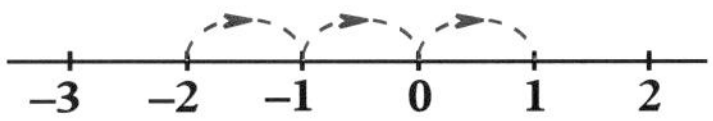

$-2 + (-1)$ Begin at -2, move 1 to the left. $-2 + (-1) = -3$

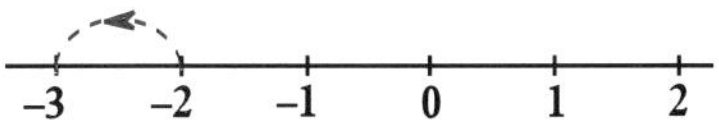

Addition and subtraction are inverse operations. To subtract, we must move in the opposite direction to that in which we move to add.

To subtract a positive number, move to the left.
To subtract a negative number, move to the right.

Examples

$4 - 1$ Begin at 4, move 1 to the left. $4 - 1 = 3$

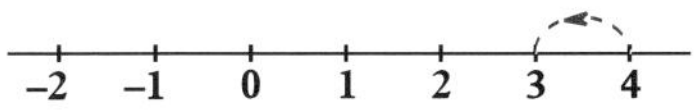

$1 - 3$ Begin at 1, move 3 to the left. $1 - 3 = -2$

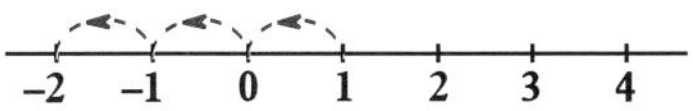

$1 - (-3)$ Begin at 1, move 3 to the right. $1 - (-3) = 4$

$-1 - (-3)$ Begin at -1, move 3 to the right. $-1 - (-3) = 2$

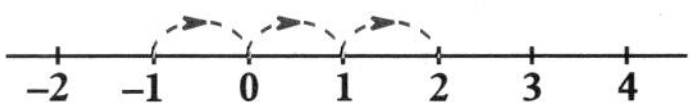

EXERCISE 6:12

Do *not* use your calculator in this exercise.

1. Find the answer to these.

   (a) 2 + (–5)   (b) –2 + (–5)   (c) 2 + 5   (d) –2 + 5

   (e) 2 – (–5)   (f) –2 – (–5)   (g) 2 – 5   (h) –2 – 5

   (i) –3 + (– 4)   (j) 5 – (–3)   (k) –8 – (–2)   (l) 4 + (–3)

   (m) –7 – 3   (n) –8 + (– 4)   (o) –3 – (–7)

2. Calculate.

   (a) –5 + 3 + (– 4)   (b) 2 + (– 4) + (–1)   (c) 3 – (– 4) + 5

   (d) –2 – (–1) + (–5)   (e) 3 + (–7) – (–2)   (f) –5 – (–2) – 4

   (g) 7 – (–2) + 5   (h) 2 + (–1) – 4

3. In a multiple-choice test +1 is given for each correct answer and –1 is given for each wrong answer. A student's score is – 4 +6.

   (a) How many correct answers did the student give?

   (b) How many wrong answers did the student give?

   (c) How many questions were there in the test?

   (d) What was the student's total score?

4. In Winchester, at 5 p.m., the temperature was 2°C. The expected temperature at midnight was –3°C.

   (a) How many degrees was the temperature expected to fall between 5 p.m. and midnight?

   (b) If the temperature at midnight was 1°C lower than expected, what was the midnight temperature?

5. Copy and complete these addition squares.

(a) 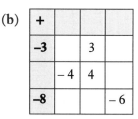 (b)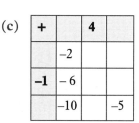

6. What are the next two numbers in these number patterns?   (a)   −14, −11, −8, −5, . . .

                                                                     (b)   7·7, 5·7, 3·7, 1·7, . . .

7. At 8 a.m. Sharon's temperature was 1·2° above normal.
    By 11 a.m. it had dropped by 2·1°.
    How far below normal was Sharon's temperature at 11 a.m.?

8. The approximate altitude (height above sea level) of some places is shown.

Place	Altitude (m)
Ayers Rock	900
Caspian Sea	−30
London	30
Nairobi	1800
Rotterdam	−5
The Dead Sea	− 400

    (a) What is the difference in altitude between London and the Caspian Sea?

    (b) What is the difference in altitude between The Dead Sea and Ayers Rock?

    (c) How much higher is Nairobi than Rotterdam?

9. (a) Cleopatra poisoned herself in 30 B.C. She was then 39 years old. In what year was Cleopatra born?

    (b) Julius Caesar was born in 100 B.C. He was assassinated in 44 B.C. How old was Julius Caesar at his death?

    (c) How much older was Julius Caesar than Cleopatra?

10.

18	19	14	9	8	7	6	5	−18
17	16	15	10	9	6	5	4	−17
16	15	14	13	10	5	2	3	−16
14	12	13	12	11	4	−13	−14	−15
−2	−1	0	1	2	3	−10	−11	−14
−3	−2	−1	0	3	−8	−9	−12	−13
−2	−3	− 4	−5	− 6	−7	− 6	−11	−12

Find a route from the pink box to the grey box.

You may move into a square only if its number is one less than the number of the square you are moving from.

You may move sideways or up or down but not diagonally.

11. Find the answer to these.

(**a**) $-3.4 + 1.8$ (**b**) $-6.8 - 2.3$ (**c**) $2.4 + (-4.2)$ (**d**) $-1.9 + (-2.3)$

(**e**) $6 + (-2.6)$ (**f**) $2.6 - (-4)$ (**g**) $6.1 + (-4)$

12. How might this addition square be completed?

+	3		
		-4	
			-5
				4

Review 1 Calculate.

(**a**) $-3 + (-5)$ (**b**) $2 - (-3)$ (**c**) $-1.6 - 0.9$ (**d**) $2.3 + (-1.4)$

(**e**) $-2 + (-5) - 4$

Review 2

City	Local time difference (hrs)
Brussels	$+1$
London	0
Mexico City	-6
Peking	$+8$
Reykjavik	0
Santiago	-4

This table gives the time difference between local time and GMT (Greenwich Mean Time).

(**a**) If it is 6 a.m. in London, what time is it in Santiago and Peking?

(**b**) If it is midday in Mexico City, what time is it in Brussels, Santiago and Reykjavik?

Review 3 Two counters are dropped onto this board. The score is found by adding together the numbers on the squares on which the counters land.
Write down all the possible scores.

-4	2
3	-1

PUZZLES 6:13

1.

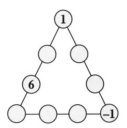

The four numbers, along each side of this triangle, must add to the same total. What might these numbers be?

2.

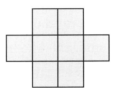

Place negative and positive numbers in these boxes so the total of each row and column is zero.

3.

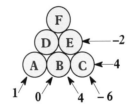

Replace the letters with numbers to give the totals shown.

4.

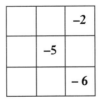

This is to be a magic square. Each row, each column and each diagonal is to add to the same number.
How might this magic square be completed?

GAME 6:14

INTEGER GAME: a game for a group or a class

Preparation A leader is chosen.

The other students each draw this diagram.

The Play The leader chooses four integers between –10 and 10. As the leader calls each one the other students must write it in one of the grey "boxes". The answer for the pink box is then calculated.

The student (or students) who have the biggest answer get 1 point.

This is repeated for a set time, perhaps 15 minutes.

The winner is the student with the most points after this set time.

PRACTICAL EXERCISE 6:15

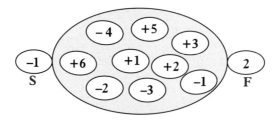

Find a route from the number labelled S (start) to the number labelled F (finish) so that the sum of the numbers on the route (including the number S) is equal to the number labelled F. You may pass through each number only once.

How many routes can you find?

Score: More than 5 Excellent
5 Very Good
3 Good
less than 3 Keep Trying

INVESTIGATION 6:16

VALUE and EULAV

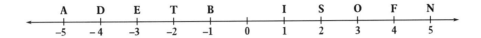

The "value" of the word NET is $5 + (-3) + (-2) = 0$.

Using the letters on the number line, **investigate** to find the three letter words which have the greatest and smallest "value".

The "eulav" of the world BE is $-1 - (-3) = 2$.

Investigate to find the two letter words which have the greatest and smallest "eulav".

PRACTICAL EXERCISE 6:17

Make up a card game or a board game.
Use positive and negative numbers in your game.

Write clear instructions for your game.
Trial the game with your group, then give it to other groups to play.

WHAT   WHEN   WHERE   WHO   HOW   WHY

What people in a hospital might use negative numbers?

When might you need to use negative numbers in your other subjects?

Where, in the media, might negative numbers be used?

Who, in the building industry, might use negative numbers?

How would the world function if we didn't have negative numbers? What might be used instead?

Why would a sailor or someone in the shipping industry need to understand negative numbers?

1. Three students did the calculation 784 – 95 on the calculator and none of them got the right answer.
   Victoria got 879, James got 698 and Thomas got 95.
   Which of these mistakes did the students make?

   A. Forgot to key =   **B.** Keyed + instead of –

   C. Reversed two of the digits on the calculator display.

2. Choose the best estimate.

   (a) 28 × 189   A. 6   B. 600   C. 6000   D. 60000

   (b) 207 ÷ 19   A. 10000   B. 1000   C. 100   D. 10

   (c) 423 ÷ 81   A. 50   B. 5   C. 500   D. 5000

   (d) 314 × 47   A. 1500   B. 150   C. 15   D. 15000

3. Positive and negative numbers are used to describe the profit and loss for each month's trading.
   If –200 means a loss of £200, explain what these mean.

   (a) –350   (b) +500   (c) 0

4. A dress costs £29.
   Nell got 5% discount.
   How much discount is this?

5. Adrian did the calculations   (a) 192 ÷ 6 = 32   (b) 83 – 15 = 68.
   What calculations could Adrian do to check his answers?

6. Which of 10, 100 or 1000 goes in the box?

   (a) $8.21 \div \square = 0.0821$ (b) $0.5 \times \square = 5$

   (c) $234 \div \square = 2.34$ (d) $6.02 \times \square = 6020$

   (e) $0.4 \div \square = 0.04$ (f) $0.03 \times \square = 30$

7. This table shows the points given for 1st, 2nd or 3rd place at the Camford Show.
   Vickers Farm got a total of 32 points in 8 events.
   How many 1st, 2nd and 3rd placings did they get?

   Is there more than one answer?

1st	**5 points**
2nd	**3 points**
3rd	**1 point**

8. Choose the correct answer for the meaning of the 7 in these.

   (a) 0.174 A. tenths   B. hundredths   C. thousandths

   (b) 1.74 A. tenths   B. hundredths   C. thousandths

   (c) 0.07 A. tenths   B. hundredths   C. thousandths

   (d) 25.257 A. tenths   B. hundredths   C. thousandths

   (e) 62.7 A. tenths   B. hundredths   C. thousandths

9. A dolphin was at –8 m i.e. 8 metres below sea level.
   How much further has the dolphin gone down (or how far has it come up) if it is now at

   (a) –10 m   (b) –5 m?

10.

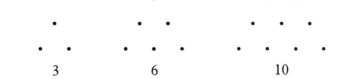

1, 3, 6, 10 are the first four triangular numbers.
Draw diagrams to find the next two triangular numbers.

11. (a) The temperature was –3°. It falls 2°. What is the temperature now?

(b) The temperature was –3°. It rises 2°. What is the temperature now?

(c) The temperature was 2°. It falls 3°. What is the temperature now?

12. Write down that part of each word indicated in the clues. You will end up with five words.
Rearrange these words to make a sentence.

    1. The last half of **tomcat.**

    2. The last $\frac{3}{4}$ of **that.**

    3. The first $\frac{3}{5}$ of **there.**

    4. The middle three-fifths of **other.**

    5. The last two-thirds of **pin.**

13. What is the missing word?

(a) Addition and _____ are inverse operations.

(b) _____ and multiplying are inverse operations.

(c) Finding a square root and _____ are inverse operations.

14. A 323cm hose is cut into 17 equal parts.

(a) Estimate the length of each part.

(b) Use long division to find the length of each part.

15. The Great Wall of China was begun in 246 B.C. It was finished 36 years later. In what year was it finished?

16. (a) Which of these is *not* the same as 0·58?

    A. 5 tenths and 8 hundredths   **B.** $\frac{5}{10} + \frac{8}{100}$ **C.** 58 tenths

(b) Which of these is the same as $\sqrt[3]{64}$?

    A. 8   **B.** $\frac{64}{3}$ **C.** 4   **D.** 262144

17. What goes in the box?

    (a) Since $37 + 9 = 46$ then $46 - \square = 37$.

    (b) $52 - 7 + \square = 52$

    (c) Since $56 \div 7 = 8$ then $8 \times \square = 56$.

    (d) $7 \times 7 \times 7 \times 7 \times 7 = 7^{\square}$

    (e) $\square$ is the square of 3.

    (f) 3 is the cube root of $\square$.

18. Copy this chart:

				O						
5	8	4	9	1	7	2	6	3	10

Use place value to do each calculation on the left. Find the answer on the right. Place your ruler so that the dots beside the calculation and its answer lie along the edge of the ruler.

The edge of the ruler will then pass through a letter. Place this letter above the number of the calculation on the chart.

For example, the answer to calculation **1.** is 600. When the ruler is placed so that the dots beside calculation **1** and 600 are both on its edge, the ruler passes through the letter **O**. The letter **O** is then written above **1** on the chart.

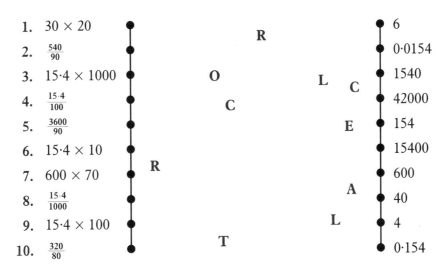

1.	30×20		6
2.	$\frac{540}{90}$		0·0154
3.	$15\cdot4 \times 1000$		1540
4.	$\frac{15\cdot4}{100}$		42000
5.	$\frac{3600}{90}$		154
6.	$15\cdot4 \times 10$		15400
7.	600×70		600
8.	$\frac{15\cdot4}{1000}$		40
9.	$15\cdot4 \times 100$		4
10.	$\frac{320}{80}$		0·154

19. 83 members of a club won £985 each on the pools.

    (a) Estimate the total they won.

    (b) Use long multiplication to find this total.

20.

On this number line, which numbers are at A, B and C?

21. The Cullinan diamond is the world's largest diamond. It weighs about 3100 carats. A carat is $\frac{1}{5}$ of a gram.

How many grams does this diamond weigh?

22. Calculate.

(a) $26\cdot2 \times 0\cdot2$ (b) $-4 + 2\cdot6$ (c) $6\cdot8 + 7 \times 0\cdot04$

(d) $2 - (-5)$ (e) $-5 + (-1)$ (f) $4\cdot1 + 2\,(11\cdot8 - 6\cdot05)$

23. Each year, about 20 million British people take a holiday abroad. Of these, about 30% go to Spain.
About how many go to Spain?

24. Copy the crossnumber. Use the clues to complete it.

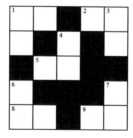

Across	**Down**
1. 4^2	1. $\sqrt{100}$
2. $7 + 2 \times 3$	3. $\frac{3}{5}$ of 60
5. 3^3	4. $3\,(5 + 4)$
8. $3\,(7 - 2)$	6. $20 - 3\,(4 - 1)$
9. The remainder when 834 is divided by 27.	7. $10 + 8 \div 2$

25. Sasha said that the sum of the cubes of 1, 2, 3, 4 and 5 was equal to the square of the sum of 1, 2, 3, 4 and 5.
Was Sasha right?

£164
Plus VAT

26. If VAT is 17·5%, what is the VAT on this microwave?

27. Copy and complete this addition square.

+		3	
			–1
	–7	–2	
–4			–8

28. John's group were making up number puzzles. John made up this one.

A number has 5 digits.

The number is between 20 and 30.

The difference between the ones digit and the tenths digit is the same as the hundredths digit.

The tens digit is the same as the thousandths digit.

The sum of all the digits is 16.

The tenths digit is three times as large as the tens digit.

Melanie got the right answer to John's puzzle. What did she get?

ALGEBRA

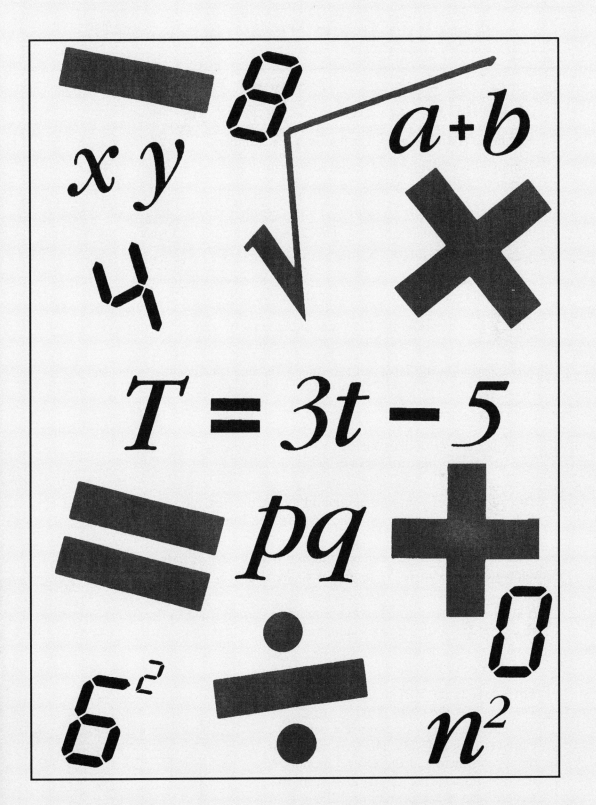

Algebra from Previous Levels

DIVISIBILITY

A number is **divisible by** 2 if it is an even number.

A number is **divisible by** 3 if the sum of its digits is divisible by 3. For instance 259104 is divisible by 3 since $2 + 5 + 9 + 1 + 0 + 4 = 21$ is.

A number is **divisible by** 4 if the number made from the last two digits is. For instance, 7532 is divisible by 4 since 32 is.

A number is **divisible by** 5 if its last digit is either 5 or 0.

A number is **divisible by** 6 if it is divisible by both 2 and 3. That is, if it is an even number and the sum of the digits is divisible by 3.

A number is **divisible by** 8 if the number made from the last three digits is divisible by 8. For instance, 259104 is divisible by 8 since 104 is.

A number is **divisible by** 9 if the sum of its digits is divisible by 9.

SPECIAL NUMBERS

A **prime number** is divisible by just two numbers, itself and 1.
The first few prime numbers are 2, 3, 5, 7, 11, 13.

The **multiples** of a number are found by multiplying the number by each of 1, 2, 3, 4, 5, 6, . . . For instance, the first few multiples of 5 are 5, 10, 15, 20.

A **factor** of a given number is a number that divides exactly into the given number. For instance, the factors of 20 are 1, 2, 4, 5, 10, 20.

A **square number** is made when a number is multiplied by itself. For instance, since $2 \times 2 = 4$ then 4 is a square number.

COORDINATES

The **x-axis** is the horizontal axis.
The **y-axis** is the vertical axis.
The **coordinates** of a point are a pair of numbers such as (5, 3). The first number is the x-coordinate and the second number is the y-coordinate. For the point P(5, 3), the x-coordinate is 5 and the y-coordinate is 3.

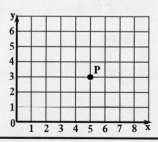

REVISION EXERCISE

1. (a) Use your calculator to find the answers to these.

$$21 \times 11 =$$
$$221 \times 11 =$$
$$2221 \times 11 =$$
$$22221 \times 11 =$$
$$222221 \times 11 =$$

   (b) Use the number pattern in the answers to (a) to find the answer to 222222221×11.

2. Copy this chart.

T $\underline{\hspace{1.5em}}$ $\underline{\hspace{1.5em}}$ $\underline{\hspace{1.5em}}$ $\underline{\hspace{1.5em}}$ $\qquad$ $\underline{\hspace{1.5em}}$ $\underline{\hspace{1.5em}}$ $\underline{\hspace{1.5em}}$ $\underline{\hspace{1.5em}}$

(1, 7) (8, 4) (6, 5) (2, 3) $\qquad$ (3, 2) (8, 4) (8, 6) (2, 3)

$\underline{\hspace{1.5em}}$ $\underline{\hspace{1.5em}}$ $\underline{\hspace{1.5em}}$ $\underline{\hspace{1.5em}}$ $\qquad$ $\underline{\hspace{1.5em}}$ $\qquad$ $\underline{\hspace{1.5em}}$ $\underline{\hspace{1.5em}}$ $\underline{\hspace{1.5em}}$ $\qquad$ $\underline{\hspace{1.5em}}$

(7, 1) (0, 5) (1, 7) (5, 0) $\qquad$ (3, 6) $\qquad$ (8, 4) (5, 6) (2, 8) $\qquad$ (6, 3)

Fill in the chart by finding the letter beside each coordinate.
T is filled in for you.

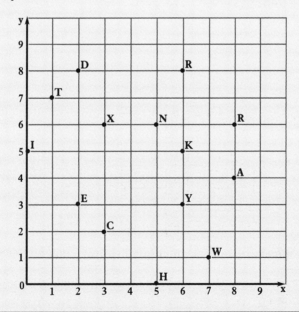

3.

| 1266 | 6144 | 3378 | 4200 | 2204 | 4143 |

   (a) Which numbers in the box are not divisible by 3?

   (b) Which are not divisible by 4?

   (c) Which numbers in the box are not divisible by either 6 or 8?

119

4. Copy these factor trees.
   Fill in the numbers in the boxes.

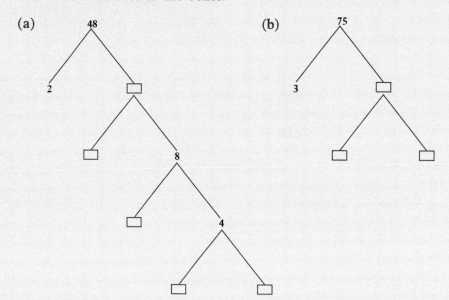

(a) 48

(b) 75

5. What is the next number?

   (a) 4, 8, 12, . . .   (b) 1, 4, 9, . . .   (c) 16, 25, 36, . . .

   (d) 12, 15, 18, . . .

6.

+	1	2	3	4	5
1	2	3	4	5	6
2	3	4	5	6	7
3	4	5	6	7	8
4	5	6	7	8	9
5	6	7	8	9	10

There are many number patterns in this addition table.

In the dotted square "box", the numbers on each diagonal (8 and 10, 9 and 9) add to the same number.
Is this true for all square "boxes"?

In the dotted rectangular "box", the numbers read clockwise, beginning at the top left, are 3, 4, 5, 6, 5, 4, 3. Do all rectangular "boxes" have a similar number pattern?

What other number patterns can you find in this addition table?

120

7. A recipe for cooking beef says "cook for 20 minutes per kg plus 30 minutes more".
   How long would you cook a piece of beef which weighs

   (a) 2kg   (b) 1·5kg?

8.

8	9	70	6	13	18	10	36	23	21	25	4	16
31	22	46	52	24	40	2	39	19	29	7	38	37
45	50	1	15	34	53	63	54	27	51	12	30	20
43	5	41	32	26	35	14	33	48	17	3	57	47

   Copy this grid of numbers.
   Shade the squares with   (a) factors of 36

   (b) multiples of 7

   (c) factors of 50

   (d) multiples of 11.

9.   10   FOR NUMBER = 1 TO 5
          20   PRINT 3 * NUMBER
          30   NEXT NUMBER
          40   END

   Write down the output from this program.
   Write a sentence to say what this program does.

10. Which 1-digit numbers are neither prime numbers nor square numbers?

11. Draw up a set of axes.
    Have x from 0 to 12. Have y from 0 to 10.
    Join these points in order. (1, 2) (1, 10) (6, 10) (11, 2) (11, 10) (1, 2) (6, 10) (11, 10)
    Now join these points in order. (11, 2) (1, 2) (11, 7)
    How many triangles are there altogether in your drawing?

12. This BASIC program will draw a rectangle.

```
10   MODE 1
20   MOVE 200, 300
30   DRAW 900, 300
40   DRAW 900, 700
50   DRAW 200, 700
60   DRAW 200, 300
70   END
```

Write a program in BASIC (or LOGO if you prefer) that will draw a triangle.

13.

Ellen drew these matchstick "stables".
A formula for finding the number of matchsticks needed to draw any of these is "multiply the number of matchsticks along the bottom by 4, then add 2".

Use this formula to find the number of matchsticks in the next "stable" in this pattern of "stables".

Check your answer by drawing the "stable" with 5 matchsticks along the bottom.

14. In the list 13, 14, 21, 35, 56 all the numbers, except 13, are multiples of 7.
Which number does not fit into these lists? Explain your answers.

(a)   1, 2, 3, 7, 17, 19   (b)   6, 24, 25, 36, 60

(c)   1, 2, 4, 9, 16, 25

15.   I am a prime number.
                      I am less than 30.
         The sum of my digits is a square number.

                    What number am I?

16. Write a program to calculate and print the first 20 square numbers.

17.

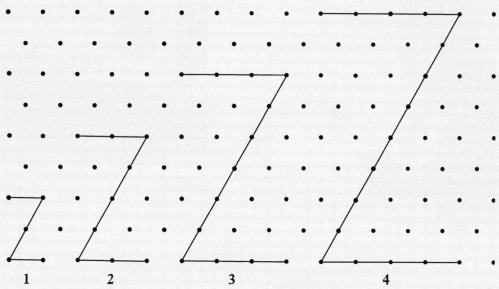

(a) 5 dots are needed to draw shape **1**.
    How many dots are needed to draw each of the other Z shapes?

(b) How many dots will be needed for the 5th Z in this pattern?

(c) How many dots will be needed to draw the 10th Z?

AROUND and ABOUT

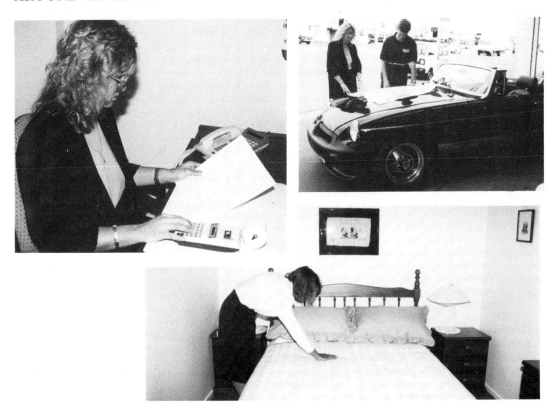

DISCUSSION EXERCISE 8:1

- Jane and James worked out how much it would cost for petrol on their journey from Horsham to Glasgow. Their car uses 1 litre of petrol every 15 kilometres. They first worked out how many litres they would use.

  To do this they used the formula   Litres needed $= \frac{\text{kilometres travelled}}{15}$.

  Then they used the formula   Cost = Litres needed × Price per litre.
  What other things might Jane and James want to work out?
  For which of these might they use a formula? **Discuss.**

- Emma calculated her weekly wage. The formula she used had things such as the overtime she worked. What other things might be in Emma's formula? **Discuss.**

- A cleaner in a hotel used the formula   Sheets = 2 × Beds   to decide how many sheets to take from the linen room. What other formulae might be used by other staff at the hotel? **Discuss.**

124

Using SYMBOLS for EXPRESSIONS and FORMULAE

```
10  FOR NUMBER = 1 TO 3
20  PRINT NUMBER + 7
30  NEXT NUMBER
40  END
```

This program is worked through as follows.

At line 10, NUMBER is given the value 1.
At line 20, NUMBER + 7 is calculated as $1 + 7 = 8$ and then 8 is printed.
At line 30, the program goes back to line 10.

At line 10, NUMBER is now given the value 2.
At line 20, NUMBER + 7 is calculated as $2 + 7 = 9$ and then 9 is printed.
At line 30, the program goes back to line 10.

At line 10, NUMBER is now given the value 3.
At line 20, NUMBER + 7 is calculated as $3 + 7 = 10$ and then 10 is printed.
At line 30, the program does not go back to line 10 as there is no NEXT NUMBER. The program now goes on to line 40.
At line 40, the program ends.

DISCUSSION EXERCISE 8:2

Program 1

```
10  FOR NUMBER = 1 TO 3
20  PRINT NUMBER + 7
30  NEXT NUMBER
40  END
```

Program 2

```
10  FOR N = 1 TO 3
20  PRINT N + 7
30  NEXT N
40  END
```

What is different about these two programs?
What is printed out by each of these programs? **Discuss.**

Both NUMBER + 7 and N + 7 are **expressions**.
NUMBER + 7 is an expression which is partly written in words. To be fully written in words it would be "NUMBER ADD ON SEVEN" or "ADD SEVEN TO NUMBER".
N + 7 is an expression which is written in **symbols**. SEVEN is written as 7, ADD is written as +, NUMBER is written as N.
Expressions written completely in symbols, like N + 7, are the types of expressions we use in algebra.

DISCUSSION EXERCISE 8:3

Program 3

```
10  FOR NUMBER = 1 TO 3
15  SUM = NUMBER + 7
20  PRINT SUM
30  NEXT NUMBER
40  END
```

Program 4

```
10  FOR N = 1 TO 3
15  S = N + 7
20  PRINT S
30  NEXT N
40  END
```

What is printed out by these programs? **Discuss.**

At line 15 of each of the above programs we have a **formula**.
Both SUM = NUMBER + 7 and S = N + 7 are formulae.

When we have named an expression, we have written a formula.
In the formula SUM = NUMBER + 7, the expression NUMBER + 7 has been named as SUM.
In the formula S = N + 7, the expression N + 7 has been named as S.

WRITING EXPRESSIONS and FORMULAE

Worked Example   A piece of Blackpool rock is x centimetres long. Dale breaks off a bit that is 2 centimetres long.

(a) Write an expression for the length that is left.

(b) Write a formula for the length that is left.

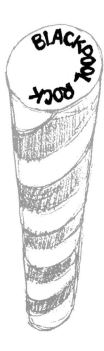

Answer (a) An expression for the length that is left is x – 2.

(b) We must name this expression to get our formula. We will name it L. Then the formula is L = x – 2.

Worked Example Boxes like this come in different heights.
The height of this one is h.
Write a formula for the height of another of
these boxes if its height is three times the
height of the one shown.

Answer An expression for the height of this other box is 3 × h.
A formula for the height is H = 3 × h.

In arithmetic 3 × 7 is the number twenty-one, 37 is the number thirty-seven.
In arithmetic 3 × 7 is not the same as 37.

In algebra 3n is the same as 3 × n. We can, and usually do, omit the
multiplication sign.

Example The formula H = 3 × h is usually written as H = 3h.

Notice that in the formulae L = x – 2 and H = 3h, small letters were used for the
expressions and capital letters were used to name the expression. This is also usual.

EXERCISE 8:4

1. There are 20 seats in each row in a theatre.
    How many seats are there in

    (a) 2 rows   (b) 5 rows   (c) 10 rows   (d) n rows?

2. Each box of maths. books has 10 books.
    How many books are there in

    (a) 2 boxes   (b) 10 boxes   (c) x boxes?

3. Theatre tickets cost £12 each.
    What is the cost of

    (a) 2 tickets   (b) 5 tickets   (c) t tickets?

4. Alex is 12 years old. How old will he be in

    (a) 5 years time   **(b)** 10 years time   **(c)** c years time?

5. There are n coins in this pile. Write an expression for the number of coins in a pile that has

    (a) 2 more coins

    (b) 5 fewer coins

    (c) four times as many coins

    (d) half as many coins

6. Using x to represent a number, write expressions for the following.

    (a) the sum of the number and 3   **(b)** three less than the number

    (c) three times the number   **(d)** four more than the number

    (e) half the number   **(f)** twice the number

7. Jars like the one shown come in different heights. The height of this one is h cm. Write a formula for the height, H, of a jar if its height is

    (a) twice the height of the one shown

    (b) four times the height of the one shown

    (c) two centimetres more than the one shown

    (d) three centimetres less than the one shown

    (e) three centimetres less than twice the height of the one shown

    (f) two centimetres more than three times the height of the one shown.

8. There are n coins in this pile.
Write a formula for V, the total value (in pence) of these n coins if

(a) they are all 10p coins

(b) they are all 20p coins

(c) they are all 50p coins.

Review 1 £5 is the cost of an all day pass on the Wendover buses.

What does it cost to buy   (a) 3 passes   (b) 30 passes   (c) t passes?

Review 2

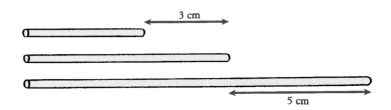

The middle straw is of length x.

Write expressions for the length of   (a) the top straw

(b) the bottom straw.

Review 3

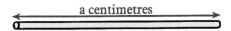

The length of this straw is **a** centimetres.

Write a formula for the length, L, of other straws if they are

(a) three times as long as this straw

(b) two centimetres shorter than this straw

(c) three centimetres longer than this straw

(d) half as long as this straw

(e) one centimetre less than twice the length of this straw.

USING FORMULAE

This is the same program that was on **page 126.**

At line 15, N is first replaced by 1.
Then S = N + 7 becomes S = 1 + 7
$$= 8$$

Program 4
```
10  FOR N = 1 TO 3
15  S = N + 7
20  PRINT S
30  NEXT N
40  END
```

The formula S = N + 7 was used to find S when N = 1.

Replacing a letter with a number is called **substituting in a formula.**

Worked Example   S = N + 7. Find the value of S when N = 3.

Answer S = N + 7   If N = 3, then S = 3 + 7
$$= 10$$

Worked Example   The formula H = 3h – 2 gives the height, H, of jars.
Find the height of a jar for which h = 5.

Answer H = 3h – 2   If h = 5, then H = 3 × 5 – 2
$$= 13$$

Worked Example | **C = 0·18n + d** |

This formula gives the charge C (in £) made by Mindy's Hire for the hire of glasses.
n is the number of glasses hired and d is the deposit.
If fewer than 50 glasses are hired then d = £5.
If 50 or more glasses are hired then d = £10.

(a)   Ann hires 25 glasses. What does Ann pay?

(b)   What does Cameron pay if he hires 95 glasses?

Answer (a)   C = 0·18n + d   If n = 25, d = 5 then C = 0·18 × 25 + 5
$$= £9·50$$

(b)   C = 0·18n + d   If n = 95, d = 10 then C = 0·18 × 95 + 10
$$= £27·10$$

EXERCISE 8:5

1. A car salesman earns £200 a week basic salary and an extra £100 for every car he sells. His weekly salary (**S**) is given by the formula $\boxed{\mathbf{S = 200 + 100n}}$ where **n** is the number of cars he sells. How much is his weekly salary if in that week he sells

    (a) 4 cars   (b) 3 cars   (c) no cars   (d) 1 car?

2. An LP record plays for 20 minutes and a single for 7 minutes. $\boxed{\mathbf{t = 20a + 7b}}$ gives the total playing time if **a** is the number of LPs played and **b** is the number of singles played. Use this formula to find the total playing time of

    (a) 1 LP and 4 singles   (b) 2 LPs and 3 singles.

3. The distance a frog jumps depends on the temperature. The warmer it is, the further it jumps. $\boxed{\mathbf{D = 3 + 2T}}$ is a formula that Jamie worked out for the distance **D** (in cm) that his frog could jump if the temperature was **T** degrees. Find the distance that Jamie's frog could jump if the temperature was

    (a) 10°   (b) 15°   (c) 20°.

4. $\boxed{h = \dfrac{28-a}{2}}$ is thought to be a formula which gives the number of hours of sleep that a child needs.
    h is the number of hours of sleep.
    a is the age, in years, of the child.

    Copy and complete this table.

a	2	4	6	8	10	12
h	13					

5. Delia's fish and chip shop sells fish at £1·75 a piece and chips at 60p a scoop.

   (a) Copy and complete this price list.

   (b) The cost of each take-away meal of fish and chips is given by the formula

   $$\text{Cost} = 1\text{·}75f + 0\text{·}6c$$

   f is the number of pieces of fish and **c** is the number of scoops of chips. Using this formula, find the cost of 10 pieces of fish and 3 scoops of chips.

DELIA'S		
Fish	**Chips**	**Price**
1	1	£2·35
2	1	£4·10
3	2	
3	3	
4	3	
4	4	
5	4	

6.

$$\text{Cost} = 55 + 35\,(h - 1)$$

This is the formula which gives the cost (in £) of each of the cars that Darryl is hiring for his wedding. **h** is the number of hours for which the cars will be hired.

How much will it cost to hire each car for 3 hours?

7. $S = 20 + 4t$ is a formula which gives the distance, **S** metres, travelled in **t** seconds by a car going downhill.

   What distance is travelled in   (a) 10 seconds   (b) 1 minute?

8. Jon set up a circuit and found that the formula $V = 5I$ gave the voltage, **V** volts, when the current was **I** amps.

   Find the voltage when the current was   (a) 10 amps   (b) 5 amps.

Review 1 A live-in nanny is paid £5 an hour. Each week £30 is taken for board. The nanny's weekly earnings are given by the formula $\boxed{\textbf{E = 5h – 30}}$ where **h** is the number of hours worked in that week.
Find this nanny's earnings for a week in which 45 hours were worked.

Review 2 Rose works in a clothing factory. She does the finishing sewing of sweatshirts; sewing on the ribbing at the cuffs, neckband and waistband. She is paid on a bonus system and her hourly wage (in £) is given by

$\boxed{\textbf{Hourly wage = 3·45 + 0·15n}}$ where **n** is the number of sweatshirts

over 44 that she finishes in 1 hour. What is her hourly wage if she finishes

(a) 44 sweatshirts   (b) 52 sweatshirts   (c) 40 sweatshirts?

PUZZLES 8:6

1. Replace each of the letters with one of the digits 0, 1, 2, 3, 4, 5, 6, 7, 8, 9 so that the additions are correct.

(a)
```
  S O M E
+   C A N
---------
  H E A R
```

(b)
```
    S U N
+ B U R N
---------
F E V E R
```

(c)
```
  F O U R
+ F I V E
---------
  N I N E
```

Is there more than one possible answer?

2. Replace each of the letters by one of the digits 0, 1, 2, 3, 4, 5, 6, 7, 8, 9 so that the subtractions are correct.

(a)
```
  F I V E
– F O U R
---------
    O N E
```

(b)
```
  S E V E N
–   F O U R
-----------
  T H R E E
```

Is there more than one possible answer?

FIND the NUMBER

> *I think of a number.*
> *I multiply by 4, then subtract 3.*
> *The result is 25.*
> *What is the number?*

The answer to this sort of problem can be found by using the following steps.

Step 1   Choose a number.

Step 2   Check to see if this number works.

Step 3   Repeat steps 1 and 2 until a number that works is found.

Worked Example   I think of a number.
When I multiply by 4, then subtract 3 the result is 25.

What is the number?

Answer   Try 1. $1 \times 4 = 4, 4 - 3 = 1$ The result is not 25.
Try 5. $5 \times 4 = 20, 20 - 3 = 17$ The result is not 25.
Try 10. $10 \times 4 = 40, 40 - 3 = 37$ The result is not 25.
Try 8. $8 \times 4 = 32, 32 - 3 = 29$ The result is not 25.
Try 7. $7 \times 4 = 28, 28 - 3 = 25$ The result is 25.

The number is 7.

PRACTICAL EXERCISE 8:7

1.   Make up a problem as follows.

Step 1   Begin with a whole number less than 10. For instance, 8.

Step 2   Multiply by a number less than 6. For instance, 5.
(You will now have $5 \times 8 = 40$.)

Step 3   Add a number less than 20. For instance 4.
(You will now have $40 + 4 = 44$.)

Step 4   Write your problem in words. For instance, the problem from the above is "I think of a number. When I multiply this number by 5, then add 4 the result is 44. What is the number I thought of?"

Give your problem to your group to solve.

2. Make up more problems.
    Change what you do at **Steps 2 and 3** for each problem. You may like to sometimes divide and subtract as well as multiply and add.

    Give your problems to your group, or to another group, to solve.

3. Make up "real-life" problems such as "When I subtract 3 from double my sister's age the answer is 23. How old is my sister?"

    Give your problems to another group, or to your class, to solve.

EXERCISE 8:8

1. (a) I think of a number.
        When I multiply by 4, then add 1 the result is 29.

        What is the number?

    (b) I think of a number.
        I divide by 2, then add 3. The result is 8.

        What is the number?

    (c) I think of a number.
        I add 5, then double the answer. The result is 22.

        What is the number?

    (d) I think of a number.
        I subtract 2, then multiply the answer by 3. The result is 54.

        What is the number?

    (e) I think of a number.
        I divide by 3, then double the answer. The result is 16.

        What is the number?

2. A bus began at the bus station with 24 people.
    At the first stop 4 got off and some got on.
    At the second stop, no one got off but 3 got on.
    There were then 34 people.

    How many got on at the first stop?

3. When Jenny asked Elizabeth how many books she had read in the holidays, Elizabeth replied as follows.
    "If you multiply the number of books by 3, then subtract 5 the answer will be 22."

    How many books did Elizabeth read?

4. Three added to double Bik's house number is 53.

    What is Bik's house number?

5. (a) Five is added to a number and the answer is halved. The result is 11.
        What is the number?

    (b) Eight is taken from a number and the answer is doubled. The result is 30.
        What is the number?

6. At Covent Garden station the number of passengers halved. At the next station 23 got off and 7 got on. There were then 25 passengers.

    How many got off at Covent Garden?

7. Samantha and Barbara worked out that if they multiplied Barbara's house number by 5, then divided by 2 they would get Samantha's house number.

    If Samantha's house number is 20, what is Barbara's?

Review 1 I think of a number.
          I double it, then subtract 5.
          The result is 13.

          What is the number?

Review 2 Zeke welded two equal lengths of steel together.
          He then cut off 3cm to get a length of 13cm.

          How long was each piece of steel that Zeke welded together?

WHAT   WHEN   WHERE   WHO   HOW   WHY

What would someone in the travel industry use formulae for?

When might an accountant in a department store use a formula?

Where, in your other subjects, could you use formulae?

Who, in your school, do you think would use formulae? What would they use these for?

How and when might an interior decorator use a formula?

Why might a cook or book publisher want to use formulae?

AROUND and ABOUT

DISCUSSION EXERCISE 9:1

Engineers often work with expressions that have letters which stand for numbers. Think of other people who work with expressions of this sort. **Discuss.**

Why do you think letters are often used instead of numbers? **Discuss.**

MULTIPLYING

DISCUSSION EXERCISE 9:2

Is ab the same as ba?   Is 3ab the same as 3ba? **Discuss.**

As part of your discussion, replace **a** and **b** with many different numbers. That is, choose a number for **a** and a number for **b**. Substitute these into ab, ba, 3ab, 3ba. Repeat, using different numbers for **a** and **b**.

Just as $2 \times a$ is written as 2a, $a \times b$ is written as ab.
$a \times a$ could be written as aa; in fact $a \times a$ is written as a^2, just as 3×3 is written as 3^2.

EXERCISE 9:3

---

1. Simplify.

   (a) $6 \times a$ (b) $x \times x$ (c) $3 \times e$ (d) $a \times w$ (e) $b \times b$

   (f) $b \times x$ (g) $4 \times x$ (h) $5 \times b$ (i) $2 \times y$ (j) $x \times y$

   (k) $a \times y$ (l) $5 \times ac$ (m) $2 \times xy$ (n) $3 \times ab$ (o) $a \times bc$

   (p) $2 \times bx$ (q) $3a \times b$ (r) $4x \times y$ (s) $bc \times xy$ (t) $ab \times cd$

   (u) $4 \times a \times c$ (v) $2 \times x \times x$ (w) $3 \times a \times b$ (x) $7a \times a$

2. Copy this chart.

5	3	6	7	1	1	7	1	6		8	2	6	3	5	4	8
				N	N		N									

   Match the expressions in **Box A** with those in **Box B** and complete the chart.
   For example, **N** is filled in as shown since expression **1.** is the same as expression **N**.

<table>
<tr><td colspan="2">Box A</td><td colspan="2">Box B</td></tr>
<tr><td>1. $3 \times h$</td><td>5. $1 \times h$</td><td>A. 3ab</td><td>I. 5a</td></tr>
<tr><td>2. $2 \times a$</td><td>6. $h \times h$</td><td>B. h</td><td>L. 2a</td></tr>
<tr><td>3. $a \times h$</td><td>7. $5 \times a$</td><td>E. ah</td><td>N. 3h</td></tr>
<tr><td>4. $5 \times a \times h$</td><td>8. $3 \times ab$</td><td>G. h^2</td><td>R. 5ah</td></tr>
</table>

Review Simplify these expressions.

(a) $p \times p$ (b) $4 \times h$ (c) $9 \times a$ (d) $q \times q$

(e) $7 \times p$ (f) $3p \times q$ (g) $2 \times ap$ (h) $cd \times ey$

(i) $5 \times b \times x$ (j) $2y \times y$

ADDING and SUBTRACTING

DISCUSSION EXERCISE 9:4

Is $a + b$ the same as $b + a$?   Is $5a + 3a = 8a$?

Is $5a - 3a = 2a$?   Is $3a + 4b = 7ab$?

Is $5a + 4b + 3a + 7b = 8a + 11b$?   Is $5a + 4b - 3a - 7b = 2a - 3b$?

Discuss. As part of your discussion replace **a** and **b** with many different numbers.

Examples

1. $5n + 6n = 11n$

2. $5n - n = 5n - 1n$
   $$= 4n$$

3. $5n + 2n + 6n = 13n$

4. $5n + 2n - 6n = 7n - 6n$
   $$= n$$

5. $5a - 2a + 3a = 3a + 3a$
   $$= 6a$$

6. $3a + a + 5m + 6m = 4a + 11m$

7. $3a + 4m + 2a + 5m = 3a + 2a + 4m + 5m$
   $$= 5a + 9m$$

8. $5a + 3m - a + 2m = 5a - a + 3m + 2m$
   $$= 4a + 5m$$

9. $5a - 4m - a + 6m = 5a - a - 4m + 6m$
   $$= 4a + 2m$$

10. $5a - 4m - a - 3m = 5a - a - 4m - 3m$
    $$= 4a - 7m$$

EXERCISE 9:5

1. Simplify these expressions.

    (a) 5n + 3n   (b) 6a – 3a   (c) 5n – 3n   (d) 5x + 2x

    (e) 5a + a   (f) 5n – n   (g) 4x + 4x   (h) 3c + 5c

    (i) 7n – n

2. (a) ⟵ x ⟶ [diagram] Two equal parts, each of length **y,** are added to each end of this diagram. The total length will then be

    A. x + y   B. x – 2y   C. x + 2y   D. 2y – x.

    (b) ⟵ a ⟶ [diagram] Two equal parts, each of length **x,** are taken off each end of this diagram. The total length will then be

    A. a – 2x   B. 2x – a   C. a + 2x   D. x + 2a.

    (c) ⟵ c ⟶ [diagram] A length **x** is added to one end and a length **b** is added to the other end of this diagram. The total length is then

    A. c + b – x   B. c – x + b   C. c + b + x   D. x + b – c.

    (d) ⟵ x ⟶ [diagram] A length **x** is added to one end and a length **y** is added to the other end of this diagram. The total length is then

    A. x + 2y   B. 2x + y   C. 2x – y   D. x + y.

    (e) ⟵ a ⟶ [diagram] A length **a** is added to one end and a length **y** is taken off the other end of this diagram. The new length is

    A. 2a – y   B. 2a + y   C. 2y + a   D. 2y – a.

    (f) ⟵ c ⟶ [diagram] A length **a** is taken off one end and a length **c** is added to the other end. The new length is

    A. a – c   B. 2c – a   C. c – 2a   D. 2c + a.

3. Copy the two columns of boxes.

   Look at the following additions and subtractions. If the answer is **wrong** shade the box beside the question. The unshaded boxes you have left at the end should make a sentence.

   For example, **1.** is **wrong** so the box is shaded as shown.

   1. $8x + 3x = 24x$ $\boxed{S}$ 13. $2x + 2x + 2x = 6x$ $\boxed{D}$

   2. $4n + 4n = 8n$ $\boxed{C}$ 14. $8a - 8a + 3a = 4a$ $\boxed{S}$

   3. $7d - 3d = 10d$ $\boxed{R}$ 15. $11b - 4b + b = 8b$ $\boxed{O}$

   4. $5x - 2x + 3x = 6x$ $\boxed{A}$ 16. $2b + b + b = 4b$ $\boxed{I}$

   5. $3n - 2n + n = 2n$ $\boxed{R}$ 17. $9x + 4x - 9x = 5x$ $\boxed{A}$

   6. $4a - a - a = a$ $\boxed{T}$ 18. $a + a + a - a = 2a$ $\boxed{N}$

   7. $8x + 2x - 3x = 7x$ $\boxed{R}$ 19. $9n - n - 4n = 4n$ $\boxed{G}$

   8. $6b + b - b = 6b$ $\boxed{Y}$ 20. $4d - 4d = 0$ $\boxed{W}$

   9. $5n - n + 2n = 7n$ $\boxed{S}$ 21. $3x - 2x - x = x$ $\boxed{T}$

   10. $7x - 3x - x = 3x$ $\boxed{O}$ 22. $9x - 5x - 4x = 0$ $\boxed{E}$

   11. $8x - x = 8x$ $\boxed{O}$ 23. $3x - x - x = x$ $\boxed{L}$

   12. $4a + a - a = 4a$ $\boxed{N}$ 24. $5a + 2a - 7a = 0$ $\boxed{L}$

4. Rebecca has 3 sandwiches and 2 apples for her lunch. Her brother James has 2 sandwiches and 5 apples.

   (a) How many sandwiches do they have between them?

   (b) How many apples do they have between them?

5. Choose the correct answer for these.

   (a) $4x + 2x + 3a + 5a =$ **A.** $14xa$ **B.** $6x + 8a$ **C.** $8x + 15a$

   (b) $4x + 2n + 2n + 6x =$ **A.** $10x + 4n$ **B.** $24x + 4n$ **C.** $14xn$

   (c) $9b + 5a - 6a - 3b =$ **A.** $12b + 11a$ **B.** $6b + 11a$ **C.** $6b - a$

   (d) $4b - 4c + 3c - b =$ **A.** $3b - c$ **B.** $3b - 7c$ **C.** $3b + c$

   (e) $7x - 4a - 6x - 3a =$ **A.** $13x + 7a$ **B.** $x + 7a$ **C.** $x - 7a$

   (f) $4n - 3d + 8n - 3d =$ **A.** $12n + 6d$ **B.** $12n - 6d$ **C.** $12n$

   (g) $6a + 3b - 4a - 2b =$ **A.** $2a + b$ **B.** $10a + 5b$ **C.** $2a - b$

Review Simplify these.

   (a) $9a + 3a$ (b) $9x - x$ (c) $9x + 2x - 7x$

   (d) $9a - 3a + 7x$ (e) $9a + 3x + 7a - 2x$ (f) $9a - 3x + 7a - 2x$

REMOVING BRACKETS

There are n twenty pence coins in this pile.
The total value of these coins is 20n pence.

Suppose another 3 twenty pence coins are added to the pile.
The total value is now $20n + 20 \times 3$.

The total value of this bigger pile can also be worked out as
follows:
There are now n + 3 coins in the pile.
Total value is $20(n + 3)$.

Then $20(n + 3)$ must be equal to $20n + 20 \times 3$
   i.e. $20(n + 3) = 20n + 20 \times 3$

This shows us how to **remove brackets.** Everything inside the
brackets must be multiplied by the number outside.

Examples   1. $2(a + 5) = 2a + 10$ 2. $2(a - 5) = 2a - 10$

3. $2(a + 5x) = 2a + 10x$ 4. $3(2a - 3x) = 6a - 9x$

5. $2(a + 5) + 3(2a + 1) = 2a + 10 + 6a + 3$
$$= 2a + 6a + 10 + 3$$
$$= 8a + 13$$

EXERCISE 9:6

1. Write without brackets.

(a) $3(x + 2)$ (b) $4(a - 5)$ (c) $5(2p + 3)$ (d) $4(3 + 2r)$

(e) $2(2a - 5)$ (f) $3(6 - 5a)$ (g) $3(4x + 1)$ (h) $5(1 - 2x)$

(i) $2(x + y)$ (j) $2(x + 3a)$ (k) $3(a - 2b)$ (l) $3(2x - 5a)$

(m) $4(2a + x)$ (n) $3(x - 3a)$ (o) $3(2y - x)$ (p) $4(6a + 5b)$

2. Remove the brackets and simplify.

(a) $3(x + 4) + 2(x + 1)$ (b) $4(a + 3) + 3(a + 2)$

(c) $2(2x + 3) + 3(x + 4)$ (d) $3(a + 5) + 2(2a + 1)$

(e) $3(a - 4) + 2(3a + 1)$ (f) $4(b + 5) + 3(1 + 5b)$

(g) $2(3x - 1) + 3(x + 4)$ (h) $2(3 - 2a) + 3(1 + 4a)$

(i) $5(3 - 2x) + 4(5x + 1)$ (j) $5a + 2(3 + a)$

(k) $3(5y + 2) - 5$ (l) $6a + 3 + 2(3a + 2)$

(m) $4(1 - y) + 2y$

3. The formula for the perimeter of a rectangle is **P = 2 (l + b)**, where *l* is the length and **b** is the breadth.

Write this formula without the brackets.

Review 1   Remove the brackets.

(a) $2(a - 7)$ (b) $3(4x + 1)$ (c) $2(a + 3b)$ (d) $5(3 - 4x)$

Review 2   Remove the brackets and simplify.

(a) $2(3a + 2) + 3(a + 7)$ (b) $5(1 - 2x) + 4(3x + 2)$

(c) $5(3x - 2) - 7$ (d) $2x + 3(2 + x)$

GAME 9:7

BRACKETS: a game for a group

Preparation Copy these cards. Make 3 of each.

3n	2n	3x	2x	−2n	−2x
6	− 6	5n	5x	n	x
3 (n + 2)	2 (n − 3)	2 (n + 3)	3 (n − 2)	3 (x + 2)	3 (x − 2)

The Game

The dealer deals 3 cards (face down) to each player; then places the next card face up on the table with the remainder of the pack face down beside the upturned card.

The object of the game is to get a set of 3 cards that make a correct statement.

For example,

− 6	3 (n − 2)	3n

is a winning set of 3 cards since $3 (n − 2) = 3n − 6$

The Play

The dealer plays first; then the other players in turn, beginning with the player on the dealer's left.
When it is a person's turn to play they may either

(1) Say the 3 cards in their hand is a winning set.

or (2) Pick up the card face up on the table if they think this card will help them get a winning set **and** discard one of the cards from their hand.

or (3) Pick up a card from the pack **and** discard one of the cards from their hand.

Rules

No card on the table may be picked up unless it is on the top of the upturned pile.
The first person to get a winning set of 3 cards scores 1 point and is the dealer for the next round.

continued . . .

. . . *from previous page*

If a player declares a winning set which is in fact not a winning set, this player loses one point.

The game is over after a set time (15 minutes is reasonable).

The winner is the person with the highest score when the time is up. Each player should keep a score card and enter a tick ✓ for each point scored or lost.

Score Card	
Points Scored	✓ ✓ ✓ ✓
Points Lost	✓ ✓
Final Score	3

WHAT WHEN WHERE WHO HOW WHY

What other times in maths. might you need to simplify expressions?

When might a landscape gardener need to simplify expressions?

Where, in your other subjects, might you need to simplify expressions?

Who, in a zoo, might need to simplify expressions?

How might an understanding of simplifying expressions help the organisers of the Olympics?

Why might people who work with money sometimes need to simplify expressions?

1. Pick-your-own fruit costs 89 pence per kg.

   What is the cost of   (a) 2kg   (b) 3kg   (c) x kg?

2. ⟦ **d = 60t** ⟧ is a formula which gives the distance, **d** in kilometres, travelled by Claire's car in **t** hours.

   How far does this car travel in   (a) 4 hours   (b) 30 minutes?

3. (a) I think of a number.
       I double this number, then
         subtract 8.
       The result is 10.

       What is the number?

   (b) I think of a number.
       I add 7, then halve the answer.
       The result is 16.

       What is the number?

4. Choose the correct answer.

   (a) $3(2a - 1) =$ A. 6a – 1   B. 6a – 3   C. 2a – 3   D. 3a

   (b) $4(3 + 5x) =$ A. 12 + 20x   B. 12 + 5x   C. 3 + 20x   D. 32x

   (c) $2(3x - 4a) =$ A. 6x – 4a   B. 3x – 8a   C. 6x – 8a   D. 8a – 6x

5. Bracelets cost £6 each.

   (a) How much do n bracelets cost?

   (b) Write a formula for the cost, C in pounds, of n bracelets.

6. In a quiz programme, the contestants begin with £x. They gain £5 for each question they answer correctly; they lose £10 for each question they answer incorrectly or are unable to answer.
Write expressions for the amount of money contestants would have if

   (a) they answer all 10 questions correctly

   (b) they do not get any of the 10 questions correct

   (c) they answer 8 of the 10 correctly

   (d) they answer half of the 10 questions correctly.

7. Jared counted the number of people in a queue for a chairlift.
After a few minutes, 7 more people had joined the queue and 3 had left.
There were then 10 people in the queue.

How many were in the queue when Jared first counted?

8. Copy this chart.

10	4	7	6	2	9	10		3	9	10	1	5	8	1	6
											C		C		

Simplify the expressions in **Box A**. Match with the answer in **Box B** and fill in the chart.
For example, $7a - 6a = a$, so **1.** matches with **C** and **C** is filled in as shown on the chart.

Box A

1.	$7a - 6a$	**6.**	$7a - 2a + a$
2.	$5 \times a$	**7.**	$a + a$
3.	$6a + 3a$	**8.**	$2(3n + a)$
4.	$a \times a$	**9.**	$4n - 5a + 2n + 6a$
5.	$5a + 2a + a$	**10.**	$3(2a - 3n)$

Box B

A.	$6a - 9n$	**I.**	$6n + 2a$
B.	$5a$	**L.**	a^2
C.	a	**P.**	$9a$
E.	$6a$	**R.**	$6n + a$
G.	$2a$	**T.**	$8a$

9. Professor Kofy found by experiment that to make "excellent" coffee in a percolator two teaspoons for each person plus three more teaspoons of coffee was needed.

   T = 2p + 3   is the formula for this.

   T is the total number of teaspoons needed and **p** is the number of people having coffee. How many teaspoons of coffee are needed for

   (a) 2 people   (b) 5 people   (c) 8 people?

10. Remove the brackets and simplify.

    (a) $2(x + 3) + 4(1 + 2x)$ (b) $5x + 3(2x + 3)$

    (c) $3(2 - 5a) + 2(3a + 5)$

11. Sarah threw the javelin x metres.
    Ann threw the javelin 13 metres further than Sarah.
    Philippa threw the javelin twice as far as Sarah.

    Write expressions for the distance   (a) Ann threw the javelin

    (b) Philippa threw the javelin.

12. Marie's lucky number is 7.
    Riffet said that if 10 was added to hers and the result divided by 2 you would get Marie's.

    What is Riffet's lucky number?

SHAPE, SPACE and MEASURES

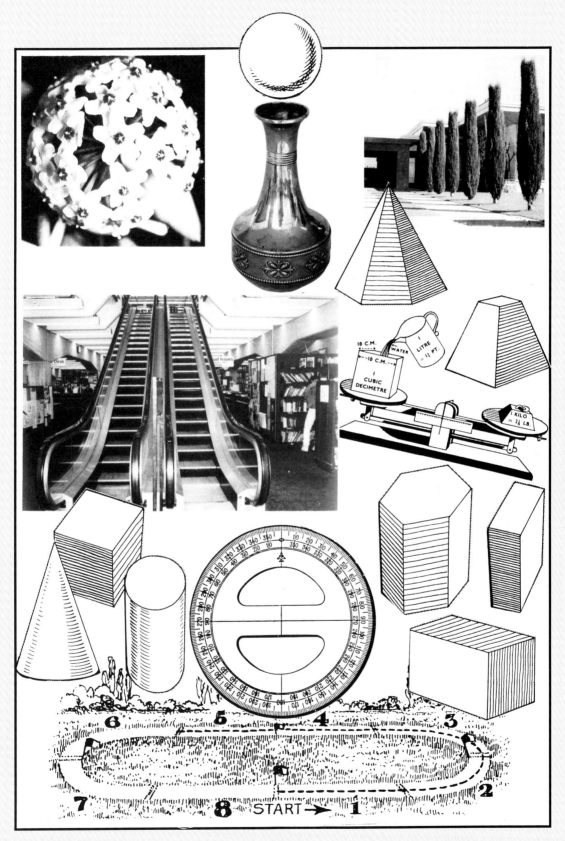

Shape, Space and Measures from Previous Levels

REVISION

LINES

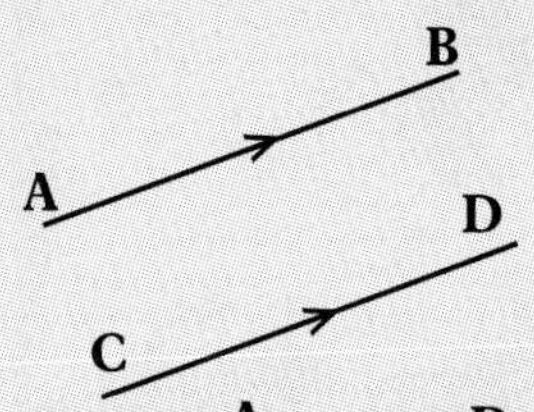

Parallel lines are always the same distance apart.
We put arrows on lines to show they are parallel.
AB // CD is read as "AB is parallel to CD".

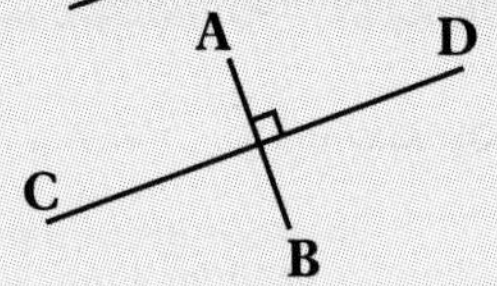

Perpendicular lines are at right angles.
AB ⊥ CD is read as "AB is perpendicular to CD".

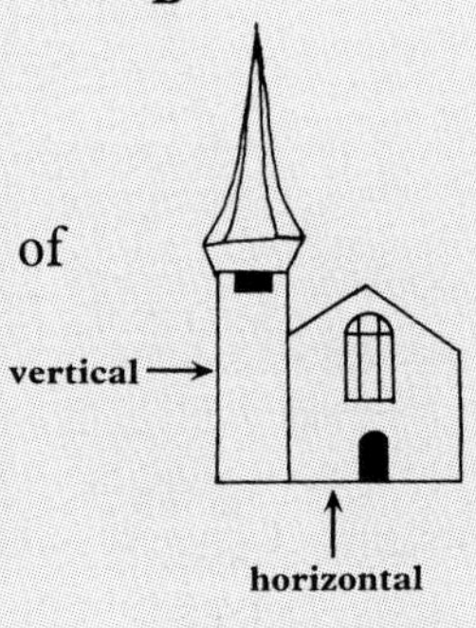

A vertical line, or surface, is perpendicular to the surface of the earth.

A horizontal line, or surface, is parallel to the horizon.

vertical →

↑ horizontal

2-D SHAPES

Triangle   Square   Rectangle   Pentagon   Hexagon   Circle

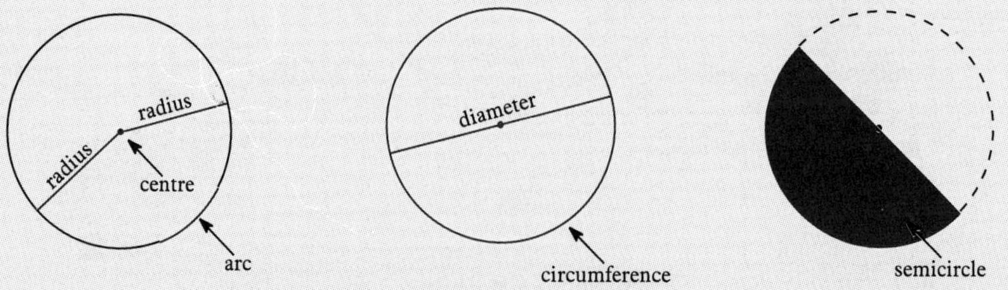

radius   radius
centre
arc

diameter

circumference

semicircle

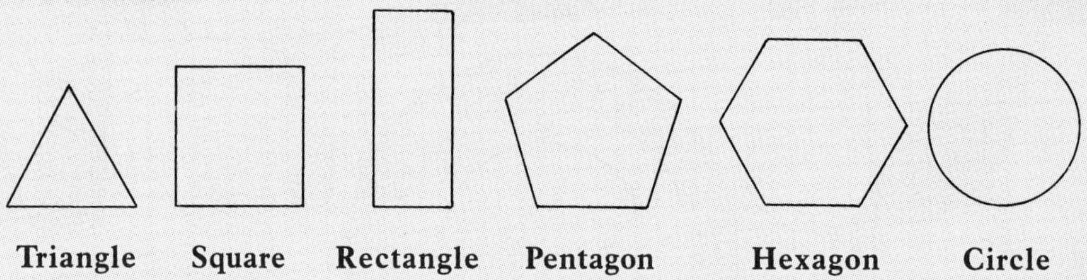

continued . . .

. . . from previous page

3-D SHAPES

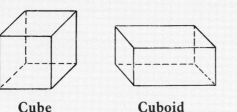 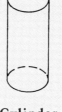 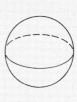

Cube	**Cuboid** **(Rectangular Box)**	**Cylinder**	**Sphere**

FACES, EDGES, VERTICES

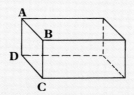

A **face** is a flat surface.
For instance, the above shape has 6 faces; a top face, a bottom face, a front face, a back face, and two side faces. One of the side faces is ABCD.

An **edge** is a line where two faces meet.
For instance, the above shape has 12 edges. Four of these are AB, DC, AD, BC.

A **vertex** is a corner where edges meet. (**Vertices** is the plural of vertex.)
For instance, the above shape has 8 vertices. Four of these are A, B, C, D.

NETS

A **net** of a 3-D shape is the shape that can be cut out of a flat piece of cardboard or paper and folded to make the 3-D shape.

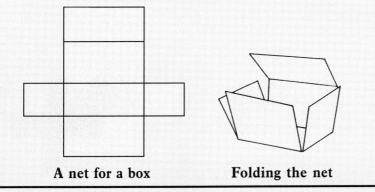 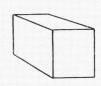

A net for a box	**Folding the net**	**The completed box**

continued . . .

. . . from previous page

CONGRUENCE

Congruent shapes are identical. They are the same shape
are the same size
have angles the same size
have sides the same length.

Congruent 3-D shapes have angles and edges and faces of the same size.

SYMMETRY

A shape has **reflective symmetry** if it can be folded so that one half fits exactly onto the other half.

For instance: This shape is symmetrical about the dotted line.
The dotted line is called a **line of symmetry**.

For instance: This shape is not symmetrical about the dotted line.

For instance: This shape is symmetrical about the shaded plane.
The shaded plane is called a **plane of symmetry**.

A shape has **rotational symmetry** if it fits onto itself more than once during a complete turn.

The number of times a shape will fit onto itself in one complete turn is called the **order of rotational symmetry**.

For instance, this shape has rotational symmetry of order 4.

continued . . .

COMPASS DIRECTIONS

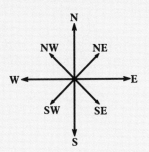

A Northerly wind blows *from* the North. A South-Westerly wind blows *from* the South-West.

TRANSLATION, ROTATION, REFLECTION

This arrow shows a movement in a **clockwise direction**.

This arrow shows a movement in an **anticlockwise direction**.

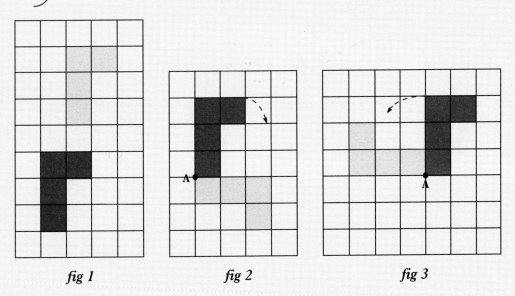

| *fig 1* | *fig 2* | *fig 3* |

fig 1 shows a **translation** (or **straight movement**). The red shape has been translated 1 square to the right and 4 squares up to the shaded shape.

fig 2 and *fig 3* show **rotation** (or **turning movement**).

In *fig 2* the red shape has been rotated clockwise about A, through $\frac{1}{4}$ turn or 1 right angle.

In *fig 3* the red shape has been rotated anticlockwise about A, through $\frac{1}{4}$ turn.

continued . . .

... *from previous page*

This diagram shows **reflection** (or **flip movement**).

The **image** of a shape reflected in a mirror line
is congruent with the shape.
Each point on the image is the same distance
from the mirror line as the corresponding point
on the shape.

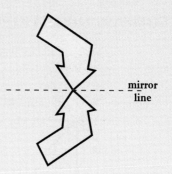

mirror
line

MEASURES

Commonly used **metric units** are:

      Length: kilometre (km), metre (m), centimetre (cm), millimetre (mm)

      Capacity: litre (*l* or L), millilitre (m*l* or mL)

      Mass: tonne (t), kilogram (kg), gram (g), milligram (mg)

CONSTRUCTIONS

Triangles may be constructed using a **compass and ruler.**

For instance, to construct a triangle with sides 5·5cm, 3cm, 3·8cm take these
steps.

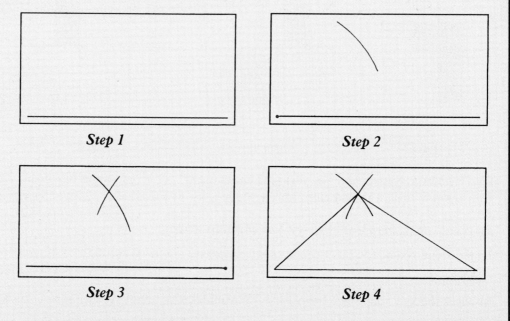

Step 1   *Step 2*

Step 3   *Step 4*

continued ...

... *from previous page*

Step 1   Draw a line 5·5cm long.

Step 2   Open the compass out to 3cm. Put the compass point on the left-hand end of the line. Draw an arc.

Step 3   Open the compass out to 3·8cm. Put the compass point on the right-hand end of the line. Draw an arc which crosses the arc drawn in Step 2.

Step 4   Complete the triangle.

Parallel lines may be drawn with a set square and ruler. The diagrams below show how to draw a line through C which is parallel to AB. (The set square is shown shaded.)

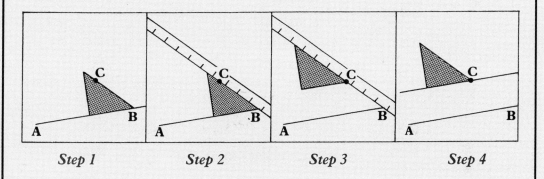

| *Step 1* | *Step 2* | *Step 3* | *Step 4* |

Step 1   Place the set square as shown.

Step 2   Place the ruler as shown.

Step 3   Holding the ruler still, slide the set square along the ruler until C is in the position shown.

Step 4   Remove the ruler. Draw the parallel line.

PERIMETER, AREA, VOLUME

The distance right around the outside of a shape is called the **perimeter**. Perimeter is measured in mm, cm, m or km.

continued ...

. . . *from previous page*

The amount of surface a shape covers is called the **area**. Area is measured in mm², cm², m² or km².

We can count squares to find area. The area of each of these squares is 1cm². Since there are 12 squares in this rectangle, its area is 12cm².

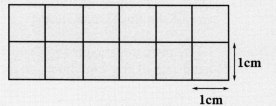

1cm

1cm

The **volume** of a shape is the amount of space it takes up. Volume is measured in mm³, cm³, m³.

We can count cubes to find volume. There are 72 cubes in this shape. If each cube measures 1cm by 1cm by 1cm, the volume of each is 1cm³. The volume of the shape is then 72cm³.

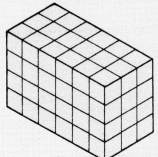

REVISION EXERCISE

1. (a) How many right angles are there in this "picture"?

   (b) How many triangles are there altogether?

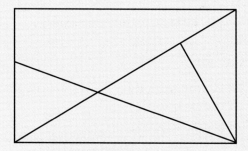

2. Items priced as follows were bought at the supermarket:

   £1·45, £3·99, £1·95, 45p, £25·68, £5·40, £1·76, £2·85, £4·99, £1·20, 97p, 99p, £1·48, £2·39, 99p, 98p

   (a) Estimate if £60 would cover the bill.

   (b) Now add to check how good your estimate was.

3.

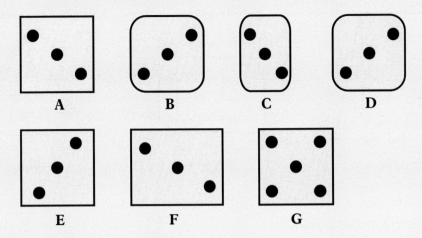

(a) Which of these are congruent?

(b) Which has no axes of symmetry?

(c) Which have rotational symmetry of order 2?

4. At an athletics meeting, the 400 metres relay times for the 4 teams competing were as follows:

	Runner 1	Runner 2	Runner 3	Runner 4
Team 1	10·31 sec	10·04 sec	10·46 sec	10·09 sec
Team 2	9·98 sec	10·68 sec	10·10 sec	10·18 sec
Team 3	10·06 sec	10·13 sec	10·24 sec	10·01 sec
Team 4	10·53 sec	10·96 sec	10·42 sec	10·18 sec

(a) Which team came first and what was the total time for the 400 metres for this team?

(b) What was the total time taken by team 2?

(c) Which team came last and in what total time?

5. How many planes of symmetry do these shapes have?

(a)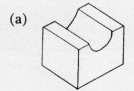

(b)

6.

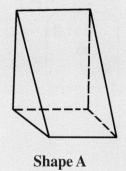

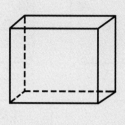

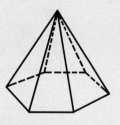

Shape A   **Shape B**   **Shape C**

(a) What is shape B called?

(b) The bottom face of shape C has 6 edges. This face is called a

   A. pentagon   **B.** hexagon   **C.** octagon.

(c) How many edges does shape C have?

(d) How many vertices does shape B have?

(e) How many faces does shape A have?

7.

kg	g	tonne	mg	*l*	m*l*	km	m	cm	mm

Which of the units in the box would be used to measure the following?

(a) the amount of paint needed to paint a room

(b) the weight of a bird's egg

(c) the length of a runway at the airport at Eastleigh

(d) the weight of a ship

(e) the thickness of the lead in a pencil

(f) the amount of cream in a cat's bowl

(g) the distance a hiker walked last weekend

(h) the mass of a leaf

8. What measurements are given by the pointers?

(a)

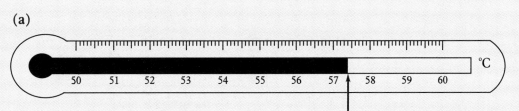

(b)

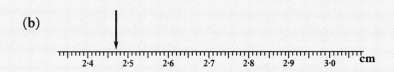

9. Each small cube measures 1cm by 1cm by 1cm.
Count cubes to find the volume of each shape.

(a)   **(b)**   **(c)**

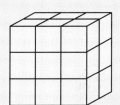   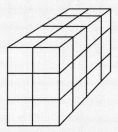   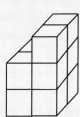

10. Write these times as they would appear on a 24-hour clock.

(a) 9·24a.m.   (b) 2a.m.   (c) 3·45p.m.   (d) five minutes to midnight

11. Write these 24-hour clock times as a.m. or p.m. times.

(a) 0400   (b) 0823   (c) 1415   (d) 2340   (e) 1700

12. (a) What is the order of rotational symmetry
of this shape?

(b) How many lines of symmetry are there?

161

13. In which direction (N, S, E, W, NE, NW, SE or SW) are the cars on these streets travelling?

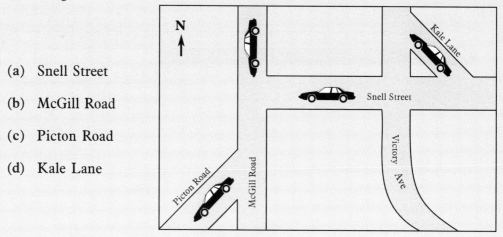

   (a) Snell Street

   (b) McGill Road

   (c) Picton Road

   (d) Kale Lane

14. Find the length of these.

   (a)

   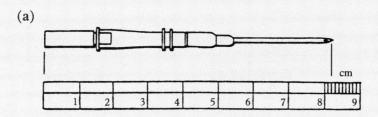

   (b)

   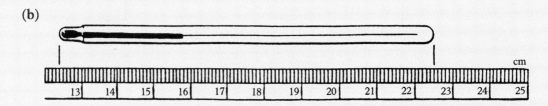

15. (a) The tiles on a bathroom wall are square.
       What is the perimeter of one of these tiles?

   15cm

   15cm

   (b) The tiles on the floor are longer than they are wide.

   These tiles have the same perimeter as those on the wall.

   Anne said they could be 16cm by 14cm. Justine gave different measurements. What might Justine have given?

16.

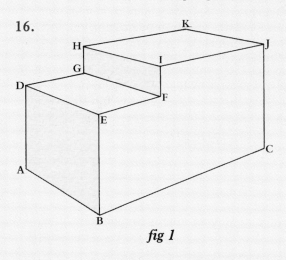

fig 1

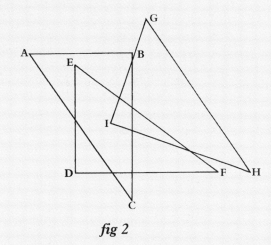

fig 2

(a) Which lines on *fig 1* are vertical?

(b) Which lines on *fig 1* are horizontal?

(c) On *fig 2*, which line is parallel to GH?

(d) On *fig 2*, which line is perpendicular to IH?

17.

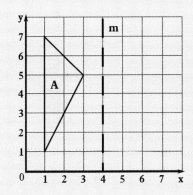

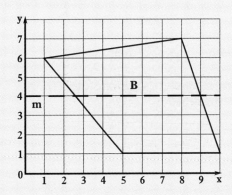

(a) Copy these diagrams.
Reflect each shape in the mirror line **m**.

(b) Write down the coordinates of the vertices of the image shapes.

163

18.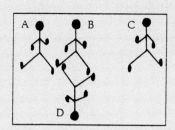

Which of the movements,
Reflection, Translation, Rotation
takes

(a) A to B

(b) A to C

(c) A to D?

19. (a) Which of these nets will fold to make a cube?

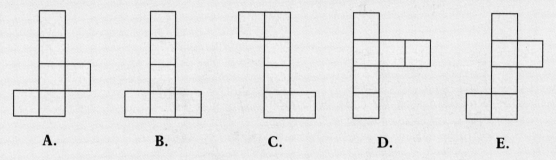

    A.   B.   C.   D.   E.

(b) Draw another net which can be folded into a cube.

20. Lucy used this pattern to make
Christmas decorations.

Count squares to estimate the area of
each decoration.

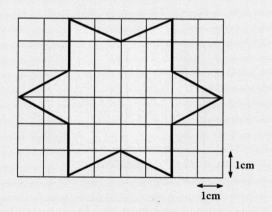

21.   6cm   5cm   4cm   3cm   2cm

Choosing three different lengths from the list for the sides, draw a triangle.
How many different triangles can you draw?

22. This shape is made from a rectangle and a triangle.

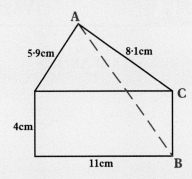

(a) Use your ruler, set square and compass to accurately construct this shape.
On your shape, measure the length of AB. Give your answer to the nearest tenth of a centimetre.

(b) Use your ruler and set square to draw the line through C which is parallel to AB.

(c) Use your ruler and set square to draw the line through A which is perpendicular to AB.

23.

Use your ruler and compass to make accurate copies of these. You could make them larger.
Use words such as semicircle, radius, arc, diameter to describe how you made the copies.

24. Trace this diagram.

Continue in two different ways to make two different patterns.

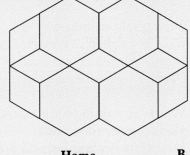

25. After the LOGO commands   RIGHT 90
                              FORWARD 400
the turtle is at B.

Where is the turtle after these further commands?   RIGHT 90
                                                  FORWARD 400
                                                  BACK 400

AROUND and ABOUT

DISCUSSION EXERCISE 11:1

- What is sold in metres?
  What is weighed in kilograms or grams?
  What is packed or measured in litres or millilitres?
  Discuss with your neighbour or group or class.

- **Merete is training for a marathon.**
  Manuel goes shopping.
  Margareta is planning and preparing for a barbeque.
  Masao is on a farm-stay holiday.
  Michal is making and painting a model aeroplane.
  Mario goes to the airport.

  Discuss what metric measures Merete, Manuel, Margareta, Masao, Michal and
  Mario would come across.

ESTIMATING MEASUREMENTS

DISCUSSION EXERCISE 11:2

- In the following "story" most of the measurements are in the wrong places. **Discuss** how to rewrite the story so the measurements are in the correct places.

On the way to the football I saw a labrador that weighed 5kg, a car that was 3cm long, a cat with a 20cm tail, a baby that weighed 40kg and a house that was 2m tall. At the football I bought a pie that was 3m thick from a man who was 6m tall.

- Write a "story", similar to the above, in which you mix all, or most, of the measurements up.
  Have the rest of your group rewrite your story.

GAME 11:3

ESTIMATION GAME – a game for a group

Choose a leader.

The leader chooses an object in the classroom and asks the other students to write down an estimate of its length, width or height.

For instance, "what is the length of the room"
               "what is my height"
               "what is the width of this calculator"?

The object is then measured.
The student whose estimate was the best becomes the leader for the next round.

Note   This game could also be played outside the classroom.

PRACTICAL EXERCISE 11:4

1. Choose two objects in the school grounds; for instance, a tree and the main gate. *Estimate* the distance between these objects.

    Use a measuring tape or a trundle wheel to measure the distance.

    How good was your estimate?

2. Repeat **1.** for other objects. Try and improve your estimation of distances.

3. Mark a point on the ground. *Estimate* a distance of 1m from this point. Place a mark here.

    Measure the distance between the two marks.

    How good was your estimate?

    Repeat until your estimate of 1m is quite good.

4. Repeat **3.** for other distances such as 2m, 5m, 10m, etc.

5. *Estimate* the mass of an object such as a brick, a bucket of water, a chair, a calculator, a pencil etc.
    Check your estimates by weighing the objects.

6. *Estimate* the capacity of a container such as a bucket, a cup, a yoghurt pottle etc.
    Fill the containers with water poured from a measuring jug to check your estimates.

7. Bring a collection of tins, packets etc. to school.
    Estimate various measurements such as height, capacity or mass. (Don't look at the labels!)

8. Work in pairs to estimate intervals of time such as 1 minute, 5 minutes etc.
    Before you begin, decide how you are going to do this.

9. Weigh 100 paper clips.
    From this measurement, work out the mass of one paper clip.

10. Repeat **9.** for other light objects such as a drawing pin or a sheet of paper.

EXERCISE 11:5

1. (a) Which is most likely to be about 5m?

   A. the width of a coach   B. the length of a tennis racquet
   C. the height of a tree   D. the height of a rose bush

   (b) Which is most likely to be about 2mm?

   A. the length of a pencil   B. the thickness of this page
   C. the diameter of a cricketball D. the thickness of a coin

   (c) The length of an eyelash could be

   A. 3mm   B. 20cm   C. 10mm   D. 10cm.

   (d) The length of a brick could be

   A. 20mm   B. 20cm   C. 200cm   D. 2m.

   (e) The distance between two cities could be

   A. 200cm   B. 200km   C. 20m   D. 200mm.

   (f) The depth of a lake could be

   A. 5mm   B. 5cm   C. 5km   D. 5m.

2. Which of km, m, cm, mm is missing?

   (a) A house is about 8 . . . high.

   (b) John's thumb is about 50 . . . long.

   (c) Brian can run about 250 . . . in one minute.

   (d) London is about 350 . . . from Liverpool.

   (e) Laura is 150 . . . tall.

   (f) Louise walks 200 . . . to school.

   (g) On her holiday abroad Rasha flew 920 . . .

3. (a) A waterbed has a mass of about   A. 700g   B. 700kg   C. 700t.

   (b) An apple has a mass of about   A. 1g   B. 10g   C. 100g.

   (c) A man could have a mass of about   A. 80kg   B. 8kg   C. 800kg.

(d)   A letter could weigh about   **A.** 1g   **B.** 10g   **C.** 10mg.

(e)   A lorry could weigh about   **A.** 500kg   **B.** 5t   **C.** 500t.

(f)   A marble could weigh about   **A.** 50mg   **B.** 5g   **C.** 50g.

4. Choose one of 20g, 250g, 1kg, 50kg, 50t, to complete these.

(a)   Kate weighed herself. The reading on the scales was . . .

(b)   The mass of a coin is about . . .

(c)   A bag of sugar weighs . . .

(d)   A large whale has a mass of about . . .

(e)   Kate bought a piece of cheese that weighed . . .

5.

Which of these has a capacity of about

(a)   300m*l*   (b)   1 litre   (c)   5m*l*   (d)   5 litres?

6. (a)   The capacity of a kitchen sink could be   **A.** 2*l*   **B.** 20*l*   **C.** 200m*l*.

     (b)   A bottle of suntan cream could hold   **A.** 10m*l*   **B.** 200m*l* **C.** 1*l*.

     (c)   The capacity of a briefcase could be   **A.** 5*l*   **B.** 50*l*   **C.** 50m*l*.

     (d)   A pot full of soup could hold   **A.** 100m*l* **B.** 1*l*   **C.** 100*l*.

     (e)   The amount of blood in an adult is about **A.** 60m*l*   **B.** 6*l*   **C.** 60*l*.

     (f)   A petrol tank of a car could hold   **A.** 50m*l*   **B.** 5*l*   **C.** 50*l*.

     (g)   The capacity of a car's engine could be   **A.** 20m*l*   **B.** 200m*l* **C.** 2*l*.

Review 1   Copy this chart.

10	12	2	8	6	4		13	5	9	7	1	11	3
											C		

Complete the chart by matching each item from **Box A** with a measurement from **Box B**.

For instance, 1 matches with **C** so **C** is filled in as shown.

Box A

1.	length of a table
2.	weight of a pencil
3.	width of a television
4.	capacity of a glass
5.	weight of a puppy
6.	capacity of a paddling pool
7.	capacity of a suitcase
8.	capacity of a bucket
9.	length of a driveway
10.	capacity of a freezer bag
11.	weight of a concrete post
12.	volume of an eye dropper
13.	weight of a garden shed

Box B

G.	200ml
T.	30kg
S.	0·75m
I.	10l
Z.	5g
S.	600ml
O.	300kg
C.	1·5m
N.	200l
I.	2ml
J.	25m
B.	2kg
E.	60l

Review 2   Choose one of km, m, cm, mm, l, ml, t, kg, g, mg to complete these.

(a)   A small parcel weighs about 200 . . .

(b)   The length of a hospital corridor is about 50 . . .

(c)   The depth of a bath is about 30 . . .

(d)   A van could weigh about 1500 . . .

(e)   The width of a wedding ring could be 5 . . .

(f)   The capacity of a wheelbarrow could be 100 . . .

(g)   Joanna sailed her yacht 50 . . .

(h)   Joanna's yacht weighs about 2 . . .

EXERCISE 11:6

1.

Estimate the lengths of these lines.

Check your estimates by measuring.

2. (a) On your page, mark two points which you estimate to be 5cm apart.
Measure the distance between the two points.
How good was your estimate?

   (b) Repeat (a) for other distances such as 9cm, 35mm etc.

3.

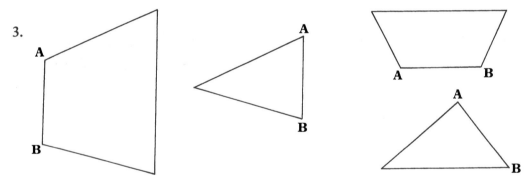

Which of the lengths marked as AB do you think is the longest?

Check your answer by measuring.

Review

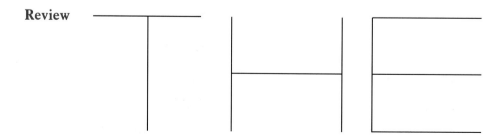

Which lines are longer, the horizontal or vertical?

Check your answer by measuring.

METRIC PREFIXES

The **basic metric units** are:

metre (m) for length, litre (*l*) for capacity, gram (g) for mass.

The **metric prefixes** are:

kilo – 1000	hecto – 100	deca – 10	deci – $\frac{1}{10}$	centi – $\frac{1}{100}$	milli – $\frac{1}{1000}$
(k)	(h)	(D)	(d)	(c)	(m)

For instance, 1 km = 1000m

$$1 \, d\mathit{l} = \tfrac{1}{10} \mathit{l}$$
$$1mg = \tfrac{1}{1000} g$$

LENGTH CONVERSIONS

For converting between the commonly used units for **length** the relationships in this list can be used.

1km = 1000m	**1m = 1000mm**	**1m = 100cm**	**1cm = 10mm**
1m = $\frac{1}{1000}$ km	**1mm = $\frac{1}{1000}$ m**	**1cm = $\frac{1}{100}$ m**	**1mm = $\frac{1}{10}$ cm**

DISCUSSION EXERCISE 11:7

- Suppose a car is 4m long.
  Discuss how to find the number of these cars in a queue that is 1km long.

- Suppose a coin has a diameter of 2cm.
  How could you find the number of these coins in a coin trail that is 1km long?
  Discuss.

- Suppose a coin is 2mm thick.
  Discuss how to find the number of these coins
  in a pile that is 40cm high.

- Suppose a wall is 5m long.
  How could you find the number of desks, 50cm wide, that would fit along the wall?
  Discuss.

- Think of things that are about 1m long. **Discuss.**

Metric units for **length** can be shown on a table.

km	hm	Dm	m	dm	cm	mm

One way of remembering this table is to use a sentence such as:

	Kings	Have	Dashed	My	Dreams	Cried	Mary
or	Keep	Him	Down	My	Dear	Cried	Mary
or	Kind	Humans	Donated	Many	Delightful	Coloured	Mobiles

We can use this table to convert from one metric unit to another.

Each unit is 10 times as large as the unit immediately to its right (1m = 10dm, 1cm = 10mm, 1km = 10hm etc.).

To convert a unit into another unit further to the right, multiply by 10 each time you move a space.

Worked Example   Write 2·4km in cm.

Answer 2·4km = 24hm = 240Dm = 2400m = 24000dm = 240000cm
or more briefly $2\cdot4\text{km} = 2\cdot4 \times 10 \times 10 \times 10 \times 10 \times 10\text{cm}$
= 240000cm

To convert a unit into another unit further to the left, divide by 10 each time you move a space.

Worked Example Convert 89mm to m.

Answer 89mm = 8·9cm = 0·89dm = 0·089m
or more briefly $89\text{mm} = \dfrac{89}{10\times10\times10}\text{ m}$
= 0·089m

Whether you use the table above or the list on the previous page depends on which you find easier to remember.

EXERCISE 11:8

1.   Kings Have Dashed My Dreams Cried Mary
    Make up a sentence of your own to help you remember the table.

2.

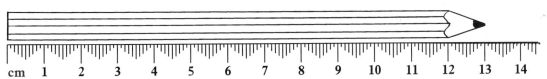

What is the length of the pencil   (a) in cm   (b) in mm?

3.

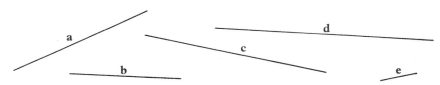

What is the length of these lines in cm?

4.   What is the length of the lines in **question 3** in mm?

5.   What is the missing unit of measurement?

(a) 7cm = 70 . . .   (b) 3m = 3000 . . .   (c) 3m = 300 . . .

(d) 2km = 2000 . . .   (e) 600cm = 6 . . .   (f) 600mm = 60 . . .

(g) 5000m = 5 . . .

6.   The High Street in Wadestown is 2km long.

How many metres is this?

7.   A swimming pool is 50m long.

How many lengths must be swum in a 2km race?

8.   Tony walks 400m to get to school each morning. He walks the same distance to get home in the afternoon.

How many kilometres does Tony walk to and from school each week? (Tony goes to school 5 days a week.)

9.

←———— 450mm ————→

How many mm wide is each of these encyclopaedias?

10. John took some measurements, in cm, for a model he was making. He decided to convert these measurements to mm. Do the conversions for him.

(a) 1cm   (b) 8cm   (c) 23cm   (d) 8·7cm   (e) 0·3cm

11. Students in science were using the measuring equipment. They measured the following lengths and then the teacher asked them to convert them all to cm. Do this for them.

(a) 1m   (b) 3m   (c) 1·2m

(d) 0·3m   (e) 0·04m   (f) 30mm

12. A textbook author decided she wanted all the lengths in her book to be in m. Convert these lengths to m.

(a) 5km   (b) 6·4km   (c) 280cm   (d) 42·6cm   (e) 19mm

13. Write these in km.

(a) 7000m   (b) 5230m   (c) 841m   (d) 20m   (e) 70·8m

14. A road race is 10000m. How long is this race, in km?

15. Find the missing numbers.

(a) 3cm = ... mm   (b) 2km = ... m   (c) 52cm = ... mm

(d) 5000m = ... km   (e) 7·6m = ... cm   (f) 4·7km = ... m

(g) 0·5m = ... cm   (h) 6852m = ... km   (i) 752cm = ... m

(j) 5·2cm = ... mm   (k) 0·48m = ... cm

16. In gymnastics the length of the beam is 5m. Kylie wanted this length in cm so she could work out her routine. How long is this beam, in cm?

17. (a) 83mm + 12cm =

     A. 95mm   **B.** 95cm   **C.** 203mm   **D.** 842cm

(b) 14·6m – 127cm =

     A. 19m   **B.** 19cm   **C.** 1333cm   **D.** 1·333m

(c) 7·3km – 576m =

     A. 15·4m   **B.** 154m   **C.** 67·24m   **D.** 6·724km

18. How many times does a cyclist need to go around a 400m track in a 2km race?

19. In gymnastics the length of the beam is 50 times its width. The length of the beam is 5m. How many cm wide is the beam?

Review 1 The widest street in the world is in Brasilia, Brazil. It is 0·25km wide. How many metres wide is this?

Review 2 What reading, in cm, is given by the pointer?

(a)

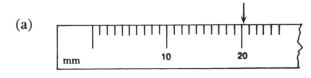

(b)

Review 3 Find the missing numbers.

    (a) 3·6km = ... m   (b) ... m = 89cm   (c) 157mm = ... m

    (d) ... cm = 26mm   (e) 6·6mm = ... cm   (f) ... m = 480cm

    (g) ... m = 50mm   (h) 386m = ... km   (i) ... mm = 2·3cm

    (j) 47·2cm = ... m

Review 4 Calculate.

    (a) 82cm + 35mm   (b) 2·3m + 405cm   (c) 2·3m − 584mm

Review 5 Max bought 2m of wrapping paper to wrap gifts. From this he cut two lengths, one of 34cm and the other of 85cm.
How much paper did he have left?

PUZZLES 11:9

1. A snail climbing up the side of a 10m high building climbs 3m every night and slips back 2m every day. On which night will the snail reach the top?

2. In the Olympic 400m hurdles there is 45m before the first hurdle and 40m after the last hurdle. The 8 hurdles between the first and the last are equally spaced. What is the distance between the hurdles?

3. If a pile of ten £5 notes is 1mm high, how much money is in a pile of £5 notes that is 1m high?

4. A motorbike travelled 30000km. Three tyres were used equally to travel this distance. For how many kilometres was each tyre used?

5. Five trees are planted in a straight line, the trees being 5m apart. How far is it from the first tree to the last tree?

6. This chain is made from 6 circular links each of which measures 24mm from outside edge to outside edge.
   Each link is made from brass 5mm thick.
   What is the length of the 6-link chain?

   24mm

7. Mike bought a 24·2cm length of chain. Each link measured 5mm from outside edge to outside edge and each link was made from gold 1mm thick. How many links were in Mike's chain?

DISCUSSION EXERCISE 11:10

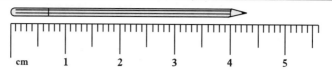

The length of this pencil is 4·3cm.

This length could also be written as 43mm or $4\frac{3}{10}$ cm or 4cm 3mm.

Discuss other ways of writing the following measurements.

8·1m   6·37m   0·9m   27cm   131cm

CAPACITY CONVERSIONS

For converting between the commonly used units for **capacity** the relationships in this list can be used.

$$1l = 1000ml \qquad 1ml = \tfrac{1}{1000}\, l$$

DISCUSSION EXERCISE 11:11

- Suppose tomato sauce comes in 1 litre bottles.
  How could you find the number of 20m*l* servings in one of these bottles? **Discuss.**

- Suppose a small bottle contains 600m*l* of wine.
  How could you find how many litres would be
  in 50 bottles? **Discuss.**

- Suppose a 40 litre tank is being filled with water using an 800m*l* container.
  How many containers full would be needed to fill the tank? **Discuss.**

- Think of things which hold about 1 litre. **Discuss.**

- Deirdre measured the capacities of some glass containers in the science laboratory.
  She wrote the capacities in both litres and millilitres.

  What numbers should Deirdre put in the boxes?

  Jar A 1*l* = ☐ m*l*   **Jar B** 3*l* = ☐ m*l*   **Jar C** ☐*l* = 5000m*l*

  Jar D ☐*l* = 4000m*l*   **Jar E** 6*l* = ☐ m*l*

Metric units for **capacity** can be shown on a table.

k*l*	h*l*	D*l*	*l*	d*l*	c*l*	m*l*

Converting from one metric unit of capacity to another, is the same as converting from one metric unit of length to another. That is, we multiply by 10's when we move to the right and divide by 10's when we move to the left.

The abbreviation for litre is sometimes written as *l* and sometimes as L.
If L is used for litre, then the units in the table would be written as kL, hL, DL, L, dL, cL, mL.

EXERCISE 11:12

1. Jugs made by "Useful Plastics" had the capacity, written in *l* and in m*l*, on the side. How many m*l* did each of these jugs have written on them?

   (a) 3 *l*   (b) 6 *l*   (c) 4·1 *l*

   (d) 5·8 *l*   (e) 0·9 *l*   (f) 0·2 *l*

2. How many m*l* of coke is there in a 1·2 *l* bottle?

3. A small can of orange juice holds 350mL. How many litres is this?

4. Calculate

   (a) 2 *l* + 175m*l*   (b) 2·5 *l* + 340m*l*   (c) 980m*l* + 0·8 *l*

   (d) 3 *l* − 147m*l*   (e) 980m*l* − 0·5 *l*.

5. (a) $3l - 250ml =$

      A. 2·5*l*   **B.** 2·75*l*   **C.** 50m*l*   **D.** 27·5*l*

    (b) $2650ml - 2·4l =$

      A. 2647·6m*l*   **B.** 24·1*l*   **C.** 0·25m*l*   **D.** 0·25*l*

6.  Bill bought a 1*l* pack of ice-cream. He used 550m*l* of this to make a frozen pudding. Was there enough ice-cream left to make another of these frozen puddings?

7. Susan has made 8 litres of grape juice. To store it she has bottles of two different sizes: 1·25*l* and 750m*l*.

    To store the juice, bottles should be filled right to the top. If as many large as small bottles are used, how many bottles are filled?

Review 1   Four friends share a 1 litre bottle of drink.

                 How many m*l* does each friend have?

Review 2   Are these statements true or false?

                 (a)   1325m*l* = 1·325*l*   (b)   35m*l* = 0·035*l*   (c)   0·74*l* = 740m*l*

                 (d)   0·4*l* = 4000m*l*

Review 3   How many 5m*l* spoons of medicine can be taken from a 0·2*l* bottle?

Review 4   Jamie made 2·2*l* of chutney. He poured this into 4 jars of the same size. If each of these jars was filled to the top, find the capacity, in m*l*, of each jar.

PUZZLES 11:13

? ?

1.  Rose needed to measure out exactly 2*l* of water. She had two containers, one that held 8*l* and one that held 5*l*. She began by filling the 5*l* container. How did she continue?

2. A large bowl, with capacity 25*l*, is full of water. Each day 3*l* of water is taken out and each night 2*l* of water is put in. When will this bowl be empty?

3. Ellen has to put exactly 6*l* of water into her goldfish bowl. She has three containers filled with water. One holds 7*l*, one 5*l* and the other 4*l*. Using the water from these containers, how can she pour exactly 6*l* into her goldfish bowl? She has no other containers. She is not allowed to refill the containers from a tap. She is not allowed to tip any water out.

4. Jimmy has 4 containers which, when full, will hold 2*l*, 3*l*, 4*l* and 5*l* of wine. At the beginning the 3*l* and 5*l* containers are full. By pouring wine from one container to another, show how to get 2*l* of wine into each of the containers in as few moves as possible.

5.

Three winemakers had between them 21 barrels, 7 of which were empty, 7 half-full of wine and 7 full of wine. These barrels were divided between the winemakers so that each had the same number of barrels and the same amount of wine. There are two ways in which this could be done. Find them. (Let F represent a full barrel, H a half-full barrel and E an empty barrel.)

? ?

MASS CONVERSIONS

For converting between the commonly used units for **mass** the relationships in this list can be used.

1 tonne = 1000kg	1kg = 1000g	1g = 1000mg
$\frac{1}{1000}$ tonne = 1kg	$\frac{1}{1000}$ kg = 1g	$\frac{1}{1000}$ g = 1mg

DISCUSSION EXERCISE 11:14

• Suppose an average student weighs 50kg. **Discuss** how to find the number of these students who would weigh a total of 1 tonne.

• Suppose an apple weighs 50 grams. How could you find out how many kilograms 200 apples weigh? **Discuss.**

• Think of things that would weigh about 1 tonne. **Discuss.**

Metric units for **mass** can be shown on a table.

kg	hg	Dg	g	dg	cg	mg

Converting from one metric unit of mass to another is the same as converting from one metric unit of length to another. That is, we multiply by 10's when we move to the right and divide by 10's when we move to the left.

EXERCISE 11:15

1. What is the missing unit of measurement?

(a) 3kg = 3000 . . .   (b) 3t = 3000 . . .   (c) 6000g = 6 . . .

(d) 5000kg = 5 . . .   (e) 4000 . . . = 4kg   (f) 4000 . . . = 4t

(g) 3000mg = 3 . . .   (h) 4g = 4000 . . .

2. A 1 kg box of breakfast cereal is enough for 25 servings.

   How many grams is each of these servings?

3. Sweets cost 45p for 200g.

   How much do these sweets cost per kg?

4. What reading, in grams, is given by the pointers?

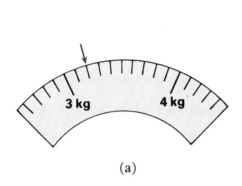

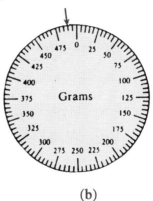

(a)

(b)

5. Maryanne wanted to divide up some food she had bought in bulk. To do this she needed to convert the masses into grams. Convert these to g.

   (a) 2kg   (b) 3·5kg   (c) 0·8kg

   (d) 0·05kg   (e) 2·534kg

6. A science experiment asked for all masses to be in kg. Colleen had weighed everything in g. Convert these to kg for her.

   (a) 3000g   (b) 5140g   (c) 743g   (d) 38g   (e) 427·4g

7. Tina needed 1·2kg of tomatoes. She had 560g in one bag and 575g in another. Did Tina have enough?

8. One tablet weighs 50mg. How many grams do 25 weigh?

185

9. Find the missing numbers.

    (a) 8000kg = ... tonne

    (b) ... g = 7820mg

    (c) 3·1t = ... kg

    (d) 240mg = ... g

    (e) 490g = ... kg

    (f) ... mg = 3·2g

    (g) ... t = 780kg

    (h) ... kg = 8924g

10. Yuri's baby brother was very small. He weighed just 1300g.
    How many kg did this baby weigh?

11.

IDEAL BODY WEIGHT CHART			
Height (m)	Weight (kg)		
	Small	Medium	Large
1·53–	48–56	53–61	57–67
1·58–	51–59	55–64	60–71
1·63–	53–62	58–67	62–74
1·68–	56–65	61–69	65–77
1·73–1·78	59–67	63–72	68–80

This chart gives the range in weight for women with a small, medium or large frame.

(a) Are these statements true or false?

   A. A medium framed woman of height 1·65m should weigh between 58kg and 67kg.

   B. A small framed woman of height 1·70m who weighs 55kg is underweight.

   C. A large framed woman of height 1·54m who weighs 59kg is overweight.

(b) What is the ideal weight range of a small framed woman of height 1·68m?

(c) What is the ideal weight range for a medium framed woman of height 1·75m?

(d) Anna, who is 1·60m tall, weighs 65kg. She is neither underweight nor overweight.
     Is Anna a small or medium or large framed woman?

12. (a) 5340g + 6·2kg =

     A. 115·40g   **B.** 11·540kg   **C.** 5402g   **D.** 5960g

  (b) 4·1 tonne + 575kg =

     A. 46·75 tonne   **B.** 4·675 tonne   **C.** 579·1kg   **D.** 579·1 tonne

  (c) 2g+76mg =

     A. 2·76g   **B.** 2076g   **C.** 2076mg   **D.** 276mg

13. Kate was trying to lighten the load she was to carry on the hike. She took a tin of soup, which weighed 432g, from her food bag. The weight of her food bag was 3·2kg before the soup was taken out. What was its weight after?

14. Imran had a number of items on the balance he was using in the Science laboratory. These items had masses of 2g, 2·5g, 350mg, 65mg, 810mg.
What was the total mass of all of these?

Review 1   Write

     (a) 3kg in g   (b) 7·6kg in g   (c) 145·8g in kg

     (d) 820mg in g   (e) 3415kg in tonne   (f) 2·4t in kg.

Review 2   (a)   The weight of a Citroen CX 22 TRS is 1275kg. What is the weight of this car in tonnes?

           (b)   The weight of a duvet is 2·1kg. How many grams does this duvet weigh?

           (c)   Joe's cat weighs 3500g. How many kg is this?

Apples	2·6 kg
Bananas	500 g
Lemons	1150 g

Review 3   What is the total weight of this fruit?

PUZZLES 11:16

1. 100kg of potatoes are given to 100 people. Each adult gets 3kg, each teenager gets 2kg and each small child gets 0·5kg. How many adults and teenagers and small children were there? (There are many answers to this problem. Find as many as you can.)

2. Dennis has just three weights. By using some of them, or all of them, he can weigh any number of kilograms of apples from 1kg to 13kg on the sort of balance shown here.

   What weights has Dennis got?

3. Shalome is given nine £1 coins, one of which is fake. This fake coin looks the same as the others but it is lighter. Shalome is allowed to keep all the coins if she can find the fake one by just 2 weighings on a balance such as that shown in the previous question. She is not allowed to use any weights during her weighing. Is she able to keep the coins?

4. Annabel, Belinda and Cushla are sisters. One of them is 13, another is 12 and the youngest is 11. Together, the three girls weigh 153kg. Belinda weighs 45kg. The 11-year-old weighs 5kg less than the heaviest of the sisters. Cushla weighs more than her 12-year-old sister and Annabel weighs less than her 13-year-old sister. Find the age and the weight of each of these sisters.

5.  Bill, Beth and Bert have to cross a river in a rowboat which can carry a maximum load of 140kg. Bill weighs 100kg, Beth weighs 50kg and Bert weighs 75kg. They all have rucksacks. Bill's weighs 40kg, Beth's weighs 15kg and Bert's weighs 25kg. How do they cross the river if none of them will leave their rucksacks with any of the others?

MIXED CONVERSIONS

EXERCISE 11:17

---

1. Copy and complete this crossnumber. If decimal points are needed give them a full space.
   23 Across is completed for you.

Across	Down
1. cm in 14·35m	1. m*l* in 0·12*l*
4. cm in 37mm	2. mm in 0·048m
6. mm in 2·8cm	3. mm in 5·2cm
7. kg in 0·239t	4. m in 0·39km
9. m*l* in 0·048*l*	5. g in 0·074kg
12. g in 0·707kg	8. cm in 3·74m
14. m in 564cm	10. m in 8·05km
16. cm in 7·35m	11. kg in 3460g
17. m*l* in 3·142*l*	13. m*l* in 7·7*l*
18. mm in 3cm	15. mm in 6·2cm
19. t in 9090kg	17. g in 3·425kg
21. m in 0·026km	18. cm in 31mm
23. cm in 41mm	19. g in 9870mg
24. mm in 3·4cm	20. kg in 0·932t
26. m*l* in 0·05*l*	22. cm in 6·07m
27. cm in 0·38m	23. cm in 4·3m
28. g in 0·523kg	25. mg in 0·43g
29. m in 7070mm	28. mm in 5·6cm

2. A speed skating track is 0·4km long.
   How many metres is this?

3. An encyclopaedia weighs 2560g. What is this weight in kg?

4. A large tin of tomato sauce holds 2·61*l* of sauce. How many m*l* of sauce is in this tin?

5. A class made a mural using 3 sheets of paper with lengths 42cm, 45cm and 87cm.
   How long was the mural? (Answer in m.)

6. A recipe for a fruit punch has
     1·4*l* of orange juice,
     750m*l* of pineapple juice and
     3*l* of lemonade.
   How many litres of punch does this recipe make?

Review 1 The weight of an unloaded Range Rover is 1·956 tonne. Find the loaded weight of this Range Rover once the Weston family and their luggage are in. Their luggage weighs a total of 124kg. The weights of the family are: Mr. Weston – 68kg, Rashni – 56kg, Michael – 62kg, Mrs. Weston – 54kg.

Review 2 To keep in shape Charlotte swims 1km twice a week. If the pool is 40m long, how many lengths does Charlotte swim each week?

Review 3 How many 300m*l* glasses could you fill from a 1·2*l* bottle of ginger ale?

WHAT   WHEN   WHERE   WHO   HOW   WHY

What metric measurements would a chef use?

When would a gardener use metric measures?

Where, in a hospital, are metric measures used?

Who uses metric measurement in their jobs?

How does an understanding of metric measurement help you in other subjects?

Why is an understanding of metric measurement important to a chauffeur?

Imperial Measures. Time Measure

AROUND and ABOUT

DISCUSSION EXERCISE 12:1

- What, in this country, is measured in pints or gallons?
  Where, in everyday life, do you find lengths and distances measured in inches, feet, yards, miles?
  What is weighed in ounces or pounds or stones or tons?
  Compared with the 24-Hour clock, how often is the 12-Hour clock used?
  Discuss with your neighbour or group or class.

- **Hien is helping on her family farm.**
  Shalome is helping at a holiday camp.
  Alex is helping at his athletics club.
  Megan is helping to care for her baby brother.
  Barry is helping to plan and prepare for a dinner party.
  Bonny is helping to care for the animals at the RSPCA.
  Tim is helping out at his mother's car sales business.

  What imperial measures will Hien, Shalome, Alex, Megan, Barry, Bonny and Tim be likely to use? **Discuss.**

  What activities, where time needs to be measured, might Hien, Shalome, Alex, Megan, Barry, Bonny and Tim either help to organise or take part in? **Discuss.**

191

IMPERIAL MEASURES for Length, Capacity, Mass

This is a list of the **imperial units** in everyday use.

Length: inch (″), foot (′) yard, mile

Mass: ounce (oz), pound (lb), stone, ton

Capacity: pint, gallon

Length	1 mile = 1760 yards	**Mass** 1 ton = 160 stone
	1 yard = 3 feet	1 stone = 14 lb
	1 foot = 12 inches	1 lb = 16 oz
	Capacity 1 gallon = 8 pints	

Worked Example   Write 5′4″ in inches.

Answer   5 feet = 12 × 5 inches
                       = 60 inches
            Then 5′4″ = 60 inches + 4 inches
                       = 64 inches

Worked Example   A large punch bowl holds 19 pints of punch. How much is this in gallons and pints?

Answer Firstly, divide 19 by 8 to find the number of complete gallons.
We get 2 complete gallons.

These 2 gallons are 8 × 2 pints = 16 pints.
We still need another 3 pints to get the original 19 pints.

The punchbowl holds 2 gallons 3 pints.

When **adding** measurements which are given in mixed units (e.g. adding 3 lb 5oz to 2 lb 12 oz), begin by adding the units separately (e.g. to add 3 lb 5oz and 2 lb 12oz, begin by adding the lbs and the oz separately).
The same applies when **subtracting or multiplying**.
When **dividing**, it is wise to convert the measurement so that it is given in the smaller unit (e.g. to divide 2 lb 12oz by 4, begin by writing 2 lb 12oz in oz).

192

Worked Example   A recipe for making apple strudel uses 2 lb 12oz of apples. Michael was using this recipe to make strudel for his family. He was going to double the recipe. What quantity of apples should he use?

Answer   Michael needs 2×2 lb 12oz of apples.

2×2 lb $= 4$ lb 2×12oz $= 24$oz
                                                                    $= 1$ lb 8oz

Hence Michael needs 4 lb $+$ 1 lb 8oz $= 5$ lb 8oz of apples.

Note   The working for this problem could be set out as follows:
$2 \times (2$ lb 12oz$) = 4$ lb 24oz
Since 24oz $= 1$ lb 8oz, then 4 lb 24 oz $= 5$ lb 8oz.

Worked Example   Add together $3'4''$ and $5'10''$.

Answer   Firstly, add the feet to get $3' + 5' = 8'$
Now add the inches to get $4'' + 10'' = 14''$ or $1'2''$

So $3'4'' + 5'10'' = 8' + 1'2''$
                                $= 9'2''$

Note   The working for this problem could be set out as follows:

$$\begin{array}{r} 3' \ 4'' \\ + \ 5' 10'' \\ \hline 8' 14'' \end{array}$$

Since $14'' = 1'2''$, then $8'14'' = 9'2''$.

Worked Example   Dina had enough money to buy 2 lb 12oz of sweets. She divided these between herself and her three friends so that they all had the same weight. What weight of sweets did each get?

Answer   Firstly, write 2 lb 12oz in ounces.

2 lb $= 2 \times 16$oz or 32oz, so 2 lb 12oz $= 44$oz
44oz is to be divided between 4 people.

Each person gets $\dfrac{44}{4}$ oz or 11oz.

Worked Example   Andy weighed 11 stone 4 lb before he went on a diet. On this diet he
lost 1 stone 10 lb. How much did he then weigh?

Answer   Firstly subtract the stones to get 11 stone – 1 stone = 10 stone.
Now subtract the pounds i.e. 4 lb – 10 lb. We have a problem since we cannot
take 10 away from 4. To avoid this problem we begin again, this time writing
11 stone 4 lb as 10 stone 18 lb.

We now have to subtract 1 stone 10 lb from 10 stone 18 lb.
Subtract the stones to get 10 stone – 1 stone = 9 stone.
Now subtract the pounds to get 18 lb – 10 lb = 8 lb.
Then 11 stone 4 lb – 1 stone 10 lb = 9 stone 8 lb.

Andy then weighed 9 stone 8 lb.

The working for this problem could be set out as follows:

	11 stone	4 lb			10 stone	18 lb
−	1 stone	10 lb		−	1 stone	10 lb
					9 stone	8 lb

Note   Another way of doing this problem is to convert both the 11 stone 4 lb and the
1 stone 10 lb to lbs, then subtract, then convert the answer back to stones and lbs.
This is shown as follows:

$$11 \text{ stone } 4 \text{ lb} - 1 \text{ stone } 10 \text{ lb} = 158 \text{ lb} - 24 \text{ lb}$$
$$= 134 \text{ lb}$$
$$= 9 \text{ stone } 8 \text{ lb}$$

EXERCISE 12:2

1. A landscape gardener measured up a garden. She decided to convert the following
measurements into inches. What answers did she get?

    (a) 2'3"   **(b)** 5'1"   **(c)** 2 yards   **(d)** 1 yard 2 feet 3 inches

2. Write these lengths in feet or feet and inches.

    (a) 74 inches   **(b)** 26"   **(c)** 96 inches   **(d)** 39"   **(e)** 3 yards

3. A dairy worker wanted these capacities converted into pints. What answers did he get?

    (a) 2 gallons   **(b)** 8 gallons   **(c)** 1 gallon 5 pints   **(d)** 5 gallons 1 pint

4. A farmer measured his milk in pints and then converted into gallons and pints for his record book. What did he write in his record book for the following?

   (a) 20 pints   (b) 160 pints   (c) 50 pints   (d) 900 pints

5. For a graph, the following need to be in pounds. Write them in pounds.

   (a) 2 stone   (b) 10 stone   (c) 3 stone 4 lb   (d) 9 stone 6 lb

6. Jo-Ann wanted to divide up some packets of sweets into smaller ones. To do so, she converted the masses to ounces. How many ounces did she get for the following?

   (a) 2 lb   (b) 10 lb   (c) 3 lb 4oz

7. A family weighed themselves in pounds. Convert their weights to stones and pounds.

   (a) 100 lb   (b) 250 lb   (c) 112 lb   (d) 73 lb

8. Flour was weighed in ounces. Convert these quantities of flour into pounds and ounces.

   (a) 25oz   (b) 80oz   (c) 36oz   (d) 40oz

9. If gold is worth £206 an ounce how much is half a pound of gold worth?

10. Jake's bathroom scales weigh in pounds. On these scales Jake weighs 124 lb. How heavy is he in stones and pounds?

11. How many pints are needed to fill a 5 gallon bucket?

12. Each of Gemma's paces is 1 yard long. She measures the length of a classroom by "pacing it out". She estimates this room to be $6\frac{1}{2}$ paces long.
    If Gemma's estimate is accurate, how long is this classroom in feet and inches?

13. Grapes are priced at £3·20 per lb. What is the cost of 6oz of these grapes?

14. Calculate.

    (a) $4'5'' + 5'6''$ (b) $6'7'' + 2'5''$ (c) $5'9'' + 3'8''$

    (d) $2'9'' + 0'5''$ (e) $2'6'' + 5'9''$ (f) $6'5'' - 1'3''$

    (g) $4'7'' - 2'9''$ (h) $5'5'' - 1'8''$ (i) $7'1'' - 3'5''$

    (j) $2 \times (3'5'')$ (k) $5 \times (2'3'')$

15. Calculate, giving the answer in simplest form.

    (a) 4 lb 5oz + 2 lb 12oz   (b) 6oz + 14oz   (c) 5 stone 10 lb + 6 stone 8 lb

    (d) 7 lb 5oz – 2 lb 8oz   (e) 12 lb + 11 lb   (f) 8 stone 4 lb – 3 stone 9 lb

    (g) 18 lb 4oz – 3 lb 12oz   (h) 6×10 lb   (i) $3 \times (4$ stone 11 lb$)$

    (j) $(2$ lb 4oz$) \div 9$

16. Four students each run one "leg" of a 1 mile relay race. How many yards does each student run?

17. Liquid is poured into a bucket from a 2 pint measuring jug. How many measuring jugs full must be poured in if a total of 4 gallons of liquid is needed in the bucket?

    Think of a practical reason to do this.

18. Relah weighs 9 stone 2 lb. Jacqui weighs 7 stone 9 lb. How much heavier is Relah than Jacqui?

19. Mrs Patea bought 2 yards of material to make 4 cushion covers. Her first step in making these was to cut the material into four equal lengths. How long was each of these? (Answer in inches.)

20. Emma decided to weigh her cat. She first weighed herself on the bathroom scales. Her weight was 8 stone 5 lb. She then held the cat in her arms. The scales now showed 9 stone 2 lb. How heavy was Emma's cat?

21. The end of Jessie's 6′ tape was missing. The greatest length it could measure was now 5′8″. Jessie used this tape to measure the distance between her front gate and her front door. She found this distance to be three lengths of her tape plus an extra 19 inches.

What is the distance between Jessie's front gate and her front door?

Review 1   The weight of a Queen size waterbed is about 1500 lbs.
How heavy is this waterbed in stones and pounds?

Review 2   The furlong is a measure of length used in horse racing.
There are 8 furlongs in a mile.
How many yards are there in each furlong?

Review 3   A bridge is 12′3″high. If a lorry of height 9′10″ drives under this bridge, how much room is left above the lorry?

Review 4   Seven buckets of water are taken from a 40 gallon tank. If each bucket of water holds 20 pints, how much water is left in the tank?

Review 5   A family needs 2 lb of strawberries for pudding.
Strawberries bought in 8oz packs cost £1·25.
"Pick-your-own" strawberries cost £1·99 per lb.
How much would this family save if they picked their own?

INVESTIGATION 12:3

OTHER IMPERIAL MEASURES

There are imperial measures of capacity other than pints and gallons.
There are imperial measures of mass other than ounces, pounds, stones, tons.
There are imperial measures of length other than inches, feet, yards, miles.

Continued . . .

. . . from previous page

1. Take just one of these other imperial measures e.g. the furlong or the hundredweight or the bushel etc. **Investigate** this measure. Before you begin your investigation write down questions such as:

   Is this measure still used?

   Who uses (or used) this measure?

   Why is it not commonly used today?

   Answer your questions as part of your investigation.

2. Take one part of British life, early this century. **Investigate** the imperial units used.

   You could consider investigating   Horse Racing

                                             Building

                                             Plumbing

                                             Farming

                                             Nursing

                                             The hotel industry

                                             The manufacturing of jewellery

3. Take one part of British life today. **Investigate** the imperial units used.

   You could consider investigating something from the list given above.

TIME MEASURE

There are 60 seconds in 1 minute.

There are 60 minutes in 1 hour.

There are 24 hours in 1 day.

There are 30 days in April, June, September and November.

There are 31 days in January, March, May, July, August, October and December.

There are 28 days in February if the year is not a leap year.

There are 29 days in February if the year is a leap year.

There are 12 months in 1 year.

All years that are divisible by 4 are leap years, except centuries which are leap years only if they are divisible by 400.

For instance, 2000 and 2008 will be leap years; 1982 and 1900 weren't leap years.

EXERCISE 12:4

1. **(a)** How many days are there between March 1st and May 3rd, not including these dates?

   (b) How many days are there between July 30th and September 20th, including both these days?

   (c) How many days were there between February 15th and March 15th in 1988, not including these days?

   (d) How many days will there be between February 15th and March 15th in 2001, not including these days?

2. **(a)** Which of the following were leap years?

   1886   1900   1939   1947   1956   1968   1972   1987   1990

   (b) Which of these will be leap years?

   2000   2001   2010   2116   2118   3000

3. Ash Wednesday is the first day of Lent, coming $6\frac{1}{2}$ weeks before Easter Sunday. In the year 2000 Easter Sunday will be on the 23rd April.
   What date will Ash Wednesday be in the year 2000?

4. A long distance swimmer swam from England to France and return in 42 hrs and 5 min. If this swimmer left England on August 18th at 8·40 a.m. at which time and on what date did she arrive back in England?

5. On May 5th 1961 Alan Shepard became the first American in Space. 291 days later John Glenn became the first American to orbit Earth. On what date did he do this?

6. It takes 23 hr 56 min 4 sec for the Earth to make one complete rotation on its axis. It takes 24 hr 37 min 23 sec for Mars to make one complete rotation on its axis. How much longer does it take for Mars to make one rotation?

7. About how long would it take to spend one thousand pounds at a penny a minute?

    A. 7 days   **B.** 70 days   **C.** 7 years   **D.** 70 years

Review 1   The first woman to orbit Earth was Valentina Tereshkova in the Vostok 6. She was launched on June 16th, 1963 at 9·30 a.m. (Greenwich time). She returned after 2 days, 22 hours and 46 minutes. When did Valentina land back on Earth?

Review 2   In the ARABIAN NIGHTS, Shahrazad told the Sultan a different story every night for 1001 nights. If she told the last story on September 28th 887, when did she tell the first story?

PUZZLES 12:5

? ?

1. When Angie asked her mother what year she was born, her mother replied "The sum of the last two digits is the same as the number of months in a year and the product of all four digits is the number of hours in twelve days." When was Angie's mother born?

2. This clock shows the correct time at 1·00p.m. on May 5th. The clock loses 20 minutes a day. When will it next show the correct time?

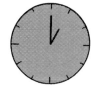

12-HOUR and 24-HOUR TIME

3a.m., 4·15p.m., are written as 12-Hour times.

0300, 1615 are the same times as the above, written as 24-Hour times.

1615 may also be written as 16·15 or as 16:15.
We read 1615 as "sixteen fifteen" or as "sixteen fifteen hours".
We read 1600 as "sixteen hundred hours".

When adding or subtracting times, it is wise to add or subtract the hours and minutes separately.

Worked Example   On Saturday, Dale practised the guitar from 11·40a.m. until 1p.m. and then from 4·25p.m. until 5·15p.m.
For how long did Dale practise on Saturday?

Answer   From 11·40a.m. until 1 p.m. is 1 hour 20 minutes.
From 4·25p.m. until 5·15p.m. is 35 minutes + 15 minutes.
Total hours = 1 hour   Total minutes = 20 + 35 + 15
= 70 minutes
= 1 hour 10 minutes
Total time = 1 hour + 1 hour 10 minutes
= 2 hours 10 minutes

EXERCISE 12:6

1. A chocolate cake, which must cook for 40 minutes, is put in the oven at a quarter to eleven. At what time must it be taken out?

2. A tennis match which lasted 55 minutes finished at 3·03p.m. At what time did this match begin?

3. An episode of Coronation Street began at 7·34p.m. and finished at 8·01p.m. How long was this episode?

4. Rose practised twice each day at the snooker table. In the morning she practised from 7·45a.m. until 8·20a.m. In the evening she practised from 7·45p.m. until 8·55p.m.

    For how long did she practise each day?

5. Copy this chart.

6	9	5	3	4	3	11		12	3	1		12	10	2	7	5	3	9	9	3		2	4	6	7	8
										D																

Match the times on the clock faces in **Box A** with a time from **Box B**. Fill in the chart.

For example, clockface **I** matches with time **D** so **D** is filled in as shown.

Box A

1. Morning	2. Morning	3. Evening	4. Afternoon
5. Morning	6. Morning	7. Evening	8. Evening
9. Morning	10. Morning	11. Evening	12. Afternoon

Box B

A	1·50p.m.
D	0300
E	9·25p.m.
F	3·05a.m.
G	2000
I	4·05p.m.
M	6·15a.m.
N	2140
O	0545
R	12·15a.m.
S	2355
T	9a.m.

6. A late night horror film was recorded on a video. The video began recording at 21:30 and finished at 00:10. How long was this?

7. This table shows the time-clock settings for Rari's central heating.

    (a) How long is the heating on in the morning?

    (b) How long is the heating on in the afternoon?

    (c) How long is the heating on for altogether during one day?

On	Off
0645	0840
1115	1300
1500	2130

8. At 2359 hours on 15th April, 1912 the TITANIC hit an iceberg. She sank 121 minutes later. When did she sink?

9. This table gives the time taken to run the 800m by the competitors in a women's international athletics meeting. The times are as shown by the electronic score board where a time of 2·05·72 means 2 minutes and 5·72 seconds.

Heat 1		Heat 2		Heat 3		Heat 4		Heat 5	
Competitor Number	Time	Competitor Number	Time	Competitor Number	Time	Competitor Number	Time	Competitor Number	Time
27	2·05·72	82	2·09·72	219	2·12·14	149	2·01·74	118	2·09·54
207	2·07·31	103	2·08·14	63	2·07·32	234	2·04·87	89	2·04·32
341	2·08·42	38	2·05·70	109	2·07·49	151	2·11·13	143	2·07·41
159	2·06·74	128	2·04·14	213	2·09·31	334	2·09·10	115	2·04·28
24	1·58·90	378	1·59·93	85	2·05·24	138	2·03·46	32	2·05·37
59	2·04·12	64	2·10·01	307	2·04·88	220	2·06·15	235	2·00·04
247	2·10·04	13	1·59·98			31	2·01·14		

(a) Give the times in minutes and seconds of competitors 115 and 85.

(b) Which competitor ran the 800m in 2 min 4·32 sec?

(c) The first three in each heat plus the fastest loser overall go into the final. List the 16 competitors who go into the final.

10. The following is a lecture timetable for the subjects Sylvia has chosen to study at Polytechnic this year.
The abbreviations are M – Monday, T – Tuesday, W – Wednesday, Th – Thursday, F – Friday.
There are two streams for each subject, Stream A and Stream B. Sylvia chose Stream B for all her subjects except Accounting.

SUBJECT	STREAM A	STREAM B
Accounting	M, Th 10 – 11	T, Th 4 – 5
Biology	M, W 10 – 11	T 4 – 5, Th 11 – 12
Economics	T, F 11 – 12	M, W 9 – 10
Mathematics	W 10 – 11, F 9 – 10	T, F 10 – 11
Biology Lab.	M or T or Th 2 – 6	W 2 – 6

Make a timetable for Sylvia.
Have the days along the top and the times down the side.

11.

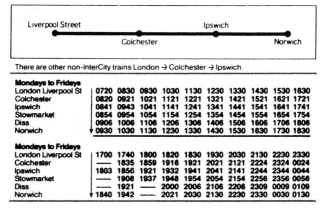

London – Colchester – Ipswich – Norwich

There are other non-InterCity trains London → Colchester → Ipswich.

Mondays to Fridays

London Liverpool St	0720	0830	0930	1030	1130	1230	1330	1430	1530	1630
Colchester	0820	0921	1021	1121	1221	1321	1421	1521	1621	1721
Ipswich	0841	0943	1041	1141	1241	1341	1441	1541	1641	1741
Stowmarket	0854	0954	1054	1154	1254	1354	1454	1554	1654	1754
Diss	0906	1006	1106	1206	1306	1406	1506	1606	1706	1806
Norwich	0930	1030	1130	1230	1330	1430	1530	1630	1730	1830

Mondays to Fridays

London Liverpool St	1700	1740	1800	1820	1830	1930	2030	2130	2230	2330
Colchester	—	1835	1859	1916	1921	2021	2121	2224	2324	0024
Ipswich	1803	1856	1921	1932	1941	2041	2141	2244	2344	0044
Stowmarket	—	1908	1937	1948	1954	2054	2154	2256	2356	0056
Diss	—	1921	—	2000	2006	2106	2206	2309	0009	0109
Norwich	1840	1942	—	2021	2030	2130	2230	2330	0030	0130

This is the Monday to Friday timetable of the InterCity train going from London (Liverpool St) to Norwich.

(a) At what time does the earliest train leave London for Norwich on Tuesdays? How long does the journey take?

The next train does not take as long. How much faster is the journey in the second train?

(b) There are two InterCity trains that differ a lot from the others. Which are they and how does each differ from the others?

(c) George needs to be in Ipswich on a Thursday night at about a quarter to nine. Which is the latest train he can catch from London?

Review 1   Murder Inc. played from 8·15p.m. until 8·50p.m. and from 9·30p.m. until 10·05p.m. and from 10·30p.m. until 11·25p.m. For how long did Murder Inc. play?

Review 2   An 180 min. video tape is used to record two programmes as shown. Will there be enough tape left to record a third programme which lasts 25 minutes?

Begin Recording	Finish Recording
09:20	10:10
15:05	17:00

Review 3

QANTAS

Flight	Day	Validity Routing		Meals	Depart/Arrive	Flying Time
QF5	- 2- - - 6-	(Until Apr 28)				
		Sydney/Melbourne		R	1300/1420	1.20
		Melbourne/Singapore	⊟	D,R	1525/2105	7.40
		Singapore/Bangkok		S	2230/2340	2.10
		Bangkok/Athens	⊟	S,B	0100/0720	10.20
		Athens/Frankfurt		R	0845/1010	2.25
QF7	- 2- - - 6-	Perth/Singapore	⊟	D	1530/2035	5.05
		Singapore/Bahrain		S,R	2215/0045	7.30
		Bahrain/London	⊟	B,R	0200/0655	6.55
QF11	- 2- - - - -	Sydney/Honolulu	⊟	D,B	1800/0715	9.15
		Honolulu/Los Angeles	⊟	L	0825/1640	5.15

(a) From this timetable, write down the Flying Time from Bahrain to London.

(b) Calculate the difference between the departure time at Bahrain and arrival time at London.

(c) Can you explain why your answers to (a) and (b) are different?

PUZZLES 12:7

? ?

1. Scones must be cooked for exactly 11 minutes. Robin decided to time his scones using two egg-timers, one of which ran for 3 minutes and the other for 7 minutes. How did he manage this?

2. Three slices of bread are to be toasted in an old toaster in which the bread is toasted on one side and then has to be turned over to toast the other side. The toaster holds two slices of bread at once. If each side of the bread takes 2 minutes to toast, show how to toast both sides of the three slices of bread in 6 minutes.

3. In three minutes time it will be three times as many minutes to 9 o'clock as it was past 8 o'clock nine minutes ago. What is the time now?

4. The digit 1 is often displayed on a digital clock. The digit 9 is not displayed as often. In a 12 hour period of time, for how many more minutes is at least one "1" displayed than at least one "9"?

? ?

PRACTICAL EXERCISE 12:8

1. Use bus and train timetables to plan an itinerary for a tourist.
   Have the tourist visiting many different places.

2. Use train and plane timetables to plan a journey you would like to take.

3. Look at a day's TV programmes.
   You could compare the time, on different channels, for news programmes, nature programmes, sports programmes etc.

   Use the programmes published in a newspaper or in TV magazines.

4. Investigate the time taken up by advertisements during different types of TV programmes.

5. Learn to use a stopwatch.
   Use the stopwatch to time another student either walking or running or jogging or cycling.

6. Do a project on mathematics in sport.

   You could investigate record times for athletics events at U.K. level or Commonwealth level or Olympic level.
   You could investigate how it is decided who competes in which heats when heats are needed.

WHAT   WHEN   WHERE   WHO   HOW   WHY

What imperial measures are used in farming?

When would a chemist use imperial measures?

Where do you use imperial measures in your other subjects?

Who, in their job, would often measure time?

How would an understanding of imperial measures be of use to a town planner?

Why would knowing about imperial measures help someone from Europe?

Metric and Imperial Equivalents

AROUND and ABOUT

DISCUSSION EXERCISE 13:1

Eduard and Laure have come with their parents from France to spend a holiday in England and Scotland.
They arrive at Gatwick Airport early one morning.
They hire a car and drive to Salisbury.
In Salisbury they book into self-catering accommodation.
In the early afternoon they go to the supermarket.
In the evening they go ten-pin bowling.
The next morning they drive to Stonehenge.

Discuss what imperial measures Eduard and Laure would have met so far.
Discuss what metric measures they would use instead of imperial measures.

Continue their holiday so Eduard and Laure do many different things. As they do each different thing, **discuss** all the unfamiliar measures they come across and what measures they would use instead.

MASS EQUIVALENTS

> **1kg is about 2 lb**
> **1 lb is about 0·5kg or 500g**

Worked Example   A recipe for fudge cake uses 8oz of butter. About how many grams is this?

Answer   1 lb of butter is about 500 grams. 8oz is $\frac{1}{2}$ lb.
$\frac{1}{2}$ lb of butter is about $\frac{1}{2} \times 500$ grams or 250g.

Worked Example   Fish is priced at £3·55 per lb. About how much per kg is this fish?

Answer   This fish is £3·55 for 1 lb.
1kg is about 2 lb. Therefore we want the price for about 2 lb.
Then, price per kg is about $2 \times £3·55$ or £7·10.

Worked Example   Ari's weight has increased from 47kg to 67kg.
Approximately how many stone has Ari gained?

Answer   Ari has gained 20kg which is about 2×20 lb.
Ari has gained about 40 lb = 2 stone 12 lb.
Ari has gained approximately 3 stone.

EXERCISE 13:2

1. Potatoes had these amounts written on the bags. Find the approximate British equivalent (i.e. imperial measure) for each.

   (a) 5kg   (b) 2kg   (c) 10kg   (d) 1500g   (e) 2500g

2. Packages to send overseas were weighed. Find the approximate metric equivalent for these.

   (a) 8 lb   (b) 2 lb   (c) 5 lb   (d) $\frac{1}{4}$ lb   (e) 12oz

3. A recipe for raspberry jam uses 6 lb of sugar. About how many kg of sugar is used?

4.

Apples	**5kg**
Pears	**250g**
Peaches	**500g**
Bananas	**250g**
Oranges	**1kg**

At the supermarket, Ruski bought the quantity of fruit shown.
Find the approximate total weight (in lbs) of this fruit.

5. Angelique has been weight-training for the last year.
During this time she has gained 1 stone 2 lb.
About how many kg has Angelique gained?

6. Steak is priced at £15 per kg.
What is the approximate price, per lb, of this steak?

Review 1 Potatoes are priced at £1·20 per kg.
What is the approximate price, per lb, of these potatoes?

Review 2 Alexis weighed her cat. Its weight was 12 lb.
About how many kg does this cat weigh?

Review 3 Tim weighs 8 stone. Jake weighs 7 stone.
About how many kg heavier than Jake is Tim?

Review 4 Tim's baby sister weighed 3500g at birth.
About how many pounds did she weigh?

CAPACITY EQUIVALENTS

> **1 gallon is about 4·5 litres**
> **1 litre is about 1·75 pints**

Worked Example A tank holds 40 gallons of water. About how many litres is this?

Answer 1 gallon is about 4·5 litres.
40 gallons is about 40 × 4·5 litres or 180 litres.
That is, the tank holds about 180 litres of water.

Worked Example A measuring jug can hold 2·5 litres.
What is the approximate capacity of this jug in pints?

Answer 1 litre is about 1·75 pints.
2·5 litres is about 2·5 × 1·75 pints or 4·375 pints.
Then, the approximate capacity of the jug is about 4·4 pints.

We could also give the answer as "about $4\frac{1}{2}$ pints" or "nearly $4\frac{1}{2}$ pints".
Either of these answers would be a reasonable approximation.

Worked Example A bucket holds 10 litres of water. About how many gallons is this?

Answer 4·5 litres is about 1 gallon.
We need to find how many lots of 4·5 litres there are in 10 litres. We do this by dividing 10 by 4·5.
Since 10 ÷ 4·5 = 2·2̇, there are 2·2̇ lots of 4·5 litres in 10 litres. Roughly, this is a little more than 2 lots. Then, 10 litres is a little more than 2 gallons.

EXERCISE 13:3

1. "Delicious Drinks" packages its juice in the following sizes. Find the approximate British equivalent i.e. imperial equivalent.

   (a) 9 litres   (b) 2 litres   (c) 5 litres   (d) 0·5 litres   (e) 13·7 litres

2. Water containers have the following capacities. Find the approximate metric equivalent of each.

   (a) 2 gallons   (b) 60 gallons   (c) 21 pints   (d) 5 pints

3. About how many litres of water can be held in an 80 gallon tank?

4. About how many litres of wine is there in an 11 pint wine cask?

Review 1   A goldfish bowl holds 4 gallons of water. About how many litres is this?

Review 2   200 litres of water are poured into a paddling pool. About how many gallons of water are poured in?

LENGTH EQUIVALENTS

> 5 miles is about 8km
> 3 feet is a little less than 1m
> 1 inch is about 2·5cm

Worked Example   Dee walked 20km. About how many miles did Dee walk?

Answer   Firstly, find how many lots of 8km Dee walked.
We do this by dividing 20 by 8. We get 2·5.

Since there are 5 miles in each lot of 8km, we now multiply by 5 to find the total number of miles.
We get $5 \times 2·5 = 12·5$ miles.
That is, Dee walked about $12\frac{1}{2}$ miles.

Worked Example   It is 158 miles from Swansea to Southampton. About how far is it in km?

Answer   Firstly, find how many lots of 5 miles there are in 158 miles.
Since $158 \div 5 = 31·6$, there are 31·6 lots of 5 miles in 158 miles.

Since there are about 8km in every 5 miles there are about
$8 \times 31·6 = 252·8$km in 158 miles.

We would give the answer as about 253km.

Worked Example   One of the corridors in the school is 25m long. About how many feet
   is this corridor?

Answer   Each metre is a little more than 3 feet.
   25m is a little more than 25 × 3 feet = 75 feet.

   That is, the corridor is a bit longer than 75 feet.

Worked Example   Kate measured her handspan as 20cm. About how many inches is
   Kate's handspan?

Answer   Firstly, find how many lots of 2·5cm there are in 20cm.
   Since 20 ÷ 2·5 = 8, there are 8 lots of 2·5cm in 20cm.

   Since there is about 1 inch in every 2·5cm,
   there are about 1 × 8 = 8 inches in 20cm.

   That is, Kate's handspan is about 8 inches.

EXERCISE 13:4

1. Distances on a map were given in km.
    Josefa wanted to convert them to miles. Approximately how many miles are there in
    the following?

    (a) 40km   **(b)** 200km   **(c)** 24km   **(d)** 98km   **(e)** 5km

2. Argene was visiting England. In her country distances were measured in km.
    Convert these distances to km.

    (a) 20 miles   **(b)** 200 miles   **(c)** 50 miles   **(d)** 12 miles   **(e)** 62 miles

3. Measurements for a theatre prop. were taken in inches and feet. Amanda needed
    these measurements in cm. Convert the following for her.

    (a) 6 inches   **(b)** 2 inches   **(c)** 18 inches   **(d)** 1 foot   **(e)** 5 feet

4. Approximately how many inches are there in

    (a) 5cm   **(b)** 10cm   **(c)** 30cm   **(d)** 1m   **(e)** 2·4m?

5. A school is 50m long. About how many feet is this?

6. Jenufa's family own a 16′ caravan.
   Find the approximate length of this caravan, in metres.

7. A book measures 25cm by 18cm.
   Find the approximate dimensions of this book, in inches.

8. A cat's tail is 8 inches long.
   About how many cm is this?

9.

Ireland

```
                                                                    Kilometres
                    402  116  166   80  315  439   37  328  113  109  309  203  212  317
      Belfast            291  248  321  196   87  439   93  452  397  198  321  190  117
         Cork                 50   35  225  351  203  240  196  134  167  214  111  204
            Drogheda              85  217  304  204  193  235  180  161  214   97  154
 250          Dublin                 246  359  153  248  158  103  240  171  132  237
  72  181        Dundalk                214  352  103  283  238  307  145  132  227
 103  154   31      Galway                  476  111  483  428  261  348  227  180
  50  200   22   53     Killarney              365  116  121  365  240  249  359
 196  122  140  135  153     Larne                 372  317  204  237  116  124
 273   54  218  189  223  133     Limerick              55  397  138  262  389
  23  273  126  127   95  219  296    Londonderry           343  111  208  335
 204   58  149  120  154   64   69  227    Omagh                 330  175   80
  70  281  122  146   98  176  300   72  231    Rosslare              153  283
  68  247   23  112   64  148  266   75  197   34     Sligo                130
 192  123  104  100  149  191  162  227  127  247  213    Tullamore
 126  200  133  133  106   90  216  149  147   86   69  205    Waterford
 132  118   69   60   82   82  141  155   72  163  129  109   95
 197   73  127   96  147  141  112  223   77  242  208   50  176   81

 Miles
```

(a) Using this distance chart find the distance in km and in miles between Belfast and Limerick.

(b) The Hannah family travel from Rosslare to Galway, via Dublin.
    How many km do they travel?

(c) On their return journey, the Hannah family travel from Galway to Rosslare via Cork and Waterford. How many miles do they travel on this return journey?

Review 1 The garage in Ana's house is 4 metres long.
What is the approximate length of this garage in feet?

Review 2 Ana's arm is 20 inches long.
Find her arm length in cm.

Review 3 Ana lives 23 miles from Manchester.
About how many km from Manchester does Ana live?

Review 4 Ana measured the length of the path around her house.
She measured this as 46 feet.
Find the approximate length of this path, in metres.

Review 5 Ana ran in a 10000m road race.

(a) How many km was this race?

(b) About how many miles was this?

EQUIVALENTS for LENGTH, CAPACITY, MASS

EXERCISE 13:5

---

1. A farmer's rucksack sprayer holds 16*l* of spray.
About how many pints of spray is this?

2. The distance between Oxford and Cambridge is 100 miles.
About how many km is this?

3. A recipe for chocolate cake has 4oz of margarine.
About how many grams is this?

4. By volume, the amount of blood in an adult is about 10·5 pints.
About how many litres is this?

5. Suzannah's and Paula's dog weighed 44kg. The vet said it had to lose at least 5kg.
How many pounds did the dog have to lose?

6. The water in a bath is 350mm deep.

(a) What is this depth in cm?

(b) Find the approximate depth of this water, in inches.

7. A washing machine holds about 30*l* of water.
    About how many gallons of water will this washing machine hold?

8. Highlife paint can be bought in 2*l* and 5*l* tins.
    About how many more pints does the larger tin hold?

9. Verity received a letter from her 11-year-old penpal Abbie.
    Abbie included a diagram of her house with the measurements in metres. Verity
    converted these to feet and inches. Abbie's diagram is shown below.
    Do the conversions.

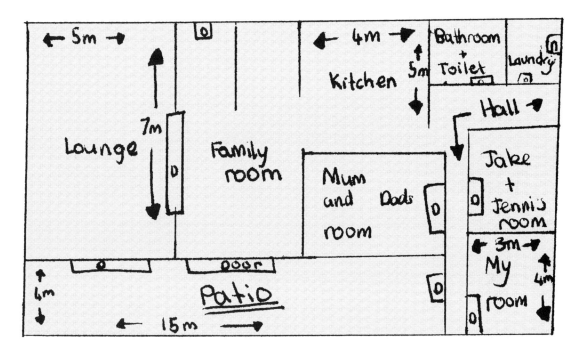

Review 1   During the last two years, Gavin's weight has increased by 13kg.
              About how many stone has Gavin gained in the last two years?

Review 2   The fuel tank on Debbie's car holds 14 gallons of petrol.
              The fuel tank on Chrissie's car holds 60 litres of petrol.
              Which car holds the most petrol?

Review 3   A marathon is 42km.
              Approximately how many miles is a marathon?

INVESTIGATION 13:6

HOW ACCURATE?

We have used the approximation: 1kg is about 2 lb.
A better approximation is: 1kg is about 2·2 lb.

Using 1kg is about 2 lb, work out the approximate weight, in stones, of a person who weighs 64kg.
Using 1kg is about 2·2 lb, work out the approximate weight, in stones, of this person.

In what situations would the approximation, 1kg is about 2 lb, not be accurate enough?
Investigate.

How accurate is the approximation: 5 miles is about 8km? **Investigate** situations where a better approximation needs to be used.
Also **investigate** the other approximations we used for length.

How accurate are the approximations: 1 litre is about 1·75 pints, 1 gallon is about 4·5 litres? **Investigate** situations where better approximations need to be used.

WHAT   WHEN   WHERE   WHO   HOW   WHY

What countries use just metric measures; what countries use some metric and some imperial measures?

When would you need to convert between imperial measures and metric measures?

Where, in industry, are both metric and imperial measures used?

Who, in their job, would need to convert between imperial and metric measures?

How and why did this country begin using metric measures?

Why would you need to convert between imperial and metric measures in your other subjects?

AROUND and ABOUT

DISCUSSION EXERCISE 14:1

-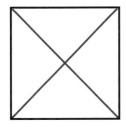

  Johnny measured the diagonal of this square to be 4cm.
  Helen measured it to be 42mm.
  Rosalie measured it to be 41·5mm.
  Who is right? **Discuss.**

- Is it possible to measure something *exactly*? **Discuss.**

-

  Rohan estimated the length of the corridor to be about 20 metres.
  How might he have done this? **Discuss.**

  When he measured it he got 32 metres. What might have gone wrong? **Discuss.**

  Janet wanted to measure the corridor as accurately as possible. How could she do this? **Discuss.**

- Think of a situation where someone has measured inaccurately and this has mattered. **Discuss.**

ACCURACY of MEASUREMENT

The **accuracy of a measurement** depends on how accurately the measuring instrument used can be read and on how accurately this is actually read.

DISCUSSION EXERCISE 14:2

-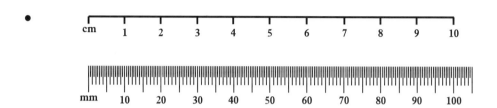

Measure the length of a small object, such as a paper clip, using both of the measuring instruments shown above.
Did everyone in your group get the same measurement using the ruler with cm divisions?
Did everyone get the same measurement using the ruler with mm divisions?

Measure the length of another small object using the ruler with mm divisions.
Measure again. Did you get the same answer both times? Would it have been easy (or was it easy) to get different answers?
Discuss possible reasons for getting different answers.
Discuss ways of measuring as accurately as possible.

- The ruler is one instrument used to measure length. What other measuring instruments are used for length? **Discuss.**

- Mass, capacity, time are other things that need to be measured. What measuring instruments are used for these? **Discuss.**

218

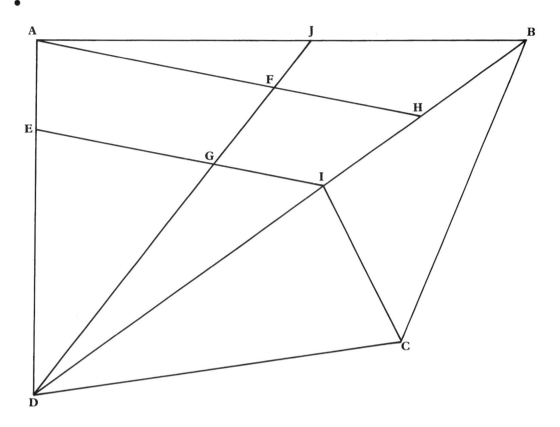

Measure the length of each of the lines.

Compare your measurements with those of the rest of your group or class or neighbour. If two students get different answers, how can you decide whose measurement is more accurate? **Discuss.**

PRACTICAL EXERCISE 14:3

Athletics events which are now timed electronically were not always timed as accurately.

Do a project on one of the following: Olympic Games
Horse Racing
Yacht Racing
Speedway

As part of your project look at the way measurements, in the topic you choose, have increased in accuracy over the years.

EFFECT of MEASUREMENT ERRORS

Sometimes an **error in measurement** is very important and sometimes it is not important. It depends on the size of the error and the particular situation.

DISCUSSION EXERCISE 14:4

- Anna measured a length to be 4cm shorter than it really was. How important would this error be in the following situations? **Discuss.**

  Situation 1   Anna was measuring the length of her room, so she could calculate the cost of buying carpet.
  Situation 2   Anna was measuring the length of a card, so she could buy a box of the right size for these cards.

  Think of some other situations where an error in the measurement of length would be important and others where it would not be important. **Discuss.**

- Abe didn't know that his watch was 5 minutes slow. How important is this in the following situations? **Discuss.**

  Situation 1   Abe has to catch the 0805 train.
  Situation 2   Abe is going to spend 20 minutes on his aerobics.

  Think of some other situations where an error in the measurement of time would be important and others where it would not be important. **Discuss.**

- **Discuss** the effect of measurement errors in these situations.

  Situation 1   A customer asks for 3·8m of dress material. The shop assistant measures wrongly and gives the customer 3·6m.
  Situation 2   A customer asks for 20·5m of curtain material. The shop assistant measures wrongly and gives the customer 20·6m.

- **Discuss** the effect of measurement errors in these situations.

  Situation 1   Natasha asked for 100 grams of caviar. She was given 150 grams.
  Situation 2   Ben was baking a chocolate cake. The recipe said 200g of butter was needed. Ben measured wrongly and used just 190g of butter.

CHOOSING the DEGREE of ACCURACY

All measurements are approximate. For instance, a length could be measured to the nearest mm or nearest cm or nearest m or nearest km. Whether we choose to give the length to the nearest mm or cm or m or km depends on how accurate we need the measurement to be.

DISCUSSION EXERCISE 14:5

- A fashion designer cuts the pattern pieces for a dress. How inaccurate can the pattern pieces be cut and still have the dress fitting well? **Discuss.**

- To build a house, what measurements are needed? How accurate do these have to be? Do some need to be more accurate than others? **Discuss.**

- Do the lengths of some sports fields and tracks need to be known more accurately than others? **Discuss.**

- Can you think of any reasons why it might be necessary to have road distances given more accurately than shown by signposts? **Discuss.**

- Think of things you or your family might buy by the length. Would you buy these things by the metre or centimetre or millimetre? **Discuss.**

- Think of things you or your family might buy by weight or volume. **Discuss** whether you would buy by the gram or kilogram or tonne or millilitre or litre.

- **Discuss** the importance of goods being the weight given (or the volume given) on the label.

Worked Example   distance between two villages
distance between two keys on a calculator
width of a river
thickness of a classroom door
depth of the sea

Which of the things in the list would be measured to the following degrees of accuracy?

(a) to the nearest mm   **(b)**   to the nearest m

(c) to the nearest km

Answer **(a)** distance between two keys on a calculator
thickness of a classroom door

(b) width of a river
depth of the sea

(c) distance between two villages

EXERCISE 14:6

1.

to the nearest gram	to the nearest kg	to the nearest tonne
to the nearest mm	to the nearest m	to the nearest km
to the nearest m*l*	to the nearest *l*	

Choose the degree of accuracy (from those in the box) to which these would be measured.

(a) the diameter of a flower

(b) the weight of a cricket ball

(c) the length of an airport runway

(d) the distance a train travels in an hour

(e) the weight of a chocolate

(f) the height of a chair

(g) the weight of a bicycle

(h) a dose of cough medicine

(i) the weight of a train

(j) the capacity of a car's petrol tank

2. Write down at least two things you would measure to these degrees of accuracy.

   (a) to the nearest hour   (b) to the nearest 5 min.

   (c) to the nearest min.   (d) to the nearest sec.

   (e) to the nearest $\frac{1}{10}$ of a sec.

3. How accurately would these be measured? Give your answer as "to the nearest . . .".

   (a) the length of a motorway

   (b) the weight of a ship

   (c) the length of a ship

   (d) the amount of tomato sauce in a bottle

   (e) the weight of a tomato

   (f) the weight of a full rucksack

   (g) the amount of water in a tank

   (h) the width of a wedding ring

   (i) the height of a mountain in Switzerland

   (j) the distance between plants in a hothouse

   (k) the length of a sailing race

Review Write down two things, other than those in **questions 1 or 3** that you would measure to these degrees of accuracy.

   (a) to the nearest m   (b) to the nearest *l*

   (c) to the nearest mm   (d) to the nearest g

   (e) to the nearest kg   (f) to the nearest m*l*

PRACTICAL EXERCISE 14:7

1. Choose five objects to weigh.
   Choose the degree of accuracy you will use.
   Compare your results with those of the other students in your group or class.

2. Choose five jars or bottles such as a tomato sauce bottle etc.
   Find the capacity of these.
   Choose the degree of accuracy you will use.
   Compare your results with those of the other students in your group or class.

3. Choose the degree of accuracy needed to measure some lengths around your school. Decide whether you need to use a trundle wheel or metre tape or ruler with cm and/or mm divisions or a micrometer screw gauge.
   Measure these lengths as accurately as possible.

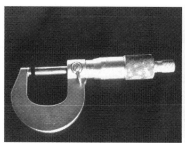  

4. Design an experiment, such as measuring reaction time, to measure small intervals of time.
   Choose the degree of accuracy you will use.

PRACTICAL EXERCISE 14:8

The pendulum clock was invented in the 17th century. Before this, time was sometimes measured using the clocks described.

The Candle Clock

Marks were made at equal distances down the side of a candle.
How close do you think these marks might be if it took 5 minutes to burn the length of candle between two marks?

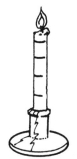

The Water Clock

A container, such as that shown, was filled with water.
The water dripped out of a hole at the bottom.
Marks were made on the inside of the container. Equal intervals of time were read off by watching the level drop from one mark to the next.
Do you think the marks should be equally spaced?

Sinking Bowl Clock
A small bowl, with a hole in the bottom, was put in a large container of water. The time it took for the bowl to sink measured a particular interval of time.

Design and make a clock to measure an interval of time, maybe 2 minutes or 5 minutes or 15 minutes.
You may like to make a candle clock or a water clock or a sinking bowl clock. You may like to make a different sort of clock.

Make your clock as accurate as possible.

WHAT   WHEN   WHERE   WHO   HOW   WHY

What situations can you think of where a tragedy might happen if something was not measured accurately enough?

When, in your other subjects, do you need to have an understanding of measurement accuracy?

Where, in a hotel, might an understanding of measurement accuracy be needed?

Who might lose their job if they did not measure accurately enough?

How important is it for these people to measure accurately?
     tailor, painter, sailor, drainlayer, farmer, mechanic, zoo-keeper

Why must doctors, nurses and chemists have a good understanding of measurement accuracy?

AROUND and ABOUT

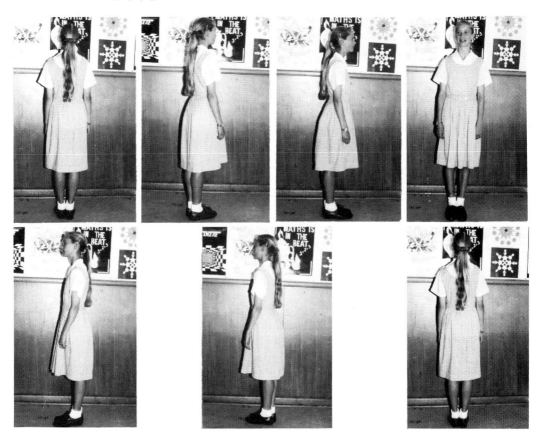

DISCUSSION EXERCISE 15:1

Stand up.
Face the front of the class.
Turn around slowly so you face the back of the class.
Keep on turning around slowly until you are facing the front again.

When you turned from facing the front to facing the front again, you turned through a complete circle.

When you turned half-way around, from facing the front to facing the back, you turned through half a circle.

How might you describe the amount of turn if you turned just a little way. That is, if you turned less than half a circle? How might you describe the amount of turn if you turned more than half-way but not quite right around? **Discuss.**

ANGLES

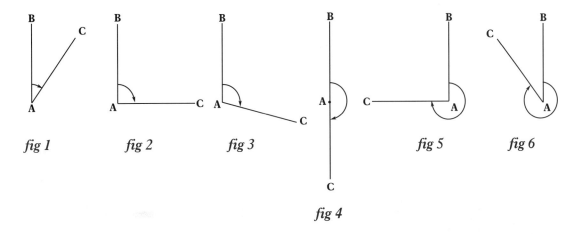

fig 1   fig 2   fig 3   fig 5   fig 6

fig 4

These diagrams show angles of different sizes.

Suppose you are standing at A looking towards B. If you turned so you were now looking at C, the angle you would have turned through in *fig 1* is quite small. In *fig 2* the angle is a bit bigger, in *fig 3* it is larger still etc.

To describe the size of an angle we use a measure called the **degree**. If we turn through a complete circle we have turned through 360 degrees. We write 360 degrees as 360°. That is, the symbol °, written at the top right-hand side of the number, is the symbol for degrees.

How big is 1°?
There are 360° in a circle.
If you turn through a complete circle in 360 equal small turns, each of these small turns will be 1°. 1° is quite small, isn't it? Try turning through a complete circle in 360 equal small turns.

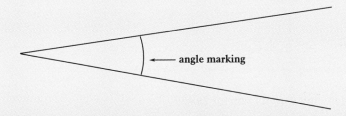

We usually mark the angle formed by two lines as shown.
The lines are called the **arms** of the angle.
The point where the arms meet is called the **vertex** of the angle.

Example

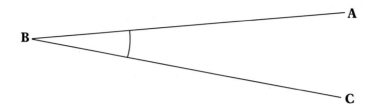

In this diagram the vertex of the angle is B. The arms of the angle are the lines AB and BC.

EXERCISE 15:2

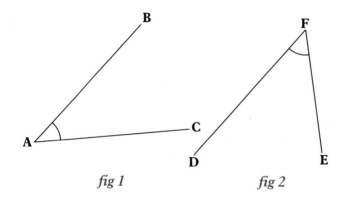

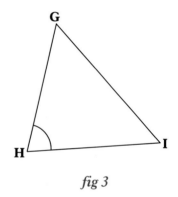

fig 1　　　　　　*fig 2*　　　　　　*fig 3*

1. For *fig 1* name (a)　the vertex of the angle

　　　　　　　　(b)　the arms of the angle.

2. Repeat question 1 for *fig 2*.

Review Are these statements true or false?

　　(a)　For *fig 3*, the vertex of the marked angle is H.

　　(b)　For *fig 3*, the arms of the marked angle are HI and GI.

MEASURING ANGLES

We measure the size of an angle with a **protractor**.
There are two sorts of protractors; a circular one and a semicircular one.

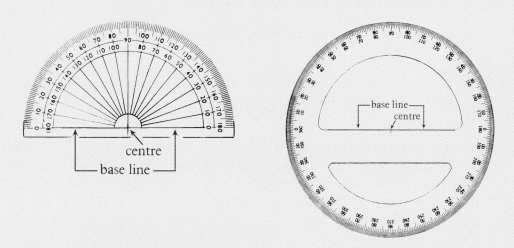

The **base line** and the **centre** have been marked on both protractors.

We use these protractors in a similar way.
Notice that they have two scales; an inside scale and an outside scale. We must take care to use the correct scale. We shall say more about which scale to use soon.

Always check that you have used the correct scale by making a rough estimate of the answer. Remember that

$$\begin{aligned}
\text{a complete circle} &= 360° \\
\text{half a circle} &= 180° \\
\text{quarter of a circle} &= 90° \\
\text{three-quarters of a circle} &= 270°
\end{aligned}$$

We use these to do a rough estimate of the size of the angle to be measured. That is, we estimate whether it is less than a quarter of a circle (i.e. less than 90°), between quarter and half of a circle (i.e. between 90° and 180°), between half and three-quarters of a circle (i.e. between 180° and 270°) or between three-quarters of a circle and a complete circle (i.e. between 270° and 360°).
Always do this estimate before measuring.

Follow these steps to measure an angle **using the protractor**.

Step 1. Estimate the size of the angle.

Step 2. Place the centre of the protractor on the vertex of the angle.

Step 3. Keeping the centre on the vertex, move the protractor around (i.e. rotate the protractor) until the base line lies along one of the arms of the angle.

Step 4. Decide whether to use the inside or outside scale. The scale to use is the one that has 0° on the arm of the angle.

Step 5. Read off the number where the other arm of the angle meets the chosen scale.

Step 6. Check this number with your estimate to make sure you have read the correct scale.

These steps are shown in the following examples.
A semicircular protractor is used in these examples. If you have a circular protractor use it in the same way, making sure that it is placed over the angle so that the base line and the 90° marking are in the same position as shown.

Examples

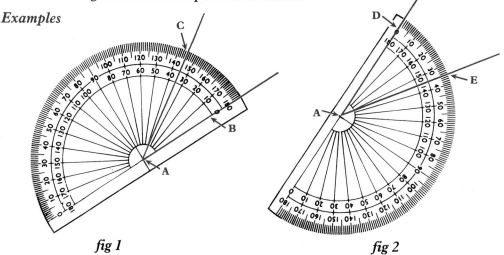

fig 1   *fig 2*

Step 1. These angles are both less than a quarter of a circle i.e. they are both less than 90°.

Steps 2, 3. The centre of the protractor (**A**) is on the vertex of the angle. In *fig 1* we have chosen to place the base line of the protractor along the bottom arm of the angle while in *fig 2* we have chosen to place the base line of the protractor along the top arm of the angle.

Steps 4, 5, 6. In *fig 1* the 0° on the protractor (**B**) is on the inside scale. This is the scale we use to measure the angle in this diagram. Read round the inside scale until we meet the other arm of the angle (**C**).

We get a measurement of 35°.
This measurement agrees with our estimate.

230

In *fig 2* the 0° on the protractor (**D**) is on the outside scale. This is the scale we use to measure the angle in this diagram. Read round the outside scale until we meet the other arm of the angle (**E**).

We get a measurement of 35°. This measurement agrees with our estimate.

The previous examples showed that we can choose to place the base line along either arm of the angle to be measured. The important thing in measuring is to read the scale that begins at 0°. This could be either the inside or outside scale.

Example

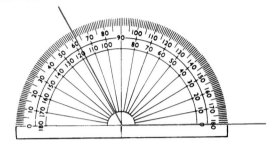

This angle is more than a quarter of a circle but less than half a circle. An estimate of its size is between 90° and 180°. The base line of the protractor is on the right-hand arm of the angle. The 0° is on the inside scale. Read round the inside scale until we meet the left-hand arm of the angle. We get a reading of 118°. This agrees with our estimate.

Measure the angle again, putting the base line of the protractor on the left-hand arm. What scale did you read this time? Did you get the same measurement as before?

EXERCISE 15:3

1. Measure the size of the angles marked **a, b, c, d, e**. Give your answers to the nearest degree.

   As a check on the accuracy of your measurement, add all 5 angles together. They should total 360°.

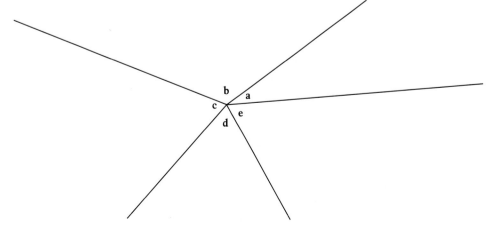

2.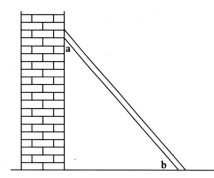

This is a diagram of a ladder leaning against a wall.

(a) Measure the angle between the ladder and the wall i.e. the angle marked as **a**.

(b) Measure the angle between the ladder and the ground i.e. the angle marked as **b**.

3. Measure the size of each of the angles inside the triangle.

As a check on the accuracy of your measurement, add all 3 angles together. They should total 180°.

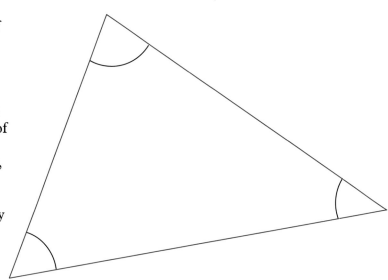

4.

Carefully trace this diagram into your book.
Measure as many angles as you can find. Write these measurements on your diagram.
Since most of the angles have short arms, you will have to extend many of the lines before you measure.

Review Draw some large triangles. Make these triangles of different shapes. Use a
sharp pencil.
Measure the three angles in each triangle as shown in **question 3**.
No matter what the shape of your triangle, the three angles should total 180°.
Use this to check the accuracy of your measuring.

INVESTIGATION 15:4

ANGLES and TIME

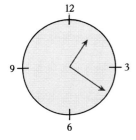

How many times do the hands of a clock make a 90°
angle in a 24-hour period of time?

The size of an angle which is greater than half a circle, i.e. greater than 180°, can be read
directly from a circular protractor. If you have a semicircular protractor take these steps.

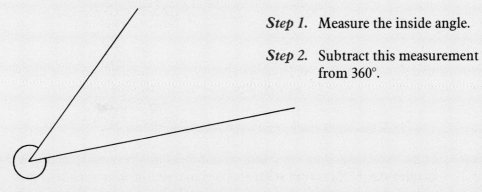

Step 1. Measure the inside angle.

Step 2. Subtract this measurement
from 360°.

Taking these steps the inside angle is measured as 43°.
The marked angle is 360° – 43° = 317°

EXERCISE 15:5

1. Measure the size of each of the marked angles.
   As a check on the accuracy of your measurement, add all four angles together. They should total 1080°.

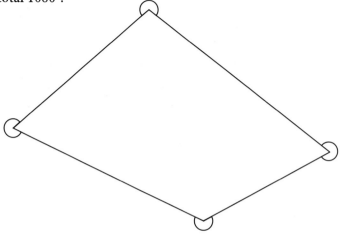

2.

Trace this diagram into your book.
Measure as many angles as you can find. Write these measurements on your diagram.
You will have to extend most of the lines to be able to measure the angles.

Review   Draw some large four-sided shapes and measure the outside angles as shown in **question 1**. No matter what shape you draw, the four outside angles should always total 1080°. Use this to check the accuracy of your measuring.

DRAWING ANGLES

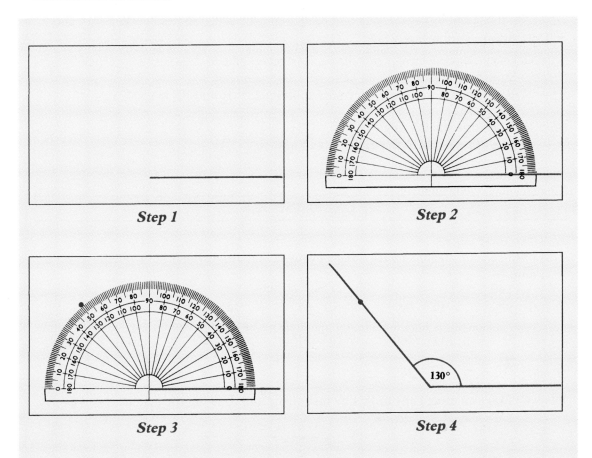

These diagrams show the steps taken to draw an angle of 130°.

Step 1. Draw a straight line. This will be one of the arms of the angle.

Step 2. Place the protractor so that the base line lies along the drawn line and the centre of the protractor is on the end of the drawn line.

Step 3. Read around the scale that begins 0° on the drawn line. Put a small mark beside 130°.

Step 4. Take the protractor away.
Through the small mark, draw the other arm of the angle.

Angles of any size, between 0° and 180°, are drawn in a similar way to that shown above.

Using a circular protractor, angles of any size between 0° and 360° may be drawn as shown on the previous page. Using a semicircular protractor, angles between 180° and 360° are drawn as follows.

Step 1. Subtract the size of the angle to be drawn from 360°.
For instance, to draw 235°, firstly subtract 235° from 360° to get 125°.

Step 2. Draw this smaller angle.
The other angle in the diagram will now be 235°.

EXERCISE 15:6

1. Draw these angles.
Compare your diagrams with those of your neighbour or the other students in your group.

   (a) 30°   (b) 80°   (c) 65°   (d) 160°   (e) 124°

   (f) 92°   (g) 200°   (h) 245°   (i) 257°   (j) 300°

   (k) 310°   (l) 281°

Review Make an exact copy of this by measuring and drawing the distances and angles.
Do not trace the diagram.

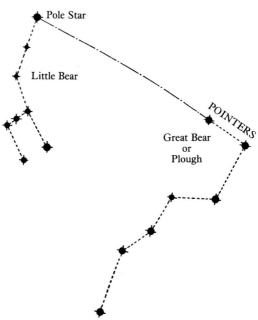

THE PLOUGH (OR "GREAT BEAR"),
THE POLE STAR AND THE "LITTLE BEAR"

PRACTICAL EXERCISE 15:7

1. **Work in pairs.** Measure your angle of vision. Your partner should stand behind you holding a pencil at your eye height. This pencil should be gradually moved forward until you can see it.

2. Draw a circle of radius 4cm.
   Mark a point on the circle and label it as 1.
   Use your protractor to mark the points 2, 3, . . . 12 which
   are evenly spaced around the circle.
   Join each point to the point that is 3 spacings further
   around the circle i.e. join 1 to 4, 2 to 5, 3 to 6, . . . 12 to 3.
   Colour the design you have made.

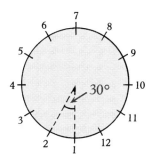

   Variation Mark off 24 equally spaced points around the circle and continue as above.

   Variation Join the points using a different spacing e.g. join each point to the point that is 4 spacings further around the circle.

   Variation Use equally spaced nails on a circular board and join the nails with thread.

3. Draw a circle of radius 5cm.
   Mark off 36 equally spaced points around the circle.
   Join 1 to 2, 2 to 4, 3 to 6, 4 to 8, . . . 18 to 36 to make a design.

   Variation Join 1 to 2, 2 to 4, 3 to 6 . . . 18 to 36 and then 19 to 2, 20 to 4, 21 to 6 . . . 35 to 34. You should get a cardioid (heart shape).

Note You may wish to begin with a larger circle and you may wish to mark off 72 equally spaced points around the circle instead of 36.
   You may wish to use equally spaced nails on a circular board and join the nails with thread.

4. Design a verandah for a house that allows no sun into the house in mid-summer but the maximum amount of sun in mid-winter.

5. Explain the use of some angle measuring instrument (other than the protractor).

6. Make a periscope.

ESTIMATING ANGLE SIZE

The best estimate you would be expected to give would be to the nearest 10°.
When estimating the size of an angle it is often helpful to compare with a right angle.

Examples The angle in *fig 1* is about one-third of a right angle i.e. about 30°.

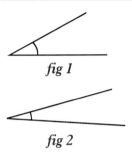

fig 1

The angle in *fig 2* is a little less than one-third of a right angle i.e. about 20°.

fig 2

DISCUSSION EXERCISE 15:8

* Estimate the size of the angle between the hands of these clocks.

  Discuss your estimates with your neighbour or group.

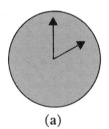 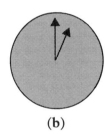 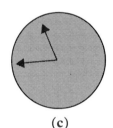 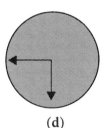

(a)   (b)   (c)   (d)

* Estimate the size of the following angles. **Discuss.**

  * What is the angle between the back of your school chair and its seat?

  * What angle does your back make with the back of the chair when you are writing at your desk?

  * At what angle to the page do you hold your pen when you are writing?

  * At what angle to the water do you dive into the swimming pool?

  * What is the angle between your arms when you are cycling?

  * At what angle to a wall does a painter usually have a ladder?

  * What is the greatest angle you can make between your thumb and each of your fingers?

  * What angle is a staircase likely to make with the floor?

- What is the angle between the broom handle and the floor as you sweep the floor?
- What angle is a wheelchair ramp likely to make with the ground?
- What is the angle between your feet when you stand?
- Ask someone in your group to put their arms up in the air. Estimate the angle between their arms.
- At what angle to the calculator do you hold your finger when you press the keys?

NAMING ANGLES

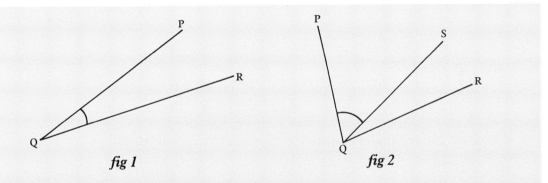

fig 1   *fig 2*

An angle can be named by the capital letter at the vertex.
In *fig 1* the marked angle can be named as the angle Q or as ∠Q. The symbol ∠ is the symbol for angle.

An angle can also be named by using three capital letters.
In *fig 1* the marked angle could be named as ∠PQR or ∠RQP. When we use three capital letters to name an angle, the first letter is the letter at the end of one of the arms, the middle letter is the letter at the vertex and the last letter is the letter at the end of the other arm.

In *fig 2* we cannot name the marked angle as ∠Q since there is more than one angle at Q. There is ∠PQS on the left, ∠SQR on the right and taking these two angles together there is the ∠PQR. Whenever there is more than one angle at a point we must use three letters to name the angle we want. The marked angle in *fig 2* may be named as either ∠PQS or ∠SQP.

Always remember that when an angle is named by three capital letters, it is the middle letter that is the vertex.

EXERCISE 15:9

1. Name the marked angles using a single letter e.g. **(a)** is ∠B.

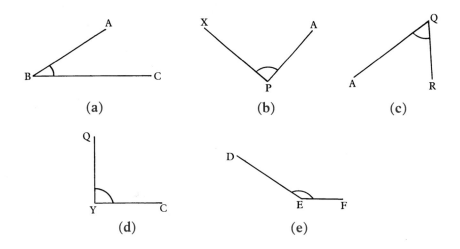

2. Name the marked angles in **question 1** using three capital letters.

3.

SAM	H ··	O ··	·· N	A ··	L ··	·· S	S ··
(a)	(b)	(c)	(d)	(e)	(f)	(g)	(h)

Copy the chart.
Name the marked angles on the diagrams below and complete this chart e.g. the angle marked in **(a)** is ∠SAM so SAM is filled in as shown.

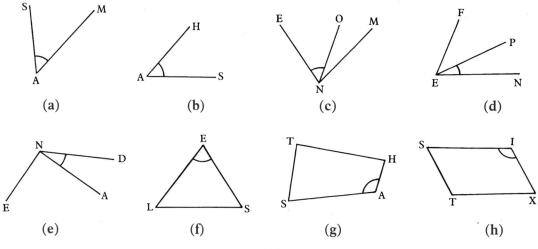

Review Name the marked angles. Use a single letter if it is sensible, otherwise use three letters.

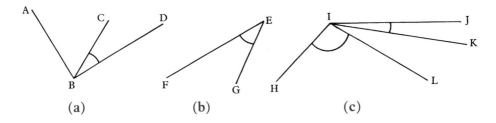

(a)   (b)   (c)

INVESTIGATION 15:10

ANGLES in the ENVIRONMENT

Choose one of the following topics and **investigate** the angles involved in the topic.
Some suggestions for the investigation are given.

Roofs. You could consider the pitch of the roofs on the houses in your street, the angles a roof makes with other parts of a building, the angles between parts of a roof etc.

Farms. You could consider the angles between fencelines, the angles through which gates swing, the angle of a loading ramp, the angle between the sides and the bottom of a trough etc.

Cars. You could consider the angles between windscreens and bonnets in various cars, the angles of seat backs, the angles through which the doors and bonnet and boot move as they are opened etc.

Clothing. You could consider the angles between seams, the angles of collar peaks, the angles in patterns for a garment etc.

continued . . .

. . . *from previous page*

Nature. You could consider trees. You could choose just one shrub or tree and consider leaves, branches, trunk, flowers etc. You could choose some different types of trees or shrubs and consider the angles between the leaves and the stems.

Sport. You could consider a sport such as cricket. You could investigate the angles between positions such as Slip and Cover.

Leisure. You could consider a leisure activity such as snooker. You could investigate the angle at which a ball must be hit if it is to be sunk. You would have to consider the balls at different positions on the table.

PUZZLE 15:11

```
                S
              S E S
            S E L E S
          S E L G L E S
        S E L G N G L E S
      S E L G N A N G L E S
        S E L G N G L E S
          S E L G L E S
            S E L E S
              S E S
                S
```

Beginning at the **A** in the centre, how many ways can the word ANGLES be spelt?

You may move up or down or sideways.

```
            S
          GLE
e.g. One way is    AN
```

TYPES OF ANGLES

A **right angle** is a $\frac{1}{4}$ turn.

A **straight angle** is a $\frac{1}{2}$ turn.

An **acute angle** is smaller than a right angle.

An **obtuse angle** is greater than a right angle but smaller than a straight angle.

A **reflex angle** is greater than a straight angle but less than a complete turn.

DISCUSSION EXERCISE 15:12

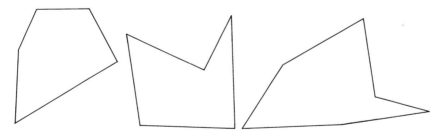

- Draw a shape with 3 acute angles and 1 obtuse angle.
  Draw a shape with 1 reflex angle, 1 right angle, 2 acute angles and 1 obtuse angle.

  Discuss your shapes with your group.

- Choose the number of sides a shape is to have.
  Decide on the types of angles the shape is to have.

  Discuss with your group how the shape can be drawn.

EXERCISE 15:13

1.

| Acute | Obtuse | Reflex | Right | Straight |

Name the marked angles, choosing from the names in the box.

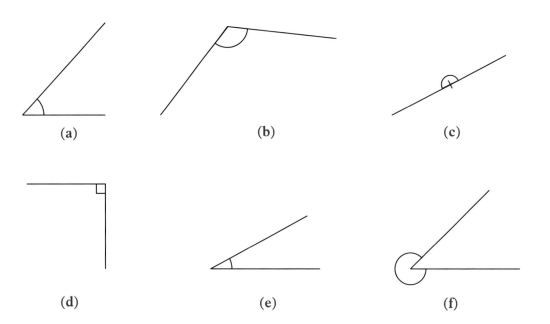

    (a)   (b)   (c)

    (d)   (e)   (f)

2. Name each of the marked angles.

(a)   (b)

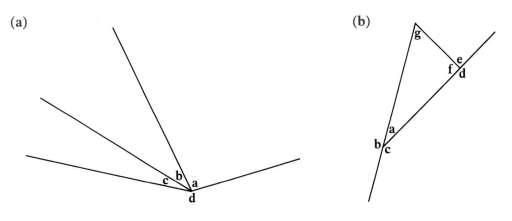

3. Copy this chart.

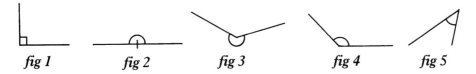

(a) Complete the chart using the following clues.

The **r** from clue **4** is shown filled in.

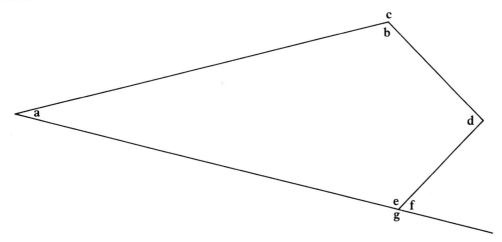

fig 1   fig 2   fig 3   fig 4   fig 5

        1. the last letter of the name of the angle in *fig 4*

        2. the last letter of the name of the angle in *fig 3*

        3. the last letter of the name of the angle in *fig 2*

        4. the first letter of the name of the angle in *fig 1*

        5. the first letter of the name of the angle in *fig 5*

        6. the first letter of the name of the angle in *fig 2*

        7. the second letter of the name of the angle in *fig 1*

        8. the fourth letter of the name of the angle in *fig 3*

(b) Read the first word on the chart from left to right.
Read the second word from right to left.

What words do you get?

Review

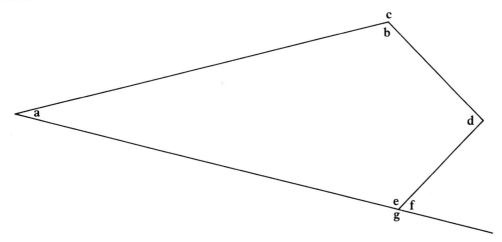

Name each of the marked angles as acute, obtuse, right, reflex or straight.

INVESTIGATION 15:14

ANGLES from PAPER FOLDING

Take a sheet of paper.
Fold it three times, opening it after each fold.

How many angles are formed by the creases?
Are they acute, obtuse, reflex or right angles?

What if you folded the sheet of paper four times?

What if you didn't open the paper after each fold?

Investigate.

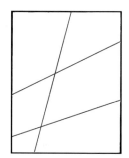

PRACTICAL EXERCISE 15:15

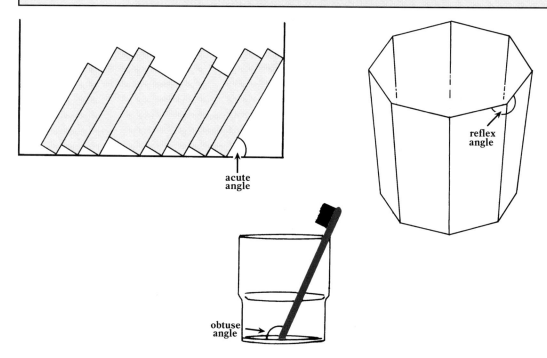

Choose one room of your home or a room in your school.
Make a list of all the acute angles you see in this room.
Make a list of all the obtuse angles and a list of all the reflex angles.

USING LOGO

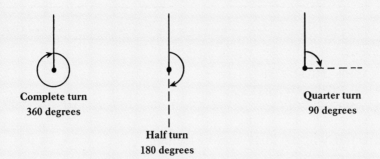

Complete turn
360 degrees

Half turn
180 degrees

Quarter turn
90 degrees

In a complete turn there are 360 degrees.
In a half turn there are 180 degrees.
In a quarter turn there are 90 degrees.

In LOGO, the turtle always begins in the centre of the screen, facing the direction shown.

The instruction RIGHT 90 tells the turtle to turn 90 degrees to the right. That is, to make a quarter turn to the right. The solid line shows the direction the turtle faces after this instruction.

The instruction LEFT 90 tells the turtle to turn 90 degrees to the left. That is, to make a quarter turn to the left. The solid line shows the direction the turtle faces after this instruction.

The instruction RIGHT 180 tells the turtle to turn 180 degrees to the right. That is, to make a half turn. The solid line shows the direction the turtle faces after this instruction.

DISCUSSION and PRACTICAL EXERCISE 15:16

- The instruction FORWARD 200 tells the turtle to move forward 200 units.

  The instructions   RIGHT 90
                        FORWARD 200
  move the turtle from H to A.

  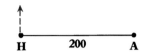

  In what direction will the turtle now be facing?
  Discuss.

- The instruction BACK 200 tells the turtle to move backward 200 units.

  The instructions   RIGHT 90
                        FORWARD 200
                        RIGHT 90
                        BACK 200
  move the turtle from H to A to B.

  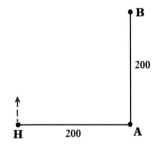

  In what direction will the turtle now be facing?
  Discuss.

- Joanne says that the instructions   LEFT 90
                                           FORWARD 400
  move the turtle from A to P.
  Neil says the instructions   RIGHT 90
                              BACK 400
  move the turtle from A to P.
  Who is right? **Discuss.**

-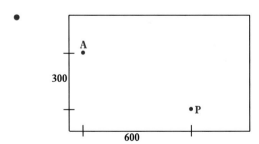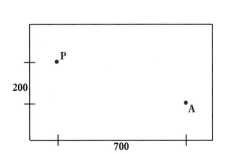

Discuss LOGO instructions which would move the turtle from A to P in each of the above.

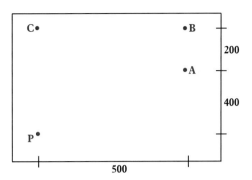

● **Discuss** LOGO instructions which would move the turtle from P to A to B to C and back to P again.

What if the turtle was to move from P to C to B to A and then back to P?

●

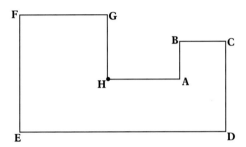

Discuss LOGO instructions which move the turtle around this route, from H back to H again.

● In LOGO, what do the instructions PU, PD, HOME, CS do? **Discuss.**

FORWARD may be written as FD	RIGHT may be written as RT
BACK may be written as BK	LEFT may be written as LT

PRACTICAL EXERCISE 15:17

Make up a journey for the turtle to follow.

Use each of these instructions at least once.

LT 90   RT 180   LT 180   RT 90   HOME   FD 400
BK 400   PU   PD

There are 90 degrees in a quarter turn.

A turn of 45 degrees is one-half of a quarter turn.

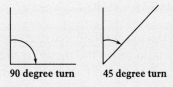

90 degree turn   45 degree turn

A turn of 30 degrees is one-third of a quarter turn.

A turn of 60 degrees is two-thirds of a quarter turn.

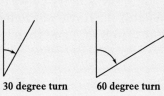

30 degree turn   60 degree turn

RIGHT 90 tells the LOGO turtle to turn 90 degrees to the right.

RIGHT 45 tells the LOGO turtle to turn 45 degrees to the right.

RIGHT 70 tells the LOGO turtle to turn 70 degrees to the right.

That is, the number after either RIGHT or LEFT gives the number of degrees the turtle must turn.

INVESTIGATION 15:18

JOURNEYS in LOGO

Investigate to find LOGO instructions which would move the turtle from H to A to B to C to D to E and back to H again.

Draw other journeys. **Investigate** to find suitable LOGO instructions.

Investigate to find LOGO instructions to draw the largest possible rectangle ABCD on the screen.

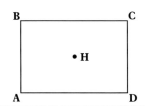

COMPASS DIRECTIONS

N 60° E means 60° East of North.

To find this direction follow these steps.

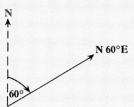

    Step 1   Face North.

    Step 2   Turn 60° towards East.

N 30° W means 30° West of North. (Face North, then turn 30° towards West.)

S 50° E means 50° East of South. (Face South, then turn 50° towards East.)

S 40° W means 40° West of South. (Face South, then turn 40° towards West.)

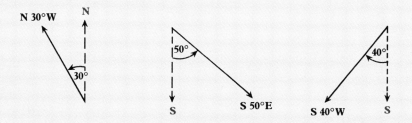

When directions are given in this way, either N or S is named first.

Example   The location of B from A can be described as:

           B is 6km from A in the direction N 56° W.

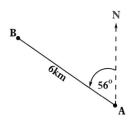

EXERCISE 15:19

1. The radius of the circle is 200m.

   Which place is 200m from P and in the direction

   (a) S 30° W

   (b) N 30° W

   (c) S 30° E

   (d) N 30° E ?

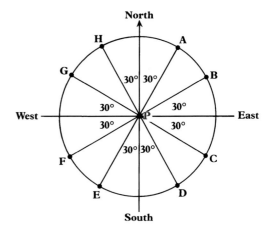

2. Describe the location of P from A.

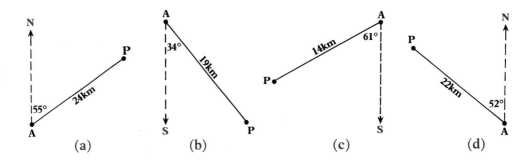

    (a)   (b)   (c)   (d)

3.

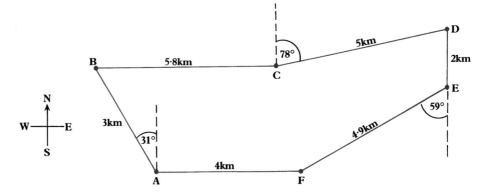

Charmaine walks from A to B to C to D to E to F and back to A again.
This journey could be described as: From A, walk N 31° W for 3km, then East for 5·8km, . . .

Finish the description of Charmaine's journey.

Review

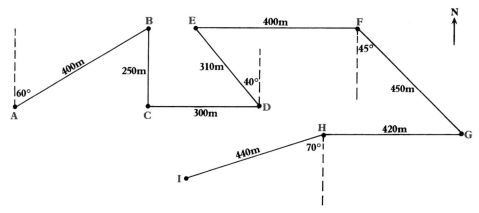

Elena begins her description of her journey from **A** to **I** as follows:
N 60° E for 400m, then South for 250m, . . .

Finish Elena's description.

WHAT   WHEN   WHERE   WHO   HOW   WHY

What sorts of angles would a builder or plumber have to measure?

When would an artist, an interior decorator or a landscape gardener estimate angles?

Where, in nature, can you find examples of angles less then 90°, between 90° and 180°, greater than 180°?

Who, in their jobs, need to be able to estimate angle size quickly?

How would an understanding of angle measurement be of help to you in a sport or hobby?

Why is an ability to draw and measure angles helpful to you in your other subjects?

AROUND and ABOUT

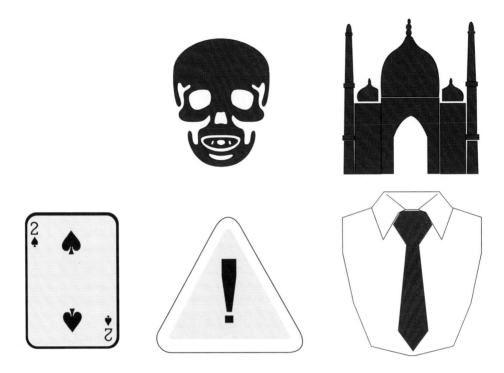

DISCUSSION EXERCISE 16:1

Look around the classroom. What shapes do you see that are symmetrical? **Discuss** with your group or class.

Imagine you are in a gym. What shapes do you see that are symmetrical? **Discuss.**

Imagine you are on your way from the front door of the school to the school gate. What shapes do you see that are symmetrical? **Discuss.**

Imagine you are on your way home from school. What symmetrical shapes do you see? **Discuss.**

Choose a place to be, other than those already mentioned. **Discuss** the symmetry of shapes in this place.

DESCRIBING SYMMETRIES of SHAPES

The **centre of rotational symmetry** is the point about which a shape must be rotated to fit exactly onto itself.

Example

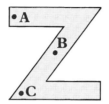

If this shape is rotated about B, it will fit onto itself twice during one complete turn; the first time after half a turn and the second time after a complete turn.
The point B is the centre of rotational symmetry.
Try this yourself.

What if you had rotated about point A or C?

What if you had rotated about some other point?

The **order of rotational symmetry** is the number of times a shape fits exactly onto itself during one complete turn.

Example   When the shape in the previous example was rotated about B it fitted onto itself twice during one complete turn.
That shape has rotational symmetry of order 2.

Example

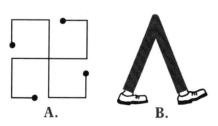

A.   B.

Trace these shapes.

Shape A has rotational symmetry of order 4.
Where is the centre of rotational symmetry for this shape?
Experiment to find it.

Shape B will fit onto itself just once during a complete turn about any point; at the end of the complete turn.
The order of rotational symmetry of shape B is 1.

Rotational symmetry can be described by giving the order of rotational symmetry.

Since all shapes will fit onto themselves at least once during a complete turn, all shapes have order of rotational symmetry of at least 1.

Reflective symmetry can be described by giving the location of the lines of symmetry. Lines of symmetry are often called **axes of symmetry.**

The number of axes of symmetry is sometimes called the **order of reflective symmetry.**

The **total order of symmetry** of a shape is the sum of the order of rotational symmetry and the order of reflective symmetry. That is, the total order of symmetry is the sum of the order of rotational symmetry and the number of axes of symmetry.

Worked Example   Describe the symmetries of these shapes.

A.   B.   C.

Answer   The axes of symmetry are shown in red.

A.   B.   C.

Shape A will fit onto itself just once during a complete turn. Shape B will fit onto itself twice and Shape C will fit onto itself 4 times.
Shape A has order 1 of rotational symmetry. Shape B has order 2 of rotational symmetry. Shape C has order 4 of rotational symmetry.

Briefly, the symmetries of the shapes can be described as:

Shape A has 1 axis of symmetry and order 1 of rotational symmetry giving a total order of symmetry of 2.

Shape B has 2 axes of symmetry and order 2 of rotational symmetry giving a total order of symmetry of 4.

Shape C has 0 axes of symmetry and order 4 of rotational symmetry giving a total order of symmetry of 4.

EXERCISE 16:2

1. Describe all the symmetries of these shapes. Include the number of axes of symmetry and the order of rotational symmetry in your description.

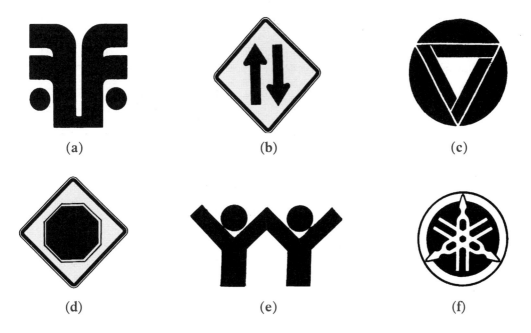

(a)   (b)   (c)

(d)   (e)   (f)

2. Describe all the symmetries of these shapes. Include the order of reflective symmetry, the order of rotational symmetry and the total order of symmetry in your description.

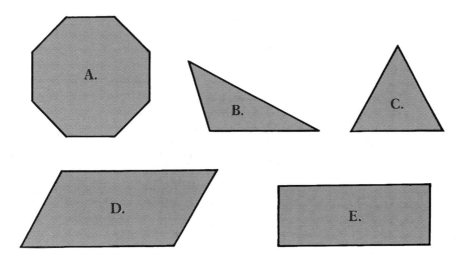

3.

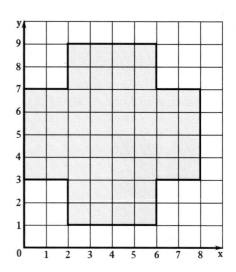

    (a) What are the coordinates of the centre of rotational symmetry of this shape?

    (b) What is the order of rotational symmetry?

    (c) How many axes of symmetry does this shape have?

4.

    (a) What are the coordinates of the centre of rotational symmetry of this shape?

    (b) What is the order of rotational symmetry?

    (c) What is the total order of symmetry?

Review 1 Describe all the symmetries of these shapes. Include the order of rotational symmetry and the number of axes of symmetry in your description.

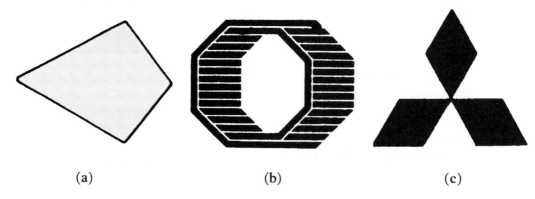

    (a)   **(b)**   **(c)**

Review 2 (a) What are the coordinates of the centre of rotational symmetry of this shape?

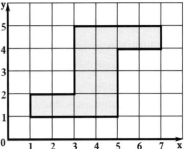

(b) How many axes of symmetry are there?

(c) What is the total order of symmetry?

PRACTICAL EXERCISE 16:3

Name the shape. One student chooses a shape in the room and talks about its symmetry. The other students in the group try to name the shape.

Draw the shape. One student draws a shape. Another student talks about its symmetry. The other students in the group try to draw this shape from the description.

Complete the shape. One student draws part of a shape and says what sort of symmetry the completed shape is to have. The rest of the group try to draw the completed shape.

PUZZLES 16:4

? ?

1. What have the capital letters A, H, I, M, O, V, W, X got in common? What other capital letter fits in this list?

2. What have the capital letters B, D, E, H, I, K, O, X got in common? What other capital letter fits in this list?

3. What have the capital letters H, O, S, X got in common? What other two capital letters fit in this list?

? ?

PRACTICAL EXERCISE 16:5

1. Choose one or more sports fields or courts and investigate symmetries. You could write your research up on a wall chart or poster.

2. Do a project on road signs. Consider the changes in these signs over the years. Look at the symmetry of these signs.

3. Design a logo for something in which you are interested, perhaps for a sports club.

4. Do a project on logos.
   You might like to make a collection of the logos used by car manufacturers or the logos that are used by businesses in your community.

5. Using LOGO on your computer, give the turtle commands to draw shapes which have different kinds of symmetry.

INVESTIGATION 16:6

SYMMETRIES

1. A piece of paper is folded in four.
   Beginning and ending on folds (as shown) a shape is cut out.
   The paper is then unfolded to get a symmetrical shape.

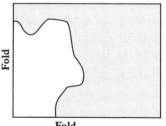

Fold

Must the symmetrical shape always have 2 axes of symmetry? Must it always have rotational symmetry of order 4? Investigate.

2.

8818	1111	8188	1881
8181	1888	8811	1118
1811	8118	1181	8888
1188	8881	1818	8111

This is a magic "magic square." **Investigate** it, looking at symmetry as well as how many different ways a total of 1998 can be found.

3. **Investigate** the symmetries in a pack of playing cards. Look at whether the arrangement of the "pips" is the same on all sets of cards.

PRISMS

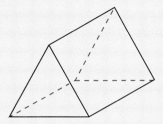 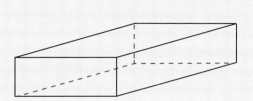

The shapes shown above are called **prisms**.

The shape on the right is also called a **cuboid** or **rectangular box**.

The shape on the left is called a **triangular prism**.

The end faces of a prism are congruent and parallel.

Imagine a slice taken through a prism, parallel to the end faces. The slice would have a face the same shape as the end faces.

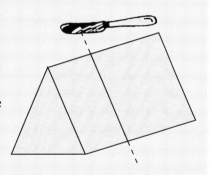

PRACTICAL EXERCISE 16:7

1.

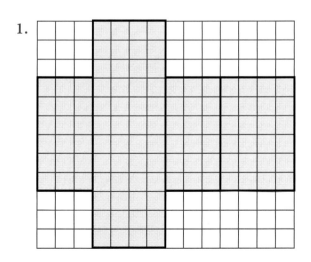 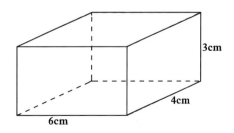

Draw the net on squared paper. Put tabs on every second edge.

Fold the net to make the cuboid.

2. Draw nets for these cuboids.

   (a) length 5cm, width 4cm, height 2cm

   (b) length 4cm, width 2cm, height 3cm

   (c) length 6cm, width 5cm, height 2cm

   Fold your nets to make the cuboids.

3. Trace this net.

   Put tabs on every second edge.

   Cut out your net.

   Fold.

   What shape does this net make?

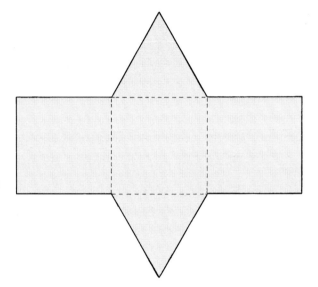

4. Draw these nets on isometric dot paper.

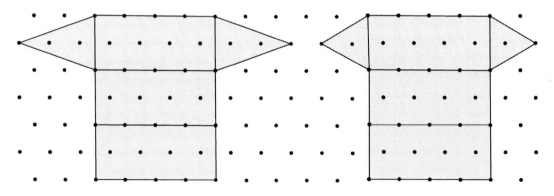

   Which net folds to make a prism?

5. Use isometric dot paper to draw the nets for other triangular prisms.

   Fold your nets to make prisms.

PYRAMIDS

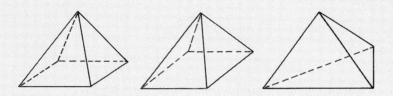

The shapes shown above are **pyramids.**

Apart from the base (the bottom) of a pyramid, all the faces meet at a point.

DISCUSSION EXERCISE 16:8

Only one of these nets will make a pyramid. Which one?
Discuss reasons why the other one will not. As part of your discussion, draw these nets and try to fold them into pyramids.

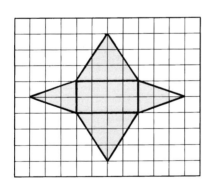
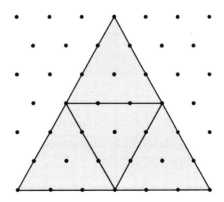

CONSTRUCTING TRIANGLES

Remember: If we are given the length of the three sides of a triangle, we can **construct** the triangle using a compass and ruler. (see **page 156**)

We may also construct triangles if we are given other information.

DISCUSSION EXERCISE 16:9

●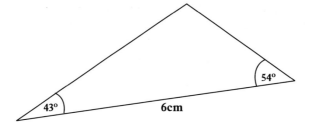

To construct the triangle sketched we could begin as follows.

Step 1. Draw a line 6cm long.

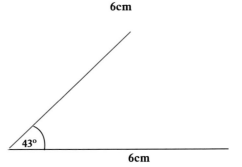

Step 2. Draw an angle of 43°.

How could we continue? **Discuss.** As part of your discussion, construct this triangle.

As a check on the accuracy of your construction, measure the third angle. It should be 83°.

● Jamie said the first 2 steps to construct this triangle should be:

    Step 1. Draw a line 6cm long.
    Step 2. Draw a line 8cm long.

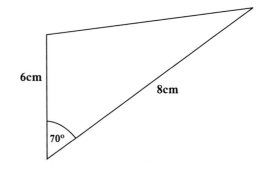

Zara said the first 2 steps should be:

    Step 1. Draw a line 6cm long.
    Step 2. Draw an angle of 70°.

Who is right, Jamie or Zara? **Discuss.** As part of your discussion, construct the triangle. As a check on the accuracy of your construction, measure the third side. To the nearest mm, it should be 82mm.

EXERCISE 16:10

1. Use your ruler and protractor to construct the triangles that are sketched. On your constructions, measure the size of the third angle.

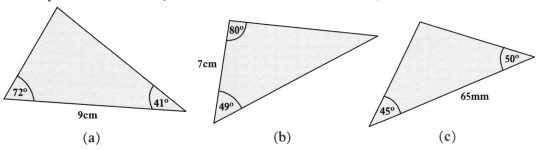

(a)   (b)   (c)

2. Construct the triangles ABC. Measure the size of the third angle on your constructions.

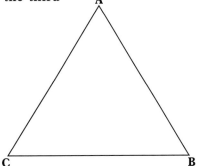

   (a) CB = 74mm, angle C = 60°, angle B = 50°

   (b) AC = 5cm, angle A = 80°, angle C = 48°

   (c) AB = 68mm, angle A = 72°, angle B = 39°

   (d) BC = 9·2cm, angle B = 62°, angle C = 42°

   (e) BC = 8·6cm, ∠ACB = 41°, ∠ABC = 36°

3. Construct these triangles.
   On your constructions, measure the length of the third side. Give this length to the nearest mm.

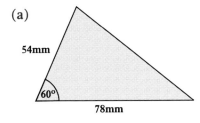
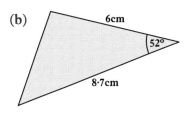

4. Construct the triangles PQR. On your constructions, measure the length of the third side.

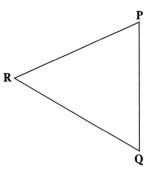

   (a) PQ = 5cm, PR = 8cm, angle P = 54°

   (b) QR = 63mm, PQ = 55mm, angle Q = 70°

   (c) PR = 8·1cm, PQ = 6·4cm, ∠RPQ = 62°

5. Contruct these triangles.
   On your construction, measure the size of angle B. Give your answer to the nearest degree.

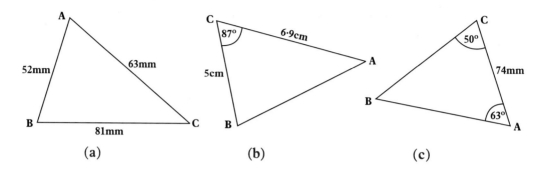

(a)   (b)   (c)

Review   Construct the triangles FGH.
On your constructions, measure the size of
angle H. Give your answer to the nearest degree.

(a)   FG = 82mm, FH = 70mm, angle F = 64°

(b)   FG = 5·1cm, FH = 7cm, GH = 7·3cm

(c)   FG = 9cm, ∠GFH = 54°, ∠FGH = 75°

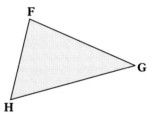

MAKING PRISMS and PYRAMIDS

DISCUSSION EXERCISE 16:11

● Will both of the nets at the top of **page 267** make this prism? **Discuss.**

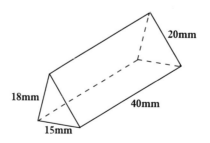

As part of your discussion, draw and fold the nets.

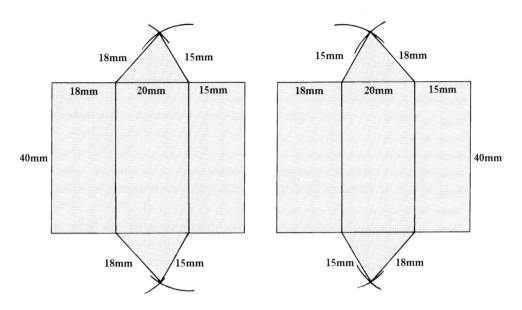

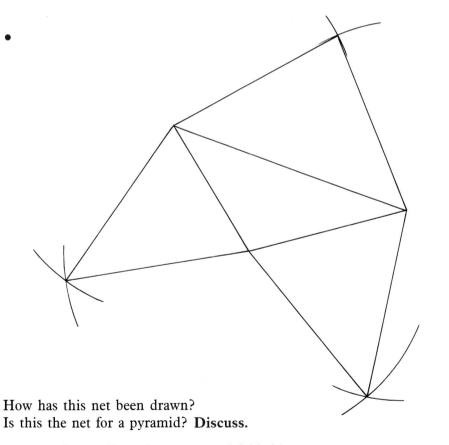

How has this net been drawn?
Is this the net for a pyramid? **Discuss.**

As part of your discussion, trace and fold this net.

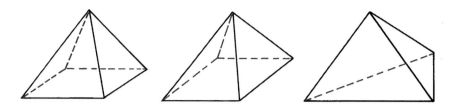

How many faces do each of these pyramids have?
What is the shape of the base (the bottom) of each? **Discuss.**

Which of the following nets would make a pyramid on a square base?
Which would make a pyramid on a rectangular base?
Which would make a pyramid on a triangular base? **Discuss.**

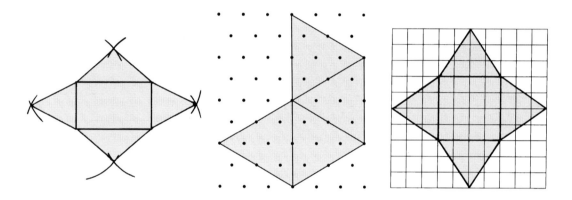

- Draw the nets shown above. Fold to make pyramids.

- **Discuss** how to draw nets for the pyramids shown below.

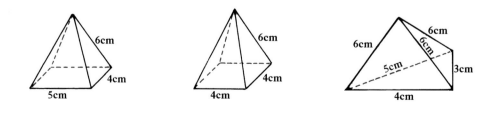

As part of your discussion, draw the nets. Fold to make the pyramids.

● This triangle shows the measurements of the end faces of the prism.

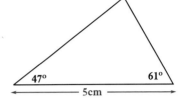

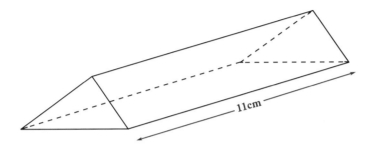

Discuss how to draw a net for this prism. As part of your discussion, draw the net and fold to make the prism.

PRACTICAL EXERCISE 16:12

---

1. Use your ruler, set square and compass to draw these nets.
   Put tabs on every second edge.

   Fold your nets to make 3-D shapes.

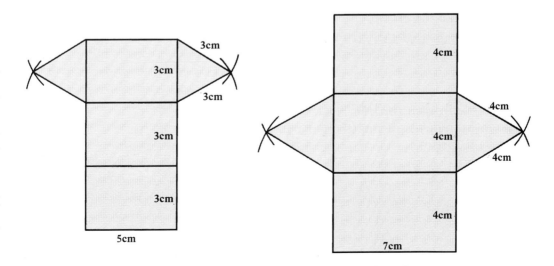

2. Make a net for each of the prisms sketched below.
   Fold your nets to make these prisms.

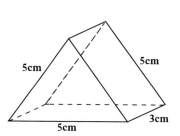

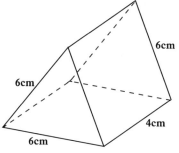

3.

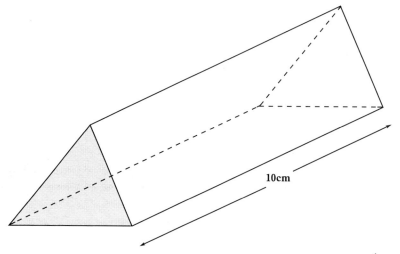

This triangle shows the end faces of the prism.
Make a net for this prism.
Fold to make the prism.

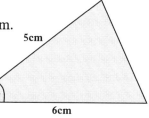

4. A triangular prism is 85mm long.
   The measurements of the triangular faces are shown.
   Make this prism.

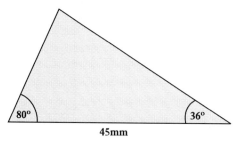

PRACTICAL EXERCISE 16:13

1. Design and make a gift box. Choose either a prism shape or a pyramid shape.
    Decide on the dimensions *before* you begin to make the box.

    You could decorate the net or you could decorate the box after you have made it.

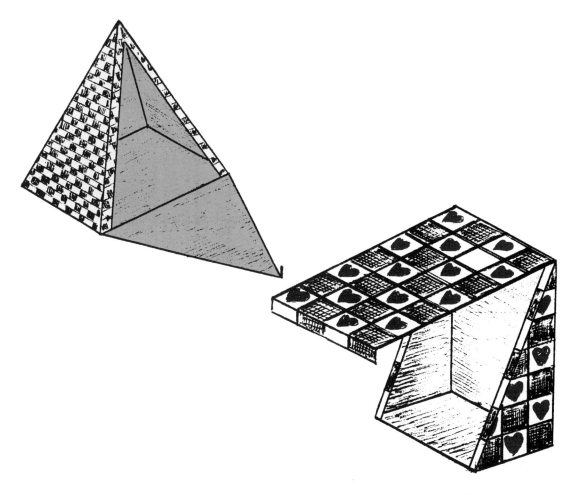

2. Design and make a container for an object which has an unusual shape.
    You could design a container for one of the following or you could choose
    something else: a stapler
                              a compass
                              a necklace
                              a watch
                              a set of 3 dice
                              a table tennis bat

SKELETON SHAPES

Skeleton shapes are shapes that consist of just edges. These can be built using Clever Sticks or by joining lengths of drinking straws with bent pipe cleaners.

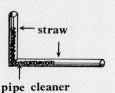

← straw

pipe cleaner

Drinking straws may be used for the edges.
Bent pipe cleaners may be used to join the edges.

INVESTIGATION 16:14

SKELETON SHAPES

What shapes can you build with 8 straws, 4 of which are 5cm long and 4 of which are 7cm long? **Investigate.**

What if you had 9 straws, all the same length?   **What if** you had 6 straws?

What if . . .

WHAT   WHEN   WHERE   WHO   HOW   WHY

What other subjects need an understanding of symmetry and 2-D and 3-D shapes?

When might a town planner use symmetry or construct 2-D and 3-D shapes?

Where, in nature, do you find examples of symmetry?

Who, in arts and crafts, needs an understanding of 2-D and 3-D shapes?

How might a knowledge of symmetry or 2-D and 3-D shapes help these people?   Architect   Builder   Landscape Gardener   Manufacturer

Why are sports fields and sports equipment usually symmetrical?

1.

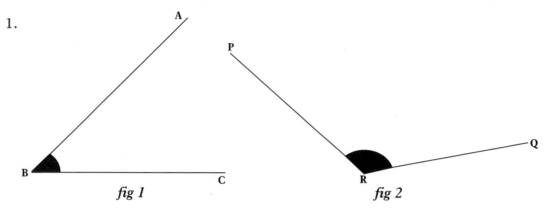

fig 1   *fig 2*

(a) Estimate the size of the marked angle in *fig 1*.

Use your protractor to measure this angle. Give your answer to the nearest degree.

(b) Is the following statement true or false?

"The angle marked in *fig 1* could be named as ∠B".

(c) Estimate the size of the marked angle in *fig 2*.

Measure this angle. Give your answer to the nearest degree.

(d) Which of these is **not** a correct name for the angle marked in *fig 2*?

     A. ∠PRQ   **B.** ∠QRP   **C.** ∠R   **D.** ∠PQR

2. What is the missing number?

    (a) 8cm = . . . mm   (b) 2000ml = . . . l   (c) 5kg = . . . g

    (d) 13g = . . . mg   (e) . . . kg = 6 tonne   (f) . . . m = 4000cm

3. A goldfish bowl holds 10 gallons of water. Jan emptied this bowl to clean it. She then poured in 20 pints of water. How many more pints of water must Jan pour in to fill this bowl?

4. Adrian measured the length of a corridor as 20·43m.
Beth measured this corridor as 20·34m.
Explain why Adrian and Beth might have got these different measurements.

5. (a) What is the order of rotational symmetry of this shape?

(b) What are the coordinates of the centre of rotational symmetry?

(c) How many axes of symmetry does this shape have?

(d) What is the total order of symmetry?

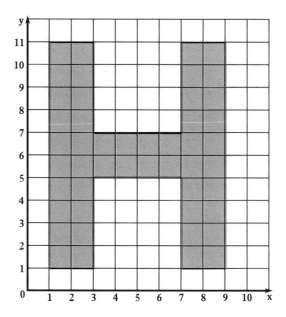

6. "May and Bell" homemade chocolates cost £1·50 for 100 grams.
About how much do these chocolates cost for 1 lb?

7. How many laps of a 400m track does Pete need to do to run a total of 6km?

8. Choose the best answer for each of these.

(a) The length of a car could be   **A.** 450mm   **B.** 450cm   **C.** 450m   **D.** 450km

(b) The length of a motorway could be **A.** 450mm   **B.** 450cm   **C.** 450m   **D.** 450km

(c) The height of a hill could be   **A.** 450mm   **B.** 450cm   **C.** 450m   **D.** 450km

(d) The capacity of the engine of a car could be   **A.** 200m*l*   **B.** 2*l*   **C.** 200*l*

(e) The capacity of a water tank could be   **A.** 200m*l*   **B.** 2*l*   **C.** 200*l*

274

(f)   The amount of lemonade in a glass could be   **A.** 200m*l*   **B.** 2*l*   **C.** 200*l*

(g) A calculator could weigh   **A.** 10g   **B.** 100g   **C.** 1kg   **D.** 1t

(h) The mass of a car could be   **A.** 10kg **B.** 100kg **C.** 1t   **D.** 10t

(i)   Time taken to run 1500m could be   **A.** 4sec **B.** 4min   **C.** 4hrs **D.** 4days

9. Manx Motors entered $1\frac{1}{2}$ hours on the time sheet for fixing the brakes on Sarah's car. They had just finished fixing them when Sarah arrived to pick the car up at 5·10p.m. At what time did Manx Motors begin to fix the brakes?

10. Adjoa was asked to name two things she would measure to these degrees of accuracy.

(a) to the nearest m   (b) to the nearest kg

(c) to the nearest m*l*   (d) to the nearest mm

(e) to the nearest *l*   (f) to the nearest g

(g) to the nearest kg

What things could Adjoa have named?

11.

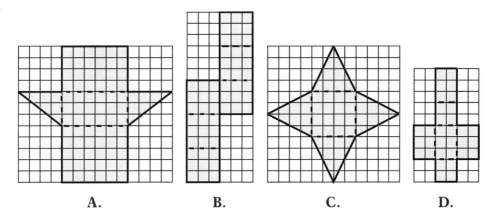

| A. | B. | C. | D. |

Which of these nets will fold to make   (a) a cube

                                         (b) a cuboid

                                         (c) a triangular prism

                                         (d) a pyramid?

12. Copy this table.

Shape	Number of axes of symmetry	Order of rotational symmetry	Total order of symmetry
A			
B			
C			
D			
E			
F			

Fill in your table for these shapes.

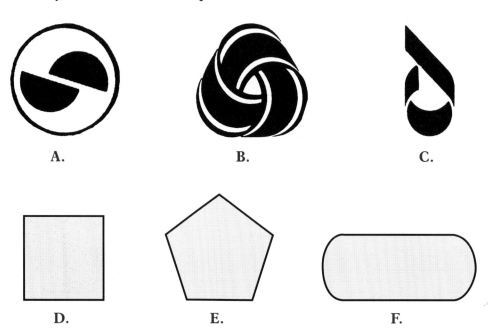

A.   B.   C.

D.   E.   F.

13. Find the missing numbers.

(a) 600ml = ... l

(b) 3m = ... cm

(c) 0·2kg = ... g

(d) 1·2l = ... ml

(e) 250mm = ... cm

(f) 1·6m = ... cm

(g) 62cm = ... mm

(h) 4840g = ... kg

(i) 0·3km = ... m

(j) 2·6t = ... kg

(k) 62cm = ... m

(l) 0·03l = ... ml

(m) 480mm = ... m

(n) 0·05g = ... mg

14.

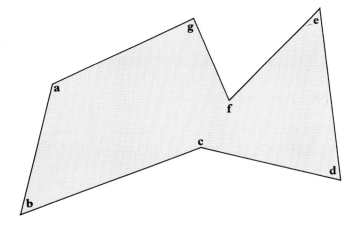

Name the angles that are (a) right angles

(b) acute angles

(c) obtuse angles

(d) reflex angles.

15. (a) A kitchen sink can hold 4 gallons of water. About how many litres is this?

(b) The capacity of a freezer is 450 litres. About how much is this in gallons?

16.

	On duty	Off duty
Mon	0800	1200
Tue	1300	1630
Wed	1430	1815
Sat	0800	1230
Sun	0600	1130

This table shows the times that Victoria began and finished work at the hospital last week.
How long did Victoria work last week?

17. The radius of the circle is 10km.
A, B, C, . . . represent villages.

(a) Which village is S 30° W of P?

(b) Copy and complete: Village J
is . . . km from P in the
direction . . .

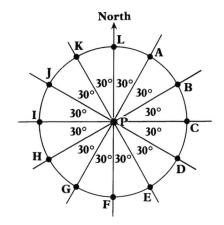

18. Six students made a mural for the classroom wall. They worked on this in pairs.
Find the completed length of this mural if the three parts measured 3'2", 2'11", 3'8".

19.

Copy and complete this crossnumber.

Across	**Down**
1. ounces in 2 lb	1. yards in 105 feet
3. inches in 4 yards	2. inches in 21'9"
6. pints in 7 gallons	3. yards in 1 mile 40 yards
7. yards in $\frac{1}{2}$ mile	4. pounds in 3 stone 6 lb
8. ounces in 9 lb 6oz	5. ounces in 25 lb
11. pence in £2·05	9. feet in 1 mile
13. pounds in 9 stone 12 lb	10. inches in 9'3"
15. inches in 2'5"	12. pence in £5·23
17. stones in 1 ton	14. feet in 12 yards
18. pints in $4\frac{1}{2}$ gallons	16. pints in 12 gallons

20. Draw nets for these.
Fold to make the cuboid and pyramid.

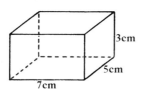 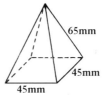

21. (a) Arlene is flying from Edinburgh to London. The luggage allowance is 15kg.
Arlene plans to take a suitcase which weighs 9kg and a box of books which
weighs 10lb.
Can Arlene take both of these?

(b) Arlene's box is 30cm long.
About how many inches is this?

(c) The distance from Edinburgh to London is about 670km.
About how many miles is this? (Give your answer to the nearest 10 miles.)

22. Use your ruler, compass and protractor to construct these triangles.

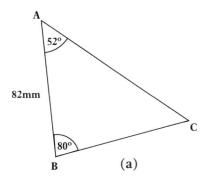

(a)

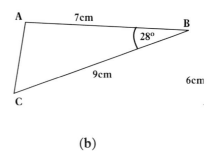

(b)

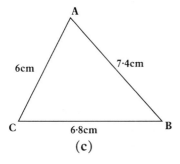

(c)

On your constructions, measure the size of angle C.

23. A loaded container weighs 4·67 tonne.
When two Honda Civic cars are taken out, the
container weighs 2·718 tonne.

How many kg does each of these cars weigh?

24. Tina weighs 8 stone 2 lb. Bridie weighs 6 stone 11 lb.
How much heavier than Bridie is Tina?

25.

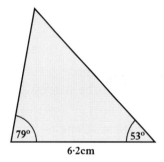

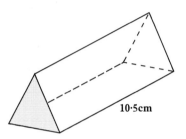

The triangle shows the shape of the triangular faces of the prism.
Draw a net and fold to make the prism.

26. (a)   What shape do these LOGO instructions draw?

        PU
        RT 30
        FD 100
        PD
        LT 30
        FD 200
        BK 100
        RT 45
        FD 140
        BK 85
        RT 70
        FD 150
        PU
        HOME

   (b)   Write LOGO instructions to draw the letter Y.

27. (a) Draw a 5-sided shape which has 2 acute angles, 2 obtuse angles and 1 reflex angle.

(b) Is it possible to draw a triangle which has an obtuse angle and a right angle?

28.

Copy and complete this crossnumber using the clues below.
Give the answer in the unit in brackets.
If a decimal point is needed, give this a full space.
For example, the answer for **1. Across** is 2·345m and this is filled in as shown.

Across

1. 2m + 34·5cm   (m)
5. 2·1cm + 6mm   (mm)
7. 1l + 40ml   (l)
8. 1m – 40cm   (cm)
9. 74·1t + 153kg   (kg)
11. 1kg – 956g   (g)
12. 3m – 558mm   (m)
14. 3·6cm + 471mm   (cm)
16. 860kg + 1·73t   (t)
18. 1·3m + 290cm   (m)
20. 2·4cm + 3mm   (cm)
21. 0·2l – 124ml   (ml)
23. 4mm + 4·9cm   (cm)
24. 28m – 655mm   (mm)
25. 1g – 866mg   (mg)

Down

1. 1·2km + 1500m   (km)
2. 312kg + 654g   (kg)
3. 5l – 460ml   (l)
4. 50t + 345kg   (kg)
6. 124mm + 64cm   (mm)
10. 1m – 58cm   (cm)
13. 18·2km + 1800m   (km)
15. 73t – 170kg   (t)
16. 0·15cm + 1·22mm   (mm)
17. 4·6m + 494cm   (m)
19. 4·6cm – 21mm   (cm)
22. 0·05g + 17mg   (mg)

HANDLING DATA

REVISION

GRAPHS and FREQUENCY TABLES

This **pictogram** shows the number of teams in a sports competition.

9 teams are playing Football.
6 teams are playing Hockey.
5 teams are playing Badminton.

Sports Pictogram

Football

Hockey

Badminton

Key: ⌂ represents 2 teams

Transport	Walk	Cycle	Train	Bus	Car	Other
Frequency	6	2	3	5	3	1

The **frequency table** shows how the students in one class come to school. This information is also shown on the **block graph** below.

Frequency is always on the vertical axis.

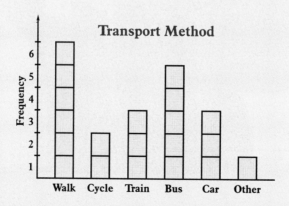

We can make conclusions from this graph.
For instance, the same number of students come to school by car as by train.

continued . . .

. . . from previous page

This **bar chart** or **bar graph** shows the number of hours of sunshine on each of the days of one week. On Monday there were 3 hours of sunshine, on Tuesday 4 hours, on Wednesday 4 hours, on Thursday 3 hours, on Friday 8 hours, on Saturday 6 hours and on Sunday 5 hours.

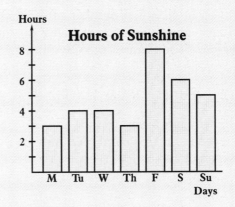

27 29 28 30 29 27 27 29 28 29 27 30 29 28 27 28 29 29 27

The figures in this list give the number of biscuits in 19 packets. These figures are summarised on the **tally chart**.

On the tally chart, a stroke is made as each figure is recorded (a diagonal stroke is used for every 5th entry). Once all the figures have been recorded, the strokes are added to get the frequency. Because this tally chart also has the frequency it can also be called a **frequency table**.

Biscuit Tally Chart

Number	Tally	Frequency
27	ℍℍ I	6
28	IIII	4
29	ℍℍ II	7
30	II	2

The data on the tally chart is graphed on this **bar-line graph**.

On the bar-line graph the height of each vertical line gives the frequency.

f stands for frequency.

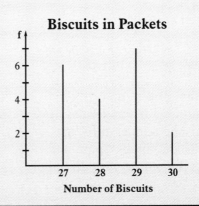

continued . . .

. . . from previous page

This data gives the number of times the letter e appears in each sentence on the last page of "The Clan of the Cave Bear".

1 2 2 1 6 10 2 8 3 3 5 5 3 1
6 7 3 9 3 4 5 2 4 9 11 15 0 8

The data has been **grouped** into 6 categories on this combined tally chart and frequency table.

e's Frequency Table

Number of e's	Tally	Frequency
0–2	⦀⦀ ⦀⦀⦀	8
3–5	⦀⦀⦀⦀ ⦀⦀⦀⦀	10
6–8	⦀⦀⦀⦀	5
9–11	⦀⦀⦀⦀	4
12–14		0
15–17	⦀	1

The information on the tally chart is graphed on this **frequency diagram**.

A frequency diagram has the bars joined as shown.

Grouped data is graphed on a frequency diagram rather than a bar graph or bar-line graph.

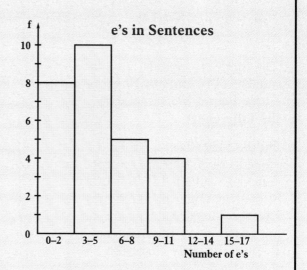

In hospital, Jane's temperature was taken every 4 hours.

At 8a.m. it was 37°C, at Noon it was 38°C, at 4p.m. it was 37·5°C and at 8p.m. it was 37·8°C.

This **line graph** shows these temperatures. It was drawn by plotting the temperatures at 8a.m., Noon, 4p.m., 8p.m. and joining the points with straight lines.

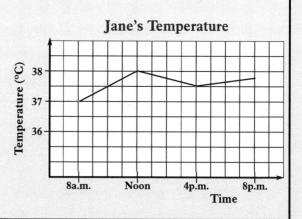

continued . . .

. . . *from previous page*

DIAGRAMS

A class was surveyed about board games played.
This **Venn diagram** shows that
  4 played both Scrabble and Monopoly
  6 played Scrabble but not Monopoly
  9 played Monopoly but not Scrabble
  2 played neither Scrabble nor Monopoly.

Scrabble	Monopoly

6   (4)   9

2

This **Carroll Diagram** tells us about the
weather in May.
It was cold and raining on 8 days, cold but
not raining on 2 days, mild and raining on
5 days, mild and not raining on 16 days.

May Weather

8	2	cold
5	16	mild

raining   not raining

This **tree diagram** can be used to
sort counters into:
red and square, red and round,
black and square, black and round.

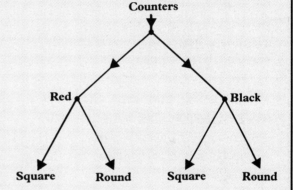

MEDIAN. MODE

The **mode** of a set of data is the value that occurs most often.
A set of data may have no mode or 1 mode or more than 1 mode.

For instance, the mode of 2, 2, 3, 3, 3, 8, 11, 15, 15, 16, 17, 17, 20 is 3.
10, 21, 15, 72, 43 has no mode.   5, 6, 3, 2, 5, 2, 1, 8 has two modes, 2 and 5.

The **median** is the middle value when a set of data is arranged in order of size.

For instance, the median of 2, 2, 3, 3, 3, 8, 11, 15, 15, 16, 17, 17, 20 is 11. To find
the median of 10, 21, 15, 72, 43 we write this data as 10, 15, 21, 43, 72 to get 21
as the median.

If a set of data has two middle values the median is halfway between these.

For instance, the median of 5, 6, 6, 8, 9, 12, 13, 15 is $\dfrac{8+9}{2} = 8{\cdot}5$.

continued . . .

. . . *from previous page*

PROBABILITY

The chance of an event happening can be described by one of:
certain, very likely, likely, unlikely, very unlikely, impossible

For instance, if today is Monday the 3rd of June:

It is certain that tomorrow will be Tuesday.
It is very likely that there will be some cloud, sometime today.
It is likely that it will be sunny sometime tomorrow.
It is unlikely to rain all day tomorrow and the next day.
It is very unlikely that it will snow tomorrow.
It is impossible that tomorrow will be Friday.

There is an **even chance** of an event happening if the chance of the event happening is the same as the chance of the event not happening.
For instance, there is an even chance of getting a head when a coin is tossed.

There is a **better than even chance** of an event happening if the event is more likely to happen than not to happen.

There is a **less than even chance** of an event happening if the event is less likely to happen than not to happen.

A game is **fair** if each player has the same chance of winning.
A game is **unfair** if one player has less chance of winning than another.

REVISION EXERCISE

1. This spinner is spun.
   Use one of "certain", "better than even chance", "even chance", "less than even chance", "impossible" to describe the likelihood of the spinner stopping on

   (a) Red   (b) Grey   (c) Yellow

   (d) 4   (e) Red 4   (f) Grey 2

   (g) a number less than 5.

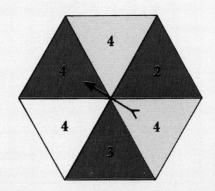

2. Denny dealt 20 cards. As she dealt each one she drew this block graph. How many cards had Denny dealt when her block graph looked like this?

The last 2 cards Denny dealt were both clubs. Copy and complete Denny's graph.

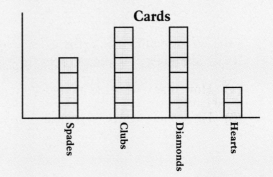

Cards

3. Put these in order of likelihood, from the least likely to the most likely.

A. The sun will set tomorrow.

B. A film star will visit your school next week.

C. Someone from your class will be late for school next Wednesday.

D. Someone from your street will go on holiday next July.

E. Someone from your class will be on TV one day.

4.

Wind Speed

This line graph shows the wind speed, at hourly intervals.

(a) What was the wind speed at 9a.m.?

(b) Estimate the wind speed at 10·30a.m.

(c) What was the greatest wind speed?
At what time was this?

(d) How much did the wind speed fall between 5p.m. and 6p.m.?

Card's Pictogram

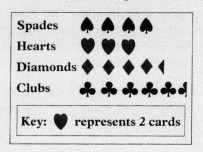

5. Julie was watching the cards as they were dealt. She drew this pictogram.

   (a) How many of these cards were clubs?

   (b) How many cards were dealt altogether?

6.

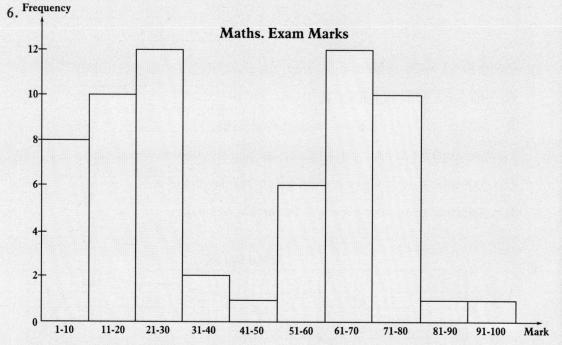

Maths. Exam Marks

This frequency diagram shows the maths. marks of the students in two classes.

(a) How many students are in these classes?

(b) Two statements that can be made about this data are "about half of the students got more than 50 marks" and "very few students got more than 80". Make two more statements about this data.

7. Set A: 8, 10, 13, 15, 15, 16, 17, 20, 22, 23, 23, 23, 26, 28, 29

   Set B: 101, 102, 102, 103, 103, 104, 105, 106, 108, 109, 111

   Set C: 2, 4, 5, 6, 9, 10, 12, 13, 14, 17, 19, 20, 22, 23

   (a) Find the mode of these sets of data.

   (b) Find the median of each set.

8. Jayne gathered data on the cars that were for sale from all the car dealers in her district. She summarised the data in this Carroll diagram.

124	74	**New**
94	65	**Used**
British	**Non British**	

   (a)   How many cars were for sale altogether?

   (b)   How many of the cars were new?

   (c)   How many of the used cars were British?

9.

Nathan is growing a plant. The table shows its height.
Copy and complete the line graph.

Week	Height (cm)
3	2
4	5
5	7
6	9
7	10
8	10

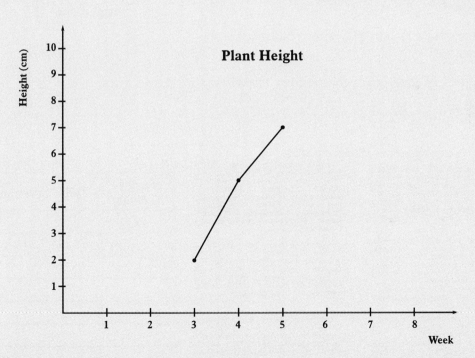

Plant Height

10. 3 1 4 0 1 5 7 4 2 2 1 3 0 1 2 1 4 1 2

This list gives the number of pets kept by the students in John's class.

Find   (a)   the mode   (b)   the median.

11. Decide if these are "certain", "very likely", "likely", "unlikely", "very unlikely" or "impossible".

   (a) You will shake hands with your favourite television star.

   (b) The Prime Minister will visit your class tomorrow.

   (c) It will get dark tonight.

   (d) You will see clouds tomorrow.

   (e) You will be 20 tomorrow.

   (f) All the students in your class will be millionaires someday.

   (g) Someone from your class will be absent tomorrow.

12. This diagram shows the number of students in Anne's class.

   (a) How many play both badminton and tennis?

   (b) How many do not play either badminton or tennis?

   (c) Which of these gives the number of students in Anne's class?

   A. 22   **B.** 20   **C.** 14   **D.** 12   **E.** 17

13. **Yesterday's football results.**

English division one: Aston Villa 3 Derby 2, Chelsea 2 Arsenal 1, Everton 2 Sunderland 0, Luton 1 Queen's Park Rangers 2, Norwich 1 Manchester City 2, Nottingham Forest 0 Crystal Palace 1, Sheffield United 4 Southampton 1, Tottenham 0 Leeds 0, Wimbledon 1 Coventry 0.

English division three: Bradford 3 Bournemouth 0, Brentford 1 Rotherham 2, Bury 1 Swansea 0, Exeter 0 Birmingham 2, Huddersfield 1 Grimsby 1, Leyton Orient 4 Tranmere 0, Preston 1 Bolton 2, Shrewsbury 0 Southend 1, Stoke 2 Chester 3, Wigan 2 Fulham 0. Played Friday: Cambridge 2 Mansfield 1, Crewe 1 Reading 0.

Scottish Premier division: Aberdeen 5 Hearts 0, Celtic 1 Dundee United 0, Hibernian 1 Motherwell 1.

Scottish division one: Brechin 0 Clyde 2, Dundee 3 Hamilton 2, Forfar 3 Raith 1, Kilmarnock 3 Clydebank 0, Morton 0 Falkirk 0.

English division two: Bristol City 2 West Bromwich 0, Charlton 1 Brighton 2, Hull 2 Bristol Rovers 0, Ipswich 0 Millwall 3, Leicester 3 Plymouth 1, Middlesbrough 2 Swindon 0, Newcastle 2 Port Vale 0, Oxford 5 Oldham 1, Portsmouth 2 Notts County 1, Watford 2 Sheffield Wednesday 2, Wolverhampton 2 West Ham 1.

English division four: Carlisle 1 Stockport 0, Chesterfield 1 Lincoln 1, Gillingham 2 Hereford 1, Scunthorpe 3 Torquay 0, Walsall 1 Doncaster 0, York 0 Darlington 1. Played Friday: Cardiff 1 Aldershot 3, Halifax 1 Peterborough 1, Northampton 0 Scarborough 2.

Scottish division two: Alloa 0 Stranraer 1, Berwick 2 East Stirling 2, Cowdenbeath 0 Arbroath 1, Dumbarton 0 Stenhousemuir 0, East Fife 2 Queens Park 1, Montrose 0 Queen of the South 0.

Number of Goals	Tally	Frequency
0		
1		
2		
3		
4		
5		

Copy and complete the tally chart.
Draw a bar-line graph to illustrate this data.

292

14. This list gives the number of words in the first 50 sentences of "Moby Dick".

3	40	15	87	8	16	6	26	25	8
30	7	8	13	4	19	35	23	4	5
4	18	1	22	1	15	8	16	5	19
2	12	27	5	38	24	12	5	22	7
37	19	37	24	9	16	36	24	31	9

Record this information on a frequency table.
Use the intervals 1–10, 11–20, 21–30, . . . 81–90.
Draw a frequency diagram for the data.

15.

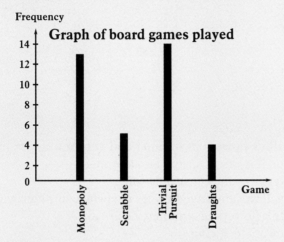

This graph shows the board games played by the students in one class.

(a) How many play Monopoly?

(b) What is the most popular game?

(c) What else can you tell from this graph?

(d) Explain why you cannot use this graph to tell how many students are in the class.

16. Ruth and Simon designed a board game for 2 players. A die was used in this game.
One of the rules was: *Each time player A throws an even number, A misses a turn. Each time player B throws a "one", B misses a turn.*

Is this a fair game? Explain your answer.

AROUND and ABOUT

*

Begonia: small; red or yellow flowers in summer and autumn; needs sun
Canterbury Bell: tall; blue flowers in spring and summer
Hollyhock: tall; red flowers in summer; needs sun
Marigold: small or tall; yellow or orange flowers in spring, summer and autumn
Sweet William: small; pink flowers in summer; needs sun
Hyacinth: small; blue flowers in spring
Daffodil: small; yellow flowers in spring
Phlox: tall; red or white flowers in summer; needs sun
Nasturtium: small; orange flowers in summer and autumn
Pansy: small; blue flowers in spring and autumn
Dahlia: tall; orange or red or white flowers in summer and autumn; needs sun

These plants could be sorted into a list of small plants and a list of tall plants.
What other lists could these plants be sorted into? **Discuss.**

* At a second-hand clothing shop, clothes were sorted into bins by colour.
  How else could clothes be sorted? **Discuss.**

* The days in July were sorted into these lists.

  Cool   3, 4, 15, 24, 25, 29, 30
  Warm   1, 6, 8, 14, 23, 26, 28, 31
  Hot   2, 5, 7, 9, 10, 11, 12, 13, 16, 17, 18, 19, 20, 21, 22, 27

How else could the days in a month be sorted? **Discuss.**

USING a DATABASE to SORT DATA

A **computer database** is a program which organises large amounts of information.

Examples of databases that your local council might use are:

a database that stores details of each person who works for the council
a database that stores details of each house in the council area
a database that stores details of all the transport companies in the council area.

Example

Habbershield Council Employees					
Name	**Department**	**Gender**	**Age**	**Salary**	**Years of Service**
A.T. Khan	12	F	19	8035	2
L.H. Oliver	03	M	52	14595	36
T.L. Patrick	09	F	34	27125	13
C.D. Stevens	03	M	28	9054	4
P. Zarifeh	22	F	18	9756	1

This could be part of a database used by the Habbershield Council.

The information in a database is in records and fields.

One line of information is called a **record**.
For instance, A.T. Khan 12 F 19 8035 2 is a record.

The **fields** on the above database are: the name of the person, the department the person works in, the gender of the person etc.

From a database many different lists can be printed out.

Example Some of the lists that could be printed out from the database shown above are:

People in Department 03	**Salary less than £10000**	**More than 10 years service**
L.H. Oliver	A.T. Khan	L.H. Oliver
C.D. Stevens	C.D. Stevens	T.L. Patrick
	P. Zarifeh	

EXERCISE 18:2

1. A bookshop put this information into a database.

Title	Science Fiction	Adventure	Romance	Horror	Price £
Roses Tomorrow	No	No	Yes	No	1·90
Secret of the Caves	No	Yes	No	No	4·20
Beyond the Blue	Yes	No	No	No	2·50
Phantom Wolf	No	No	No	Yes	1·95
Adventures of Adrian	No	Yes	No	No	2·95
Summer Holiday	No	No	Yes	No	3·45
The Doomed Mountain	No	No	No	Yes	2·85
Dark Waters	No	No	No	Yes	4·10
Clash of the Starmen	Yes	No	No	No	3·85
Hills of Gold	No	Yes	No	No	2·15
The Noon People	Yes	No	No	No	2·95

What is printed in these lists?

   (a) titles of the horror books
   (b) titles and prices of the romance books
   (c) titles of the books that were either horror or adventure
   (d) titles of the science fiction books that cost less than £3·50

2. Amanda gathered data from her friends about the board games they played.
   This is what she put into a database.

Name	Monopoly	Cluedo	Draughts	Trivial Pursuit	Chess
Marie	N	N	Y	Y	Y
Beth	Y	N	N	Y	N
Riffet	N	N	Y	Y	Y
Holly	Y	Y	Y	Y	N
Chelsea	N	Y	Y	N	N
Sarah	Y	N	Y	Y	N
Heather	N	Y	N	N	Y
Pam	Y	N	N	N	N
Amanda	Y	N	N	Y	N

Amanda printed these lists of names:

(a) those who played Trivial Pursuit
(b) those who did not play Monopoly
(c) those who played both Cluedo and Monopoly
(d) those who played either Chess or Draughts
(e) those who played Monopoly but not Trivial Pursuit.

Write down the lists that were printed.

3.

House Number	Dog	Cat	Bird	Guinea Pig	Fish	Tortoise	Rabbit	Mouse
125	1	2	0	0	0	0	0	0
127	0	1	4	0	0	1	0	0
129	2	0	0	2	0	1	0	0
131	0	1	0	0	0	0	0	3
133	1	1	0	0	0	0	2	0
135	0	0	4	0	3	0	0	0
137	1	0	0	0	0	0	0	0
139	1	1	0	0	0	0	0	1
141	1	3	0	0	0	1	1	0
143	0	0	0	0	0	0	0	0
145	3	1	0	1	0	0	0	0
147	1	2	0	0	2	0	0	2
149	2	1	0	0	0	0	0	0

Deborah surveyed some of the houses in her street. She asked about the animals the people had.
Deborah put the information onto the table shown above.
She then put it into a database.

Deborah then printed these lists of house numbers:

(a) those with cats
(b) those with cats and dogs
(c) those with no animals
(d) those with birds and cats
(e) those with a rabbit or a tortoise
(f) those with more than five animals.

Write down the lists that were printed.

Review

Name	Car	Train	Coach	Plane	Ship	Bicycle
Emma	Y	Y	N	Y	N	N
Claire	Y	N	Y	N	Y	N
Tung	Y	Y	N	N	N	Y
Robert	N	Y	N	N	N	N
Melanie	Y	N	N	N	N	N
Keith	Y	Y	Y	N	Y	Y
Mark	Y	N	Y	N	Y	Y
Scott	Y	Y	N	N	N	N
Lin	Y	N	N	Y	N	Y
Emily	N	Y	N	N	N	N

Emily gathered data on the vehicles the students in her group had travelled on in the summer holidays.

She put this data into a database. She printed these lists of names:

(a)   those who had travelled by train
(b)   those who had travelled by coach and ship
(c)   those who had travelled by plane or ship
(d)   those who had travelled by train but not by car.

Write down the lists that were printed.

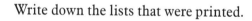

PRACTICAL EXERCISE 18:3

Arrange a visit to a place in your community which stores information in a database.

Some suggestions are: library
                        council
                        LEA
                        large bookshop
                        large manufacturer
                        school office

DISCUSSION and PRACTICAL EXERCISE 18:4

Name	Cricket	Tennis	Netball	Table Tennis	Soccer	Gymnastics
Jared	Y	N	N	N	Y	N
Michelle	N	Y	Y	N	N	Y
Amy	Y	Y	N	Y	N	N
Thomas	Y	N	N	Y	Y	N
Justin	Y	Y	N	N	N	N
Kate	N	Y	N	Y	N	Y
Meghan	N	N	N	Y	N	N

Jared's group put this information into a database.
They used the following program.

```
10   DATA   JARED, Y, N, N, N, Y, N
20   DATA   MICHELLE, N, Y, Y, N, N, Y
30   DATA   AMY, Y, Y, N, Y, N, N
40   DATA   THOMAS, Y, N, N, Y, Y, N
50   DATA   JUSTIN, Y, Y, N, N, N, N
60   DATA   KATE, N, Y, N, Y, N, Y
70   DATA   MEGHAN, N, N, N, Y, N, N
200  CLS
210  PRINT "SPORTS PLAYED"
220  PRINT : PRINT "CRICKET AND TENNIS"
230  FOR C = 1 TO 7
240  READ NAME$, C$, T$, N$, TT$, S$, G$
250  IF C$ = "Y" AND T$ = "Y" THEN PRINT NAME$
260  NEXT
270  RESTORE : PRINT
280  PRINT "NETBALL OR TABLE TENNIS"
290  FOR C = 1 TO 7
300  READ NAME$, C$, T$, N$, TT$, S$, G$
310  IF N$ = "Y" OR TT$= "Y" THEN PRINT NAME$
320  NEXT
330  RESTORE : PRINT
340  PRINT "TENNIS BUT NOT SOCCER"
350  FOR C = 1 TO 7
360  READ NAME$, C$, T$, N$, TT$, S$, G$
370  IF T$ = "Y" AND S$ = "N" THEN PRINT NAME$
380  NEXT
390  END
```

Run this program on a computer.

What extra instructions will be needed to print the list of those who play both Cricket and Soccer? **Discuss.** As part of your discussion, run the program again with these extra instructions.

What other lists could be printed? **Discuss.**

Lines 230, 290 and 350 must be changed if data is input for more students. How should these lines be changed if data is input for 10 students? **Discuss.** As part of your discussion, put in extra data using lines 80, 90, etc., and run the program again.

Gather data from your group or class. Some suggestions follow.
Rewrite the above database, from lines 10 to 200, for your data.

Decide what lists you want printed.
Rewrite the above database, from line 210, so that your lists will be printed.

Suggestions for data: TV programmes watched
take-away food likes and dislikes
types of books read
hobbies
countries visited

PRACTICAL EXERCISE 18:5

1. Use a database that your school has.

    You could choose a database that has information about Britain's geography or one that has information about schools or you could choose another database.

    Think of some questions you would like the answers to. Print out lists from the database that will help you answer these questions.

    If you are using a database about schools you may like to find the answer to questions such as:
    are there more girls' schools than boys'
    what are the names of the largest schools in the country
    were there more schools built in the 1950s than in the 1970s?

    If you are using a database about Britain's geography you may like to find the answer to questions such as:
    which counties are about the same area as your county
    what is the population of each of the Cathedral cities
    what place had the highest recorded temperature last year?

2. Collect information about the students in your class.
   You could use the following questions or you could make up questions of your own.

> Are you the only child in your family?
> Are you the oldest child in your family?
> Are you the youngest child in your family?
> Are you left-handed?
> Do you have a part-time job?
> Were you born in England?
> In which month is your birthday?
> What is your "at rest" pulse rate?
> How many schools have you been to?
> What is your shoe size?
> How many animals do you own?

Put the information you collect into a database. You could then print out lists.

WHAT   WHEN   WHERE   WHO   HOW   WHY

What data might a teacher need to sort?

When, in your other subjects, might you need to sort data?

Where are databases used to sort data?

Who, in the advertising industry, might need to sort data?

How might a database be used to sort data at your local council?

Why might these people need to sort data?

   Farmer   Chemist   TV Producer   Researcher   Counsellor

AROUND and ABOUT

DISCUSSION EXERCISE 19:1

●   *The average house price is* . . .

                The average length for a 6-month-old baby is . . .

                The average wage is . . .

                The average temperature at Liverpool for July is . . .

                The average rainfall at Swansea is . . .

Think of other examples where the word average is used.
Discuss with your group or class.

● Roseanne wanted to know which tennis team at her school had played best.

   Tim wanted to know if he had improved his scores in gymnastics this year.

   Roseanne and Tim would have to compare data to find the answers to their questions.
   What other situations can you think of when we need to compare data? **Discuss.**

MEAN. RANGE

Christine   **John**   **Deirdre**   **Allan**   **Lisa**

These photos show the number of Easter eggs given to 5 children.

By sharing the Easter eggs equally between the children we find the **mean** number of Easter eggs given to each child.

Christine   **John**   **Deirdre**   **Allan**   **Lisa**

Altogether the children were given 20 Easter eggs. If these were shared equally between the children each would have 4.
The mean number of Easter eggs given to each child is 4.

The **mean** is often called the **average**.
We could say that the average number of Easter eggs given to the children is 4.

The largest number of Easter eggs given to any of the children was 8.
The smallest number of Easter eggs given to any of the children was 2.

The **range** is the difference between these. That is, the range of the number of Easter eggs given to the children is 8 – 2 = 6.

Deirdre   **Christine or Lisa**

The **mean** is found by adding together all of the data and then dividing by the number of data values.

The **range** is the difference between the biggest and smallest data values.

Worked Example This data gives the points scored by the horses in a show.

$$78 \quad 59 \quad 74 \quad 64 \quad 75 \quad 82 \quad 71 \quad 77 \quad 88 \quad 78 \quad 67 \quad 69$$

Find (a) the mean number of points scored

(b) the range of the points scored.

Answer (a) Mean $= \dfrac{78+59+74+64+75+82+71+77+88+78+67+69}{12}$

$= 73 \cdot 5$

(b) Range $= 88 - 59$
$= 29$

Worked Example £12565   £8030   £9500   £7650

These figures give the salaries of the people in one house.
Find the average salary of these people.

Answer Average Salary $= \dfrac{12465+8030+9500+7650}{4}$

$=$ £9436·25

EXERCISE 19:2

1. Calculate the mean.

(a) 2, 2, 3, 4, 4, 4, 5, 5, 7, 7, 8, 9

(b) 2, 3, 7, 11, 12, 19, 23, 25, 29, 31, 36

(c) 4, 7, 7, 7, 7, 8, 8, 9, 10, 10, 11, 13, 14, 14, 15

(d) 22, 19, 14, 16, 27, 11, 32, 41, 17, 43

(e) 5, 4, 2, 7, 11, 5, 6, 2, 4, 4

(f) 4, 3, 1, 6, 10, 4, 5, 1, 3, 3

(g) 3, 1, 2, 5, 6, 2, 3, 4, 7, 8, 1, 2, 1, 3, 1, 1

(h) 30, 10, 20, 50, 60, 20, 30, 40, 70, 80, 10, 20, 10, 30, 10, 10

2. Find the range of the data in **question 1**.

3. The number of goals scored by a football team in 15 matches is shown below.

    3   0   1   0   0   2   1   2   0   3   0   4   0   1   1

    Find (a)   the range of this data

    (b)   the mean number of goals scored in each match.

4. | | | | | | |
    |---|---|---|---|---|---|
    | 34 | 48 | 38 | 54 | 45 | 49 |
    | 45 | 49 | 39 | 57 | 44 | 30 |
    | 46 | 38 | 42 | 45 | 51 | 39 |
    | 47 | 49 | 38 | 49 | 32 | 48 |

    These figures give the number of grapes on bunches.

    (a)   What is the mean number of grapes on these bunches?

    (b)   What is the range?

5. Find the mean and range of these lists of data. Round the answer to the nearest whole number.

    (a)   3, 4, 4, 5, 6, 9, 13, 14, 16, 17 ,19, 21

    (b)   1, 1, 1, 1, 1, 3, 3, 3, 4, 5, 6, 7, 7, 8, 8

    (c)   102, 105, 108, 101, 98, 106, 105, 110, 123, 103

    (d)   12, 1, 8, 6, 2, 4, 14, 10, 15, 7, 6, 3, 6

    (e)   13, 2, 9, 7, 3, 5, 15, 11, 16, 8, 7, 4, 7

Review   75   62   61   58   85   84   74   60   68   71
             73   64   59   75   82   65   69   63   87   57

   This data gives the marks in a maths. test.

   (a)   What is the mean mark?

   (b)   What is the range of these marks?

DISCUSSION EXERCISE 19:3

- Three meals have an average price of £5.
  What might these meals be priced at? **Discuss.**

- In 5 tests, Tina's average mark was 66.
  What might Tina's marks be? **Discuss.**

- Ben's marks for his first 4 maths. tests were   72   64   63   69.
  What was Ben's average mark?
  What mark does Ben need to get in his next test to raise his average to 70? **Discuss.**

USING the $\bar{x}$ CALCULATOR KEY

Example   To find the mean of 3, 5, 9, 12, 13 key as follows.

$\boxed{\text{MODE}}$ $\boxed{\cdot}$ $\boxed{3}$ $\boxed{x}$ $\boxed{5}$ $\boxed{x}$ $\boxed{9}$ $\boxed{x}$ $\boxed{12}$ $\boxed{x}$ $\boxed{13}$ $\boxed{x}$ $\boxed{\text{SHIFT}}$ $\boxed{\bar{x}}$ to get answer of 8·4

Notes
- Pressing $\boxed{\text{MODE}}$ followed by $\boxed{\cdot}$ gets the calculator ready to calculate statistical functions. (sd will appear on the screen.)
- Pressing $\boxed{x}$ stores each value input into the memory.
- Pressing $\boxed{\text{SHIFT}}$ $\boxed{\bar{x}}$ tells the calculator to calculate the mean of the values it has stored in the memory.
- If another mean calculation is to be done before the calculator is turned off, $\boxed{\text{SHIFT}}$ followed by $\boxed{\text{SAC}}$ must be pressed to clear the memory of earlier values input.
- Pressing $\boxed{\text{SHIFT}}$ $\boxed{n}$ at any stage, gives the number of values entered. This can be used as a check at the end to make sure all values have been entered.

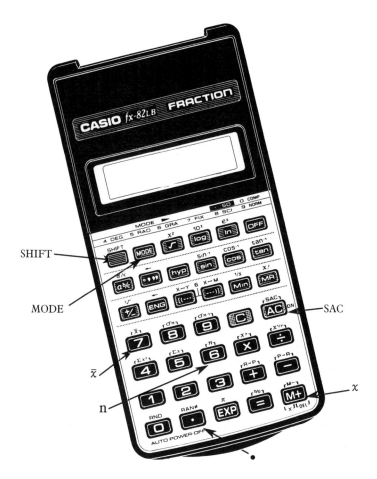

EXERCISE 19:4

1. Use your calculator to find the mean of these.

   (a) 3, 3, 4, 5, 6, 7, 7, 7, 8, 8, 9, 11, 13
   (b) 2, 5, 7, 4, 3, 2, 5, 7, 8, 11, 6, 10, 7, 4, 9
   (c) 4·6, 5·1, 5·3, 7·4, 5·9, 6·7, 7·2, 6·8, 5·4, 8·3
   (d) 24, 27, 35, 41, 62, 65, 71, 74, 75, 76, 76, 83, 85, 92, 100, 106
   (e) 0·3, 0·5, 0·2, 0·4, 0·3, 0·1, 0·8, 0·9, 0·7, 0·6
   (f) 1·3, 1·5, 1·2, 1·4, 1·3, 1·1, 1·8, 1·9, 1·7, 1·6
   (g) 0·9, 1·5, 0·6, 1·2, 0·9, 0·3, 2·4, 2·7, 2·1, 1·8
   (h) 96, 90, 82, 75, 73, 66, 66, 65, 64, 61, 55, 52, 31, 25, 17, 14

2. This data gives the height (in metres) of 11 boys.

   1·60   1·65   1·71   1·72   1·52   1·45   1·60   1·58   1·54   1·67   1·67

   What is the mean height?

Review This list gives the marks in an Aural test.

72	68	74	53	78	49	74	82	94	97
63	58	75	48	58	68	71	74	57	63
96	87	73	65	81	97	63	65	64	72

   What was the mean mark?

DISCUSSION EXERCISE 19:5

This table gives the runs made by a cricket team in 10 matches.

Runs scored in each of 10 matches										
A. Jacobs	42	29	0	34	55	31	19	0	49	72
N. Phipps	24	72	64	51	25	18	0	5	64	32
B. Yeoman	18	24	35	0	8	29	17	0	2	9
T. Manning	0	0	47	38	51	32	34	36	41	0
L. Khan	24	36	48	25	52	1	41	17	18	26
Y. Zarifeh	31	19	21	0	0	31	0	0	82	79
P. Freshman	16	15	20	22	14	3	0	17	21	19
T. Young	21	17	16	23	5	48	21	18	16	25
B. Eadie	6	0	19	11	24	0	13	2	3	17
M. Mahon	8	24	31	0	11	5	15	0	17	9
D. Brightling	1	3	5	24	21	2	7	16	21	42

Find the batting average of each player.
Which player had the smallest range? Which player had the greatest range?
Who would you choose to bat first? In what order would you have these players bat?
Discuss.

COMPARING DATA

The **mean, median** and **mode** are all measures of **average**.

Remember: The mode is the value that occurs most often.
The median is the middle value when a set of data is written in order of size.

DISCUSSION EXERCISE 19:6

Which of the mean, the median, the mode would be the most useful in the following situations? **Discuss.**
a photographer arranging people for a photograph
a teacher analysing test marks
a footwear retailer doing a stocktake

Discuss other situations where one of the mean, the median or the mode would be more useful than the others.

Suppose the range of a set of data is 7. The data could go from 2 to 9 (as A shows) or from 14 to 21 (as B shows) or from 18 to 25 (as C shows) or . . .

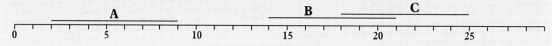

That is, although the range shows how spread out the data is it does not show where the data is located on a number line.

Also, although average gives us an idea of where the data is located it does not show how spread out the data is. For instance, the sets of data 1. 2, 3, 15, 16, 16, 2. 1, 2, 15, 29, 45 and 3. 13, 14, 15, 16, 18, all have the same median but very different ranges.

DISCUSSION EXERCISE 19:7

Could a set of data be well described by giving the range and the median? **Discuss.**

Could a set of data be well described by giving just the mean? **Discuss.**

If the range is large, would the median describe the location of the data better than the mean? **Discuss.**
What if the range was small? **Discuss.**

In what situations would the mode and range describe a set of data well? **Discuss.**

DISCUSSION EXERCISE 19:8

- Ten students were given 2 different maths. tests. The results were:

Test 1	42	55	47	61	59	71	49	53	65	61
Test 2	54	49	63	63	58	48	68	61	48	58

What can you tell from this data? **Discuss.**

Why might these sets of data need to be compared? **Discuss.**

-

This data gives the salaries of workers in two different offices.

Office A	£9500	£11485	£8250	£16400	£7050
Office B	£8250	£9500	£12560	£13400	£11340

What can you tell from this data? **Discuss.**

Why might these sets of data need to be compared? **Discuss.**

- In 8 matches the Beaford Netball team scored the following goals:

  34   41   33   48   42   33   36   38

  In 6 matches the Westways Netball team scored the following goals:

  47   29   52   34   42   28

What can you tell from this data? **Discuss.**

Why might these sets of data need to be compared? **Discuss.**

- Think of other sets of data which might need to be compared. **Discuss.**

  As part of your discussion, **discuss** reasons why the sets of data might be compared.

Worked Example   **Team A**   2   2   6   2   1
                   Team B   7   2   3   3   2   2   2   3

This data gives the number of goals scored by two hockey teams in their matches.
Compare the scoring record of these teams.

Answer   **Team A**:   mean $= \dfrac{2+2+6+2+1}{5}$

$= 2{\cdot}6$

range $= 6 - 1$
$= 5$

Team B: mean $= \dfrac{7+2+3+3+2+2+2+3}{8}$

$= 3$

range $= 7 - 2$
$= 5$

Both teams have the same range.
Team B has the higher mean.
We could say that Team B has the better scoring record.

DISCUSSION EXERCISE 19:9

In the previous worked example we used the range and mean to compare two sets of data.
Would it have been better to have used the range and mode?
Would it have been better to have used the range and median?
Discuss.

EXERCISE 19:10

1. **A. Mann**   81   76   79   85   89   78   74   83   74   87
    B. Prebble 79   88   87   76   91   73   74   76

This data gives the golf scores of two players.

(a)   Find the mean golf score for each player.

(b)   Find the range of scores for each player.

(c)   Who do you think is the better golfer? Why?

310

2. The data below gives the number of words in each sentence in the first paragraph of two novels.

Novel A	7	9	15	13	4	8	9	11	3	8	13	14	17	18
Novel B	8	18	4	16	12	10	5	8	7				

    Write a sentence or two comparing these sets of data.
    Use the mean and the range in your comparison.

3. The rainfall (in mm) at five places, during one week, is given below.

Andover	4	0	5	24	3	0	0
Cardiff	3	0	4	0	16	0	11
Coventry	1	9	7	12	8	2	5
Richmond	0	0	5	18	6	0	8
Stirling	3	5	7	2	4	12	7

    Which place had (a) the smallest mean daily rainfall for the week

    (b) the greatest range in rainfall

    (c) the smallest range in rainfall

    (d) the greatest median daily rainfall?

    Which place do you think had the best climate during the week in which these readings were taken? Make some statements using your answers to the above questions.

Review This data gives the number of children in the families of the students in 2 classes.

Class 1   2 1 3 2 5 3 1 3 4 4 2 1 5 3 2 2 4 1 3 5 6 3 1
Class 2   1 3 6 1 1 2 2 1 4 2 3 2 1 1 2 1 2 3 2 1 1

Write a sentence or two comparing these sets of data. Use the means and ranges in your comparison.

Would you make the same conclusions if you used the range and median? Explain your answer.

Would it be better to use the range and mode rather than the range and mean? Explain your answer.

PRACTICAL EXERCISE 19:11

Collect some data. Some suggestions are given below.

Make conclusions about the data by finding one or more of: the mean, the median, the mode, the range.

Suggested data: midday temperatures at different places on one day

hours of sunshine, in your area, each day for 20 days

number of students in classes at your school

goals scored, in matches last season, by two football teams

height of students in your class and another class

price of cars for sale at two different car sales showrooms

WHAT   WHEN   WHERE   WHO   HOW   WHY

What examples of mean and range might you find in the newspaper?

When might averages be used by the media to give a false impression?

Where, in your other subjects, might you use mean and range or need to compare data?

Who, in their job, might need to calculate means and ranges or compare data?

How might data about the weather be used to predict weather patterns?

Why might these people need to compare data?
School Teacher   Farmer   Manufacturer

AROUND and ABOUT

Road plans approved by residents

A traffic-calming scheme of road humps has been given the thumbs up by many residents in Wessex Road, Didcot.

Around 35 people attended an exhibition of the plans and submitted mostly favourable comments.

A senior engineer in Oxfordshire County Council's road safety group, Mr Anthony Kirkwood, said: "At least 75-80 per cent were in favour of the scheme although some were concerned about the need for additional parking restrictions on the road."

The county council is awaiting responses from emergency services and South Oxfordshire District Council and Didcot Town Council.

The scheme involves about nine humps, 12 feet long, at intervals of about 70 metres. The intention is to slow down traffic in a road that has a history of accidents.

Survey highlights city pollution

Carbon monoxide levels in Oxford city centre are up to six times the recommended guidelines.

A two-day survey carried out at Carfax in Oxford this week recorded levels of more than 50 parts per million of the gas produced by car exhaust fumes.

The World Health Organisation (WHO) recommended limit is 8.5 parts per million.

Levels of nitrogen dioxide, which can cause respiratory problems and asthma, were higher than last year.

The gas, which eats at the stonework of buildings, is still above recommended EC guidelines of 135 microgrammes per cubic metre.

Benzene, which increases the risk of leukaemia, was also found. Other gases, such as ozone, toluene and sulphur dioxide were found to be at normal levels, but Mr Steve Read of Enviro-Technology, which carried out the monitoring, said the levels would be much higher during the summer.

The findings have shocked environmental health officers, who are concerned by the level of pollutants.

Trial of new vaccine in Oxford

Oxford researchers will tell Government scientists today that they soon hope to go ahead with a meningitis vaccine trial on 10,000 young babies in the Oxford area.

A hundred babies born in Oxford have already been given the new vaccine during the summer. The results are expected to be announced at the end of the year.

If the first trial proves successful the researchers will go ahead with a far bigger trial starting in April.

Professor Richard Moxon of the John Radcliffe Hospital and his research registrar, Dr Robert Booy, hope to vaccinate 10,000 babies from February onwards in the Oxford area.

DISCUSSION EXERCISE 20:1

- Data would be collected before the articles on the previous page were written. What data would be collected? **Discuss.**

- Write down examples of data that could be collected
    about the class
    about the school
    about other subjects you are studying
    about sporting events
    about hobbies
    about the local community.

  Discuss your examples with other members of your group or class.

- We can often collect data to test a statement.
  For example, Imran may think that most of the students at his school have brown eyes. He tests the statement "most students at Fairview School have brown eyes" by doing a survey.

  Make a statement, similar to Imran's, that you could collect data to test. It could be about the school, the community etc.
  Discuss your statement with your neighbour or group or class.

INTRODUCTION

There must always be a reason for **collecting data.** We may just be interested to know how many cars travel along a road, or the council may want to know whether a pedestrian crossing is needed.

Whatever the reason for collecting the data, we should **organise the data** so we can clearly see patterns or trends. This can be done by showing the data on a **frequency table** or **graph** or by putting the data into a **computer database.** The graphs could also be drawn and printed by the computer.

Once the data has been organised in this way, we can then write or talk about the patterns or trends i.e. we can **analyse the data.**

COLLECTING DATA

Data may be collected as a **list**.

Example   The number of pens and pencils in the pencil cases of 21 students could be collected as 15, 27, 9, 15, 14, 13, 6, 11, 15, 21, 6, 10, 12, 11, 9, 18, 13, 8, 12, 10, 24.

Data may be collected on an **observation sheet**.
A **tally chart** makes a good observation sheet. On a tally chart, the data can be organised as well as collected. Having a column for **frequency** helps to organise the data. Before we use a tally chart as an observation sheet, we need to have a good idea of the smallest likely observation and the greatest likely observation.

Example   The number of pens and pencils in the pencil cases of some students is to be recorded on a tally chart. If we think that no pencil case will have fewer than 3 or more than 30 pens and pencils, our tally chart could be:

PENS and PENCILS in PENCIL CASES		
Number	Tally	Frequency
3		
4		
5		
.		
.		
.		
.		
.		
29		
30		

We may group the data. For the previous example we may decide to use the categories 0-4, 5-9, 10-14, 15-19, 20-24, 25-29, 30-34.

Notice that each category is the **same width**. If you group data, always make each category the same width. This will make it easier for you to analyse the data. The categories are often called **class intervals**.

Example   Using the categories 0-4, 5-9, etc., the tally chart for the previous example could look like:

PENS and PENCILS in PENCIL CASES		
Class Interval	Tally	Frequency
0–4		0
5–9	丅卄丄	5
10–14	丅卄丄 ||||	9
15–19	||||	4
20–24	||	2
25–29	|	1
30–34		0

Sometimes we do not have numbers in the first column on our tally chart. We can have actual items or descriptions of items.

Example   Mei-Lin noticed that nearly all the houses in her street had red front doors. She wondered if this was so for all the streets in her area.

Mei-Lin made the statement "Most houses in my area have red front doors". She decided to do a survey to see if her statement was correct. The observation sheet she designed could look like:

COLOUR of FRONT DOORS in SWAYTHLING		
Colour	Tally	Frequency
Red		
White		
Blue		
. . .		

Example Siobhan was collecting data on the maths. equipment that the students in her class had on their desks. She designed an observation sheet, listing on it all the items of maths. equipment she thought students would have.

Her observation sheet could have been:

MATHS. EQUIPMENT on DESKS		
Item	Tally	Frequency
Calculator Pencil Compass		

Example Mrs Millar wanted to know what maths. equipment the students in her class had. Alex designed an observation sheet to collect this data. This sheet listed the names of the students down the left and the maths. equipment across the top. He used ticks and crosses as he collected the data; a tick if a student did have that maths. equipment and a cross if the student didn't.

His observation sheet could have been:

	MATHS. EQUIPMENT					
Name	Calculator	Pencil	Compass	Textbook	Ruler	Protractor
Belen	✓	✓	✗	✓	✓	✗
Joana	✓	✓	✓	✗	✓	✓
Andrew	✓	✓	✓	✓	✗	✓
. . .						

DISCUSSION EXERCISE 20:2

- Write down at least 2 examples of data collection where it would be sensible to use a "tick and cross" observation sheet, similar to that used above. **Discuss** with your group or class.

- Write down at least 3 examples of data collection where it would be sensible to use a tally chart as an observation sheet. **Discuss**.

- Write down at least 1 example of data collection where it would be sensible to collect the data as a list. **Discuss**.

ORGANISING DATA

Once data has been collected, it should be organised.

If a tally chart, with a frequency column, has been used as an observation sheet then the data has been partly organised.

If you wish, you could write up a separate frequency table. The frequency table does not have to be written vertically. It may be written horizontally.

For example,

Item	Calculator	Pencil	Compass	Protractor
Frequency	18	21	16	11

The data could now be displayed on a graph.

You might use a pictogram, a bar chart or a bar-line graph. You could get your graphs printed out by the computer.

If a lot of information has been collected about each item, such as in the last example on the previous page, the data could be put into a computer database. The data is given again below.

	MATHS. EQUIPMENT					
Name	Calculator	Pencil	Compass	Textbook	Ruler	Protractor
Belen	✓	✓	✗	✓	✓	✗
Joana	✓	✓	✓	✗	✓	✓
Andrew	✓	✓	✓	✓	✗	✓
.						
.						
.						

Records could be set up for each of the students. That is, a record for Belen, a record for Joana, a record for Andrew, etc.

The **fields** could be labelled Calculator, Pencil, Compass, Textbook, Ruler, Protractor. When you are putting the information into a database you probably won't use ticks and crosses. How you put this information in will depend on the database program that you have for your computer. You might use numbers such as 1 for a tick and 0 for a cross or you might use Y for a tick and N for a cross (Y meaning yes and N meaning no).

Once the data has been put into a database it may be organised in many ways. For instance, you might have the computer print out lists, in alphabetical order, of those students who have not got protractors or of those students who have got both a compass and a protractor.

ANALYSING DATA

By looking at the organised data we can usually make some conclusions.
These may be **general conclusions** such as "On the desks there were more calculators than protractors" or "There was about the same number of calculators as textbooks".
They may be **mathematical conclusions** such as "The mean number of pens and pencils in pencil cases was 13·3" or "Since the largest number of pens and pencils was 27 and the smallest number was 6, then the range was 21" or "Since about 70% of the front doors in my area are red, I conclude that most of the front doors are red".

Get yourself well organised before you begin your data collection.
Make decisions about
- what data you are going to collect
- how you are going to collect it
- when and where you are going to collect it.

If you are going to use an observation sheet, design it carefully.
If you are collecting grouped data, decide what class intervals you are going to need.

When you have collected the data, organise it. You could use some or all of
- frequency tables
- hand drawn graphs
- computer drawn graphs
- computer database.

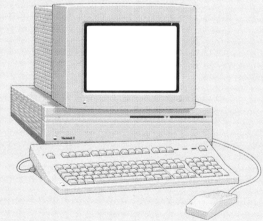

ALWAYS
- use graphs that are appropriate
- give your graphs a title
- have frequency on the vertical axis
- label the axes
- show the scale used on each axis

If you have put data into a computer database, organise it into a number of different lists and have these printed out.

When you have organised the data, analyse it. That is, write some conclusions. These could be
- general conclusions
- mathematical conclusions.

SURVEYS

DISCUSSION EXERCISE 20:3

How would you carry out the surveys suggested below? **Discuss.** As part of your discussion, talk about:

> how you would collect the data
> whether it would be useful to put the data into a computer database
> how you would organise the data
> how you would analyse the data.

Suggested Surveys

1. Number of people in cars passing the school.

2. Amount of money that the students in your class have on them.

3. Food likes and dislikes of the students in your class.

4. Goals scored by netball teams (or other sports teams) in a season or on a day.

5. Number of pages in the library books or magazines on a shelf in the school library.

6. Music likes and dislikes of the students in your class.

7. Videos (type or number) watched by the students in your class last week.

8.   Win? Lose? Draw? Home? Away?
   You could consider your local football teams or the teams in one of the national leagues.

9. Student pulse rates. You could consider the pulse rate "at rest" and/or after exercise.

10. Litter around your school. You could consider some or all of: type, place, amount, easily seen or not, recently dropped or not etc.

The steps you should take to do a survey are:

Step 1 **Decide** on the purpose of your survey.

Step 2 **Design** an observation sheet or tally chart.

Step 3 **Collect** the data on the observation sheet or tally chart.

Step 4 **Organise** the data onto tables and graphs or into a computer database.

Step 5 **Analyse** the data. That is, write some conclusions or print out some lists.

SURVEY 20:4

Carry out some surveys. You could choose to do your survey about your class or school, a hobby or sport or interest of yours, one of your school subjects or about your community. You could collect data yourself or you could get it from a newspaper or magazine or a reference book. The HMSO publications "Social Trends", "Regional Trends", "Key Data", and "Monthly Digest of Statistics" have data you might like to use.

Some suggestions for surveys were given in **Discussion Exercise 20:3.** Some more suggestions follow.
You may wish to do a survey on something not mentioned.
You may wish to make and test a statement.

More Survey Suggestions

1. Number of calculations correctly done, within 10 minutes, using a calculator.
    Collect the data from your class. Group it into categories.
    You will need to write the questions. Make them fairly easy, but have lots of them.

2. Weeds (dandelions, daisies etc.) in different parts of your school grounds. You could count the number of weeds per square metre.

3. Cars passing your school gate.
   Collect data on make, colour, number of doors, number of passengers, estimated age of car, gender of driver, estimated age of driver etc.
   What will you set up records for?
   What will your fields be?

4. Advertisements on TV.
   Collect data on the type of product, the running time, the number of times the product is mentioned, the way the advertisement is presented, the number of spoken words etc.
   What will you set up records for?
   What fields will you use?

5. Lengths of sentences on a page of a book or magazine or newspaper.
   You could collect data on the number of words in the sentences or on the total number of letters in all the words in the sentences.

6. Number of times the TV channel was changed during an evening's TV viewing.
   Collect data from your class.
   You will need to design two different sorts of data collection sheets for this survey; one sort for each student to fill in and the other for you to write on the results from all the students.

7. Articles in a newspaper or magazine.
   Collect data on the type of article (sport, business, news etc.), number of words in the article, number of words in the shortest and longest sentence, size of heading, size of type etc. Think carefully about what your fields and records will be.

8. Ask a teacher of one of your other subjects for a suitable survey topic.

INVESTIGATION 20:5

CENSUS

> What is a census?
> Who organises a census?
> When was the last full census in Britain?
> How often is a full census taken?
> Are there different sorts of census?
> How is the data gathered?
> What data is gathered?
> What is the information used for?
> Who is able to use the information?

Investigate these and other questions to do with a census.

WHAT   WHEN   WHERE   WHO   HOW   WHY

What data should a school office collect?

When would your local council want to collect data?

Where would you, or someone you know, be likely to use data from a newspaper?

Who, in a sports organisation, would need to use data?

How would a manufacturer conduct a market survey of a new product?

Why do librarians find computer databases so useful?

Pie Charts

AROUND and ABOUT

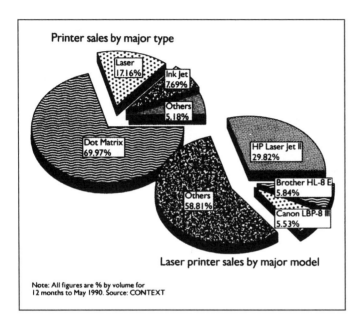

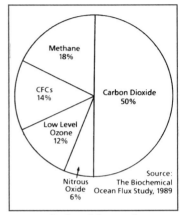

Contribution of the greenhouse
gases to global warming in the 1980s.

DISCUSSION EXERCISE 21:1

- Pie charts are graphs.
  In what ways are these different from other graphs?
  Discuss with your neighbour or group or class.

  Think of some data that could be well displayed on a pie chart.

-

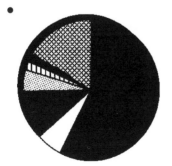 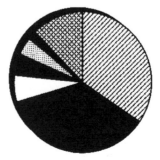 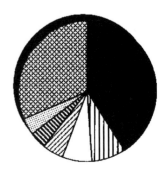

What do you think these three pie charts might represent? **Discuss**. Make up a title
for the graphs and label each section.

READING PIE CHARTS

Pie charts are circle graphs.
The circle is divided into parts.

Travel Pie Chart

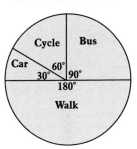

Example This pie chart shows the way students travel to school.
Since the angle at the centre of the walk part (180°) is twice as large as the angle at the centre of the bus part (90°), then twice as many students walk as catch the bus.
Since the bus angle (90°) is three times as large as the car angle (30°), then three times as many students travel by bus as by car.

Sometimes, we don't write the angles on the pie chart.

Instead we may put equally spaced marks around the outside of the circle.
This makes it easy to work out the angles.

Travel Pie Chart

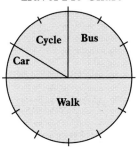

Example On this pie chart, there are 12 equally spaced marks.
There are 360° in a complete circle.
Since $\frac{360°}{12} = 30°$, there are 30° between each of the 12 marks.
The walk angle is $6 \times 30° = 180°$.
The car angle is $1 \times 30° = 30°$.
The cycle angle is $2 \times 30° = 60°$.
The bus angle is $3 \times 30° = 90°$.

Worked Example The pie chart drawn in the previous example shows how the students from Huntly College travel to school.
There are 800 students at Huntly College. How many come to school by bus?

Answer The circle is divided into 12 parts.

Of these, 3 parts show those who come by bus.

Fraction who come by bus $= \frac{3}{12}$

Number who come by bus $= \frac{3}{12} \times 800$

$= 200$

Worked Example How many of the 800 students at Huntly College cycle to school?

Answer Number who cycle $= \frac{2}{12} \times 800$

$= 133 \cdot \dot{3}$

We do not get an exact answer this time.
Round the answer to the nearest person.

That is, about 133 students cycled.

Worked Example What percentage, of the students at Huntly College, travel to school by car?

Answer Fraction who travel by car $= \frac{1}{12}$

Percentage who travel by car $= \frac{1}{12} \times 100\%$

$= 8\%$ to the nearest percent.

EXERCISE 21:2

1. Cressfield School is thinking about changing the colour of the boys' jerseys.
    This pie chart shows the colour 100 boys voted for.

    (a) What fraction voted for black?

    (b) How many voted for black?

    (c) What fraction voted for red?

    (d) How many voted for red?

    (e) How many did not vote for red?

    (f) What percentage voted for red?

Jersey Pie Chart

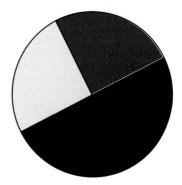

2.

Crop Pie Chart

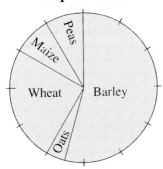

This pie chart shows the area, in hectares, planted in crops. The total area planted is 270,000 hectares.

(a) Which two crops have the same area planted?

(b) Which crop has the smallest area?

(c) How many hectares are in wheat?

(d) How many hectares are in oats?

(e) How many hectares are in barley?

3. This pie chart shows how the 503 students at Hill View College travel to school.

(a) What fraction of students walk to school?

(b) What fraction cycle to school?

(c) How many students travel by bus?

(d) How many travel by car?

Travel Pie Chart

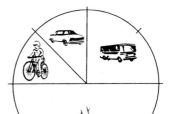

Review Paul has been working and flatting. This pie chart shows his expenses.

Expenses Pie Chart

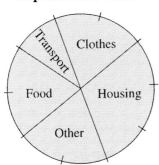

(a) What fraction did Paul spend on clothes?

(b) What fraction did he spend on transport?

(c) What fraction did Paul spend on food and housing taken together?

(d) If the total expenses for one week are £250, how much did he spend on food?

(e) Did Paul spend more on food than on clothes?

(f) What percentage of his total expenses is transport?

If we are given the size of the angle in each section of a pie chart, we can find the actual number of things represented by a section.
Once again, we do this by finding the proportion, or fraction, of the whole pie chart taken up by that section.

People in Cars

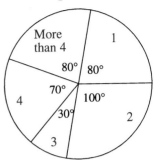

Worked Example This pie chart shows the number of
people in the cars that Danny surveyed.
Danny surveyed 600 cars altogether.
How many of these cars had 2 people in
them?

Answer There are 360° in the whole pie chart.
There are 100° in the section representing 2 people.

Fraction with 2 people $= \frac{100}{360}$

Number with 2 people $= \frac{100}{360} \times 600$

$\qquad\qquad\qquad\qquad\; = 166\cdot\dot{6}$

There were about 167 cars with 2 people.

Percentages are often written on pie charts.

Crop Pie Chart

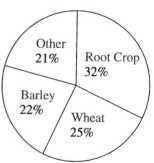

Worked Example This pie chart shows the area, in
hectares, planted in crops. If there were
200,000 hectares in crops, how many
hectares were planted in barley?

Answer Hectares in barley $= 22\%$ of 200,000

$\qquad\qquad\qquad\qquad\;\; = \frac{22}{100} \times 200,000$

$\qquad\qquad\qquad\qquad\;\; = 44,000$ hectares

Sometimes there are no angles given; there are no markings around the outside and
there are no percentages given.
In this case, we must find the angle in each section ourselves.
We do this by measuring the angles with a protractor.

Worked Example There were 6420 Christmas cards posted from a country post office. This pie chart shows where they were posted to.
How many were posted to destinations other than Britain or Europe?

Mail Pie Chart

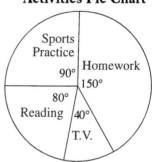

Answer Measuring the angle in the section marked "Other", we find it is 77°.
There are 360° in the whole pie chart.
Fraction of "Other" $= \frac{77}{360}$
Number of "Other" $= \frac{77}{360} \times 6420$
$= 1373$ to the nearest whole number.
There were about 1373 cards posted to destinations other than Britain or Europe.

EXERCISE 21:3

1. This pie chart shows how Daimen spent 4 hours one evening.
    How long did Daimen spend on these?

    (a) sports practice

    (b) reading

    (c) watching TV

    (d) doing his homework

Activities Pie Chart

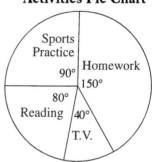

2. **Advertisements**

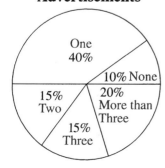

This pie chart shows the number of advertisements on the pages of a 120 page magazine.

(a) How many pages had no advertisements?

(b) How many had two advertisements?

(c) Terry looked at this pie chart and said "Most of the pages have one advertisement". Was Terry right? Explain your answer.

3. 50 small discs were put in a box. Some were white, some black, some red and the rest grey.

Alicia counted these discs and drew this pie chart.

Find the number of these discs that were **(a)** black **(b)** grey.

Disc Colour

4.

Employees and self-employed: by sex and occupation, 1988

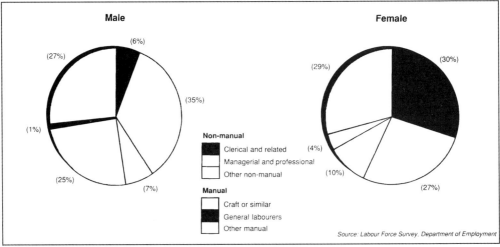

Source: Social Trends 1990

These pie charts represent about 16 million males and 12 million females.

(a) How many females were in clerical and related employment?

(b) Were there more females than males in Other non-manual employment? If so, how many more?

(c) Write about any similarities or differences between the males and females that can be clearly seen on these pie charts.

(d) The percentages on the Male pie chart add to 101%. Can you think of a reason why these do not add up to 100%?

Review 1   **Instrument Pie Chart**

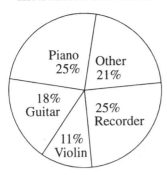

This pie chart shows the instrument learned by 200 students at the Music Academy.
How many of these students learned

(a)   the guitar

(b)   the violin

(c)   an instrument other than the piano?

Review 2   This pie chart shows the number of fiction books (F), non-fiction books (NF), magazines (M) and videos (V) loaned by the Smithfield Library last week.
Altogether there were 2800 items loaned.

Library Loans Pie Chart

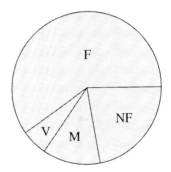

(a)   How many of these were magazines?

(b)   The librarian said that about 60% of the items loaned were fiction books. Is the librarian right?

WHAT   WHEN   WHERE   WHO   HOW   WHY

What data might scientists display on a pie chart?

When would data be better displayed on a pie chart than on a bar chart?

Where in your school, or community, have you seen pie charts?

Who in business might use pie charts?

How could the advertising industry use pie charts?

Why might a travel agent draw pie charts?

AROUND and ABOUT

DISCUSSION EXERCISE 22:1

Marcel thinks there is a good chance it will rain today.

Paula thinks there is not much chance of her winning the pools.

Jeffrey thinks it is certain he will watch TV tonight.

Andrea thinks she has no chance of going to Paris for her next holiday.

We often make predictions about the chances of an event happening.
What other events can you think of that we make predictions about? **Discuss.**
As part of your discussion make some predictions.

USING A PROBABILITY SCALE

The chance of an event happening could be described by one of: no chance, poor chance, even chance, good chance, certain.

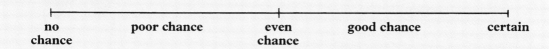

| no chance | poor chance | even chance | good chance | certain |

The chance of an event happening is also called the **probability** of the event happening.

EXERCISE 22:2

Use one of "no chance", "poor chance", "even chance", "good chance", "certain" to describe the probability of the following events happening.

1. Next year, Christmas day will be on 25th December.

2. The marble will land in Box A.

3. Your teacher will live for 200 years.

4. It will be sunny on at least one day of the summer holidays.

5. Getting a "7" when a die is tossed.

6. Next year will be 1992.

7. The next person you meet will have the same birthday as you.

8. Dealing yourself 4 Aces in a card game.

9. It will snow in Antarctica on July 1st next year.

10. You get a "Head" when you toss a coin.

11. You will win the football pools.

Review 1   It will snow in England on July 1st next year.

Review 2   The "Pizza Hut" will serve pizzas next week.

Review 3   Getting a number less than 7 when a die is tossed.

Review 4　(a) A counter dropped onto this board landing on a red section.

(b) A counter dropped onto this board landing on a yellow section.

DISCUSSION EXERCISE 22:3

Write some sentences. Use the following in your sentences.

poor chance	*good chance*	*even chance*
less than even chance	*no chance*	*better than even chance*
very unlikely	*likely*	*very likely*
unlikely	*certain*	

Discuss your sentences with your group or class.

A probability of $\frac{1}{20}$ means 1 chance in every 20.

Example　One student from Emily's class of 20 students is to be chosen to thank a visiting speaker.
If the names are put in a hat and one drawn out, each student has 1 chance in 20 of being chosen.
The probability that Emily is chosen is $\frac{1}{20}$.

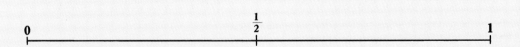

The probability of an event that is certain to happen is 1.

The probability of an event that will never happen is 0.

The probability of all other events is between 0 and 1. The more likely it is that an event might happen, the closer the probability is to 1.

334

Examples   The probability that you will be born tomorrow is 0.

The probability that the next triangle you draw has three sides is 1.

The probability that you win a prize in a raffle next year would be quite close to 0; perhaps $\frac{1}{10000}$. That is, 1 chance in 10000.

The probability that you eat a meal tomorrow would be quite close to 1; perhaps $\frac{498}{500}$. That is, 498 chances in 500.

DISCUSSION EXERCISE 22:4

- Estimate the probability of each of the following events.
  Discuss your estimates with your group or class.

  The next person you see will be 2m tall.

  You will watch a video tonight.

  Manchester United will win the next F.A. Cup.

  You will eat breakfast tomorrow.

  South Africa will win the next World Cup Cricket Series.

  You will swim the English Channel.

  The next car you see will be driven by a woman.

  You will own a car before you are 21.

  Someone in your class will get a letter tomorrow.

- Think of 5 events which have the following probabilities:

        probability of 0   probability of 1   probability of $\frac{1}{2}$
     probability between 0 and $\frac{1}{2}$ probability between $\frac{1}{2}$ and 1

  Discuss with your group or class.

- Make up some probability examples such as "The probability that it will rain tomorrow is $\frac{2}{5}$."

  Discuss your examples with your group or class. As part of your discussion, explain how you decided on the probability you gave to each event.

LISTING OUTCOMES

Example   The possible outcomes when a die is tossed are 1, 2, 3, 4, 5, 6.

Worked Example   List all the ways in which you could get a total of 4 when two dice are tossed.

Answer

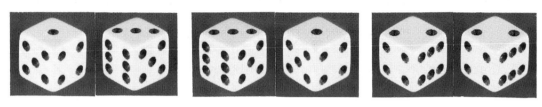

The three possible ways are shown.
These are 1, 3;   3, 1;   2, 2.

EXERCISE 22:5

1. List all the possible outcomes when a coin is tossed.

2. List all the different ways you could get a total of 5 when two dice are tossed.

3. A coin and a die are tossed together.

    Copy and complete this list of possible outcomes: H1, H2, . . .

4. A coin and a die are tossed together.

    List all the possible ways you could get a head and an even number.

5. Two coins are tossed.

    List all the ways you could get a head on one and a tail on the other.

6. Two coins are tossed.

    List all the possible ways you could get at least one tail.

7.   ① ② ③   ② ④ ⑤
         ④ ⑤   ⑥ ⑦ ⑨

    One counter is chosen from each of these piles.
    List the ways you could get (a) a total of 6
                                 (b) a total of more than 9
                                 (c) a total of less than 5.

8.

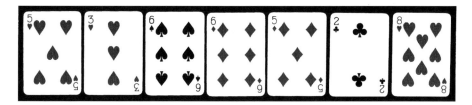

These cards are shuffled and put face down on the table. James then chooses two of the cards.

List all the ways James could choose two red cards that total 8.

Review 1 List all the ways you could get a total of 10 when two dice are tossed.

Review 2 (a) The spinner is spun once. List all the ways you could get an even number.

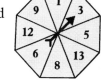

(b) List all the ways you could get a total of 9 when the spinner is spun twice.

GAME 22:6

COUNTER GAME: a game for 2 players

● ● ● ● ● ● ● ● ● ● ● ● ●

Set out 13 counters in a line.
Each player, in turn, takes either 1, 2 or 3 counters.
The player who is forced to take the last counter is the loser.

WHAT   WHEN   WHERE   WHO   HOW   WHY

What probabilities might a person going fishing estimate?

When, in a school, might the chances of an event happening be discussed?

Where, in sport, might you estimate probabilities?

Who, in their job, might need to list the outcomes of events?

How might a weather forecaster use a probability scale?

Why might words such as good chance, poor chance, better than even chance, even chance and so on, be used by people in election campaigns?

AROUND and ABOUT

DISCUSSION EXERCISE 23:1

Two football teams take the field.
The referee tosses a coin.
"Heads" calls one of the team captains. What is his chance of winning the toss?

In a game of monopoly it is Elise's turn. If she throws a 5 she will land in jail. What are her chances of not going to jail on this turn?

Jake and Jennisie are about to play a card game.
They "cut" the cards to decide who deals. Whoever gets the highest card is the dealer.
What is the probability that Jennisie will be the dealer?

Shalome and Simon decide to play ludo.
Each must throw a six to begin.
How many throws is it likely to take before Simon begins?

For each of the above events, you could make up a **Probability Experiment** to investigate the probability of that particular event taking place. For example, you could toss a coin many times to see how many times heads come up and how many times tails does.
Think of experiments that would test the likelihood of each of the other events happening. **Discuss** these with your neighbour or group or class.

PROBABILITY EXPERIMENTS

DISCUSSION AND PRACTICAL EXERCISE 23:2

1. **Work with a partner.**

   Make a circular spinner from card and a pencil as shown.
   Divide the card into 4 equal parts. Colour these Red, Blue,
   Black and Green.

   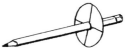

   Hold the spinner upright, with the point of the pencil on the desk.
   Make it spin, by twirling the top of the pencil.
   Record the colour of the part that is on the desk when it stops.
   Do this spinning and recording 100 times.

   Write up a tally chart, like the one shown, before you begin the spinning and
   recording.

Colour	Tally	Frequency
red		
blue		
black		
green		

   Using the results of your experiment, copy and complete:

   $$\text{Probability (red)} = \frac{\text{Number of times red was on the desk}}{\text{Total number of spins}}$$

   $$= \frac{...}{100}$$

   In the same way, find the probability of each of the other colours.

   Compare your results with the results of the other students in your group or class.
   Discuss. If there were big differences between any of the results, be sure to look for
   reasons.

   Using the results of your experiment, estimate the probability of the black part
   landing on the desk at your next spin.

   What could you use a spinner like this for? **Discuss.**

2. **Work with a partner.**

Shuffle a pack of cards.
Look at the top card and record its suit. Put the card back in the pack.
Do this 40 times.
One student could do the shuffling and the other do the recording on a tally chart
like that shown.

Suit	Tally	Frequency
♦		
♣		
♥		
♠		

Using the results of your experiment, copy and complete:

$$\text{Probability (heart)} = \frac{\text{Number of hearts drawn}}{\text{Total number of shuffles}}$$

$$= \frac{...}{40}$$

From your experiment, estimate the probability that the next time you shuffle, the
top card will be a heart.
Is your answer what you would have expected? If not, why not?
Discuss the results with other students in your group or class. Combine all the
results of your group or class. **Discuss.**

When might you need to know these probabilities?

3. **Work with a partner.**

Put 2 red, 3 white, 4 blue and 1 green counter in a paper bag.
Write up a tally chart like the one shown.
Draw out a counter, record its colour and then put it back in the bag.
Do this 50 times.

Colour	Tally	Frequency
red		
white		
blue		
green		

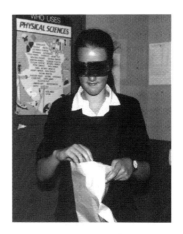

From your experiment, find the probability of drawing a red counter by completing the following:

Probability (red) $= \dfrac{\text{Number of times red was drawn}}{\text{Number of draws altogether}}$

$= \dfrac{...}{50}$

Work out the probability of drawing   (a) a white counter

                                                 (b) a blue counter

                                                 (c) a green counter.

Repeat the experiment but change roles so that each student has a turn at drawing the counters. Work out the probabilities again. Were they the same as before? If not, why not? Compare your results with other students in your group or class. **Discuss.**

Using the results of your experiment, estimate the probability of getting a blue counter the next time you draw a counter.

4. Put a small piece of plasticine on one side of a coin.
Is this a "fair" or "unfair" coin?
Toss this coin many times.
Record the number of times you get a head and the number of times you get a tail.
Use a table for the recording.
Using the results of your experiment, estimate the probability of tossing (a) a head

                                                         (b) a tail.

Discuss how the plasticine affected your results.

5. **Work with a partner.**

   One student shuffles a pack of cards. The other student then "cuts" the pack to choose a card. The card is then put back in the pack.

   Do this many times.

   Each time a picture card is chosen, record this on a tally chart like the one shown. Only record the picture cards, not the others. Keep a count of the *total* number of times you draw a card (picture or other).

	Ace	King	Queen	Jack
tally				
frequency				

   Using the results of your experiment, estimate the probability that at the next shuffle the card chosen will be **(a)** any picture card

          (b) a Jack

          (c) a King or a Queen

          (d) a card other than a picture card.

   When might it be useful to know these probabilities?

6. Do experiments which would help you to estimate the probability of each of the events given in **Discussion Exercise 23:1.**

   Before you do each experiment, make a prediction. For example, predict Elise's chances of not going to jail.
   Repeat each experiment a number of times to test your prediction.
   Keep a record of your results.
   Discuss your results with the rest of your group or class.

7. **Work in groups or with a partner.**

   Design and carry out a probability experiment. From your results estimate probabilities. You could do one of the following experiments or you could choose something quite different.

   ### Suggested Experiments

   The probability that the first student into class tomorrow is left-handed.

   The probability that the next school bell will be late.

   The probability that the next person you interview about lucky numbers will say that 7 is their lucky number.

   Number of advertisements between songs on the radio. (Estimate the probability that there will be three advertisements between the next two songs.)

Gender of car drivers. (Estimate the probability that the next car to pass the school is driven by a man.)

Types of vehicles going through an intersection. (Estimate the probability that the next vehicle is a cycle or estimate the probability that the next car is a British car or estimate the probability that the next car is white.)

Number of bags of groceries that a shopper carries (or pushes) from a supermarket. (Estimate the probability of the next shopper having just one bag of groceries.)

Age group of people using a pedestrian crossing. (Estimate the probability that the next person to use the pedestrian crossing is an elderly person.)

INVESTIGATION 23:3

COIN FLIPS

Someone once told me that if a coin was placed tails up on the thumb nail, then flicked into the air, it was likely to land tails up!
Investigate.

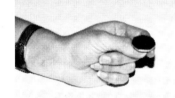

WHAT   WHEN   WHERE   WHO   HOW   WHY

What probability experiment might you do for one of your other subjects?

When would a scientist want to conduct a probability experiment?

Where, in the media, might you come across a statement that was based on a probability experiment?

Who in the horse racing industry, or in the casino business, or at a fairground might want to conduct a probability experiment?

How would you use a computer to help in a probability experiment?

Why might a manufacturer of sports balls want to conduct a probability experiment?

AROUND and ABOUT

DISCUSSION EXERCISE 24:1

For some of the probability experiments in the previous chapter (**Discussion and Practical Exercise 23:2**) we could have predicted the results. Which experiments were these? What was different about the experiments for which you couldn't predict the results? **Discuss.**

Think of some other probability experiments for which you could predict the results and some for which you couldn't. **Discuss.**

USING EQUALLY LIKELY OUTCOMES

In this chapter, we find probabilities without doing any experiments. Instead of tossing a die many times to estimate the probability of a 5 turning up, we use the fact that each of the numbers on the die is **equally likely** to turn up.

For equally likely outcomes,

$$\text{Probability of an event} = \frac{\text{Number of favourable outcomes}}{\text{Number of possible outcomes}}$$

Number of favourable outcomes means the number of ways it is possible for that event to occur.

Worked Example What is the probability of getting a 2 when a die is tossed?

Answer Possible outcomes are 1, 2, 3, 4, 5, 6. That is, there are 6 possible outcomes.
There is only one favourable outcome; getting a 2.
Probability of getting a 2 on a die $= \frac{1}{6}$.
We often use just P for probability so we may write Probability of getting a 2 as
$P(2) = \frac{1}{6}$.

In the previous worked example there was only one favourable outcome for the event we were interested in. There can be more than one favourable outcome for an event. In the next worked examples, there is more than one favourable outcome for each event.

Worked Example What is the probability of getting a factor of 6 when a die is tossed?

Answer Possible outcomes are 1, 2, 3, 4, 5, 6. That is, there are 6 possible outcomes.
Favourable outcomes are those numbers that are factors of 6.
These are 1, 2, 3, 6. That is, there are 4 favourable outcomes.

$$P(\text{factor of 6}) = \frac{4}{6} \text{ or } \frac{2}{3}$$

Worked Example A card is drawn from a pack of cards. What is the probability that it is an Ace or a Jack?

Answer There are 52 cards in a pack so there are 52 possible outcomes.
There are 4 Aces and 4 Jacks so there are 8 favourable outcomes.

$$P(\text{A or J}) = \frac{8}{52} \text{ or } \frac{2}{13}$$

Worked Example In a box of 40 counters, 7 are black. Hien closes her eyes and takes one counter. What is the probability that Hien chooses a black counter?

Answer Hien could have taken any one of the 40 counters. That is, there are 40 possible outcomes.
There are 7 black counters. If Hien takes any one of these she has chosen a black counter. That is, there are 7 favourable outcomes.

$$P(\text{Black}) = \frac{7}{40}$$

In the last worked example, Hien closed her eyes so she couldn't see which colour counter she was choosing. We could have said "Hien chooses a counter at random".

Choosing at **random** means every item has the same chance of being chosen.

EXERCISE 24:2

1. What is the probability of getting (a) a tail when a coin is tossed

   (b) a 6 when a die is tossed

   (c) an odd number when a die is tossed?

2. One card is drawn from a pack.

   How many possible outcomes are there?

3. Gafa shuffles a pack of 52 cards and then deals one card.

   What is the probability that this card is (a) a Jack   (b) a spade

                                                (c) a red card   (d) a face card

                                                (e) a picture card?

   Note: Aces are picture cards but not face cards.

4. The arrow is spun.

   What is the probability it will stop in the red part?

5. A die is tossed. Find the probability of getting

   (a) the number 3   (b) an even number

   (c) a number less than 3   (d) a number greater than 3

   (e) a number less than 7.

6. Sami has 15 socks in his drawer, 4 of which are blue. He pulls out a sock at random.

   What is the probability that the sock he has pulled out is blue?

7. There are 16 counters in a bag. Five of them are black. Miranda is blindfolded when she chooses a counter from the bag.

   What is the probability that Miranda chooses a black counter?

8. There are 50 pieces of chalk in a box. All of them are white. Mrs Patel chooses one piece at random. What is the probability that this piece of chalk is   (a) white

    (b) yellow?

9. What is the probability that your maths. teacher's birthday is on the 30th of February?

10. Kalinda has bought a raffle ticket. The first prize is a trip to Paris. 3000 tickets are to be sold. What is the probability that Kalinda wins the trip to Paris?

11. A pack of 26 cards is made, each with a different letter of the alphabet on it. What is the probability of these if one card is drawn at random?

    (a) a vowel

    (b) a consonant

    (c) a letter between L and P inclusive

    (d) a letter from the word "probability"

    (e) either a vowel or a consonant

    (f) either a vowel or a letter from the word "mathematics"

12. 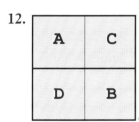 A coin is dropped onto this square. Find the probability that the coin

    (a) lands on the part marked A

    (b) lands on either the part marked C or the part marked D

    (c) does not land on B.

13. In a class raffle, 30 tickets numbered 1 to 30 are sold.

    (a) How many of these tickets have just 1 digit?

    (b) Sally has ticket 18. What is the probability that Sally wins?

    (c) Melanie bought all the tickets which had either the digit 5 or the digit 3. What is the probability that Melanie wins?

14. A roulette wheel in Amsterdam has 37 numbers from 0 to 36. Find the probability that a bet placed on the following will win.
    (a) 36   (b) the odd numbers   (c) the first dozen (1-12 inclusive)

15. A coin is tossed twice and both times tails come up. What is the probability of getting another tail if the coin is tossed again?

16. This disk is spun and darts are thrown at it.
It costs 25p to throw a dart.
If the dart lands on the black area £1 is won. If it
lands on the red area the 25p is returned. If it lands
on the grey area the 25p is lost.
Find the probability that, at any one throw,

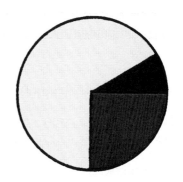

   (a)   a dart thrower will lose his or her money

   (b)   the disk operator will lose money.

17. A set of faulty traffic lights show red for 2 minutes, green for 30 seconds and amber
for 1 minute. What is the probability of a motorist finding them on green?

Review 1 Frank comes home late and must open the front door
in the dark.
His key ring has 5 keys on it.
What is the probability that he chooses the right key
at the first try?

Review 2 In the Camellia section of a flower show there are 30 camellias entered. Five
are cream, 9 are red, 11 are pink and the rest are pink and white. What is the
probability that

   (a)   a cream camellia will win

   (b)   a red camellia will win

   (c)   a camellia with some pink on it will win

   (d)   a red camellia will *not* win?

Review 3 A chocolate wheel at a fair has the numbers 1 to 25 around the outside. The
wheel is spun. What is the probability that the wheel will stop at

   (a)   the number 21

   (b)   a number with either the digit 1 or the digit 5 or both these digits

   (c)   a two digit number?

INVESTIGATION 24:3

REPLACEMENT DICE

Tim and Natasha were going to play a game that needed dice. When they looked for dice they couldn't find any.

Tim suggested they toss six coins together and count the number of heads that came up.

Natasha suggested they write the digits 1 to 6 on separate pieces of paper. These pieces of paper would be put in a bag and one piece drawn at random.

What else could be used to replace dice? **Investigate.**

Sometimes, estimates of probability can be made by looking at all the possible, equally likely outcomes. This chapter had many examples like this.

Sometimes, estimates of probability can only be made after looking at the results of a survey or experiment. Chapter 23 had many examples like this.

EXERCISE 24:4

Will a survey need to be done to estimate these probabilities?

1. The probability that the next ewe to lamb on Farnleigh Farm has triplets.

2. The probability that, on the next spin of a roulette wheel, a bet on the even numbers will win.

3. The probability that it will rain next Christmas Day.

4. The probability that the first passenger off tomorrow's 13:10 train is female.

5. The probability that the favourite will win next year's Grand National.

6. The probability of getting a prime number when a die is tossed.

7. The probability of a car having to stop at a pedestrian crossing.

8. The probability of an apple tree having fruit in its third year.

Review 1 The probability that an Ace is drawn when one card is chosen at random from a pack of cards.

Review 2 The probability that the next customer at a newsagents buys a magazine.

GAME 24:5

BOXES: a game for a group or a class

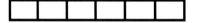

Draw a "box" of this sort in your book.

The leader calls six digits from 0 to 9 inclusive, each one different.
As each digit is called you must write it in one of the six sections of the "box". You must write each digit in a section before the next digit is called.
To win you must have made the largest possible number.

The winner becomes the leader for the next round.

WHAT WHEN WHERE WHO HOW WHY

What industries might calculate probability?

When would a scientist calculate probability?

Where in your other subjects might a knowledge of how to calculate probability be useful?

Who calculates probability in their job?

How would an understanding of how to calculate probability help you in the games you play?

Why would insurance companies need to calculate probability?

1. Trevor collected this data on the number of days the people in Aintree Street spent on their holiday last year.

13	6	16	19	23	0	5	27	31	15	14	18	7	28
15	8	14	16	19	34	14	22	17	23	30	4	19	11
4	20	22	0	15	15	12	25	18	0	7	7	18	8

(a) Find the mean number of days holiday. Give your answer to the nearest day.

(b) Find the range.

(c) Find the median of this data.

2. Describe the probability of the following events using one of:

no chance   poor chance   even chance   good chance   certain

(a) A red counter is drawn from a bag with the counters shown.

(b) A red counter is drawn from a bag with all red counters.

(c) A black counter is drawn from a bag with all red counters.

(d) Getting two sixes when two dice are tossed together.

3. A vet. is investigating if colour plays any part in cat health.
In one week the vet. saw 300 cats.
This pie chart shows what colour these cats were.

(a) What fraction of these cats were ginger?

(b) How many of the cats were ginger?

(c) How many of the cats were tortoiseshell?

Cat Colour

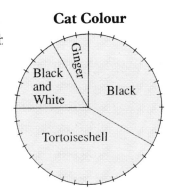

351

4. A die is tossed. Calculate the probability of getting

    (a) the number 6   (b) a number less than 5

    (c) a number which is a factor of 4   (d) a number less than 7

    (e) a number greater than 6.

5. Nawar gathered data from her friends about what they liked to drink. She then put the information into a database.

Name	Tea	Coffee	Milk	Milkshakes	Coke	Lemonade	Fruit Drinks
Huda	No	No	Yes	Yes	Yes	No	Yes
Adam	No	Yes	Yes	Yes	Yes	Yes	Yes
Denise	Yes	No	No	No	Yes	Yes	Yes
Linda	Yes	Yes	Yes	Yes	Yes	Yes	Yes
Trevor	No	Yes	No	Yes	No	Yes	Yes
Melanie	Yes	No	Yes	Yes	Yes	Yes	Yes
Charlotte	Yes	Yes	Yes	No	Yes	Yes	No
Jonathon	No	No	No	No	Yes	No	Yes
Indihar	Yes	No	No	Yes	Yes	Yes	Yes
Kate	Yes	Yes	Yes	Yes	Yes	Yes	Yes

Nawar printed the following lists:

(a) those who liked to drink milk

(b) those who liked to drink both tea and coffee

(c) those who liked lemonade but not coke

(d) those who liked either milk or milkshakes.

Write down the lists that were printed.

6. List all the ways you can get a total of 7 when two dice are thrown.

7. Choose one of the survey suggestions below.
   Design a suitable observation sheet for collecting the data.
   What sort of graph would you use for the data? Explain your choice.
   What conclusions do you think you might make from the data you collect?

Survey Suggestions

The type and number of birds you see in the school grounds or a park.

The number of letters in the surname of the students in your class.

The forearm length (elbow to fingertip) of the students in your class.

The time you spend on different activities (sport, dishes, TV, etc.) on a weekend.

8.

Near the end of a game of scrabble there are five letters left. A, E, D, T, B.
Their values are shown.
Find the probability that the next letter taken   (a)   is the letter D

  (b)   is worth 1 point

  (c)   is worth more than 1 point.

9. From a pack of cards, 7 cards are to be dealt.
   Would you need to do an experiment to estimate the probability of an Ace being dealt first?

10. What is the probability that   (a)   Sunday is a school day

  (b)   you will grow older

  (c)   the day after Saturday is Monday

  (d)   the day after Monday is Tuesday

  (e)   you will blink again today

  (f)   the sun will rise tomorrow?

11. Data on each of the following is to be collected, organised and analysed. For which of these would it be useful to use a computer database?

    (a) the subject likes and dislikes of the class

    (b) the wrist measurement of the students in the class

    (c) the magazines read by the students in the class

    (d) the aural and other marks gained by a particular year group

For those that you think should be put in a database, state what the records would be and what the fields would be.

12. A class was fund raising for charity. They decided to raffle a large box of chocolates. Tickets were bought as shown in the table.

Students	Staff	Parents
43	19	38

    (a) How many tickets were sold?

    (b) What is the probability that a student wins?

13. **Anna:**   12   15   11   14   13   18   12   9   17   16
    Beatrice: 14   13   18   21   17   19   10

Anna and Beatrice both play goal shoot for their netball teams.
The data gives the number of goals these girls have shot in matches.

    (a) Find the mean number of goals shot by each girl.

    (b) Find the range of each set of data.

    (c) Who do you think is the better goal shoot? Why?

14. Explain the steps you would take to do a survey to estimate either

        (a) the probability that the next person to come through the school gate is wearing glasses

  or   **(b)** the probability that the next advertisement you see on TV lasts for less than one minute.

15.

Public libraries: percentage of stocks and issues by major type, 1987–88

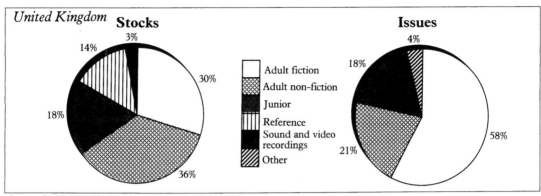

Source: Social Trends 1990

(a) There were 594 million issues made during 1987–88.
How many of these were Adult non-fiction?
(Answer to the nearest million.)

(b) Stocks were 135 million.
How much stock was Adult non-fiction?
(Answer to the nearest million.)

(c) Not all the categories shown in the Stocks pie chart are on the Issues pie chart.
Why not?

(d) What might be included in the Other category in the Issues pie chart?

16.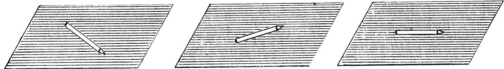

A small pencil is held above a sheet of lined paper. It is held so that it is parallel to the lines on the paper. It is then dropped.

Design a probability experiment to estimate the probability that when the pencil lands on the paper, it will still be parallel to the lines.

17. Estimate the probability of each of these. Give your estimate as a fraction. Give reasons for your estimate.

    (a) A 15-year old will win Wimbledon before the year 3000.

    (b) Someone in your class will represent Great Britain at the Olympics.

    (c) Someone in your class will have a friend to stay next month.

    (d) Someone in your class will buy an ice-cream tomorrow.

18.

    A coin is thrown from a distance and lands on the rectangle ABCD.

    Find the probability that it lands on   (a) the red part

    (b) the black part.

INDEX

ANSWERS

NUMBER ANSWERS

Number from Previous Levels

Page 14 Revision Exercise

1. C   2. 4021, 4102, 4120, 4201, 4210   3. (a) 3 (b) 2   4. (a) 484506 (b) 0·815   5. $\frac{3}{8}$
6. (a) hundreds (b) ten thousands (c) units (d) hundred thousands (e) thousands
7. 19%   8. £3·07   9. (a) 10 ; £1·10 (b) £4·43   10. (a)

+	17	43	83
24	41	67	107
19	36	62	102
38	55	81	121

(b)

×	5	3	4
8	40	24	32
6	30	18	24
9	45	27	36

(c)

+	472	579	891
77	549	656	968
234	706	813	1125
104	576	683	995

11. b and c   12. (a) 8·86 (b) 0·14 (c) 15·6 (d) 11·32 (e) £56·22
13. 35 + 17 = 52   14. (a) 345796 (b) 976543   15. (a) Rounded up; 7
(b) Rounded down; 16   16. –18°C   17. (a) 300 (b) 290 (c) 289   18. (a) 10 (b) 5
(c) $\frac{15}{20}$ or $\frac{3}{4}$ 19. (a) 19 (b) 56   20. 70   21. £3·80   22. (a) 427 – 398. This is the only
answer.   (b) One possible way is 298 + 734. There are other possible answers.
23. (a) 350 (b) 700 (c) 70 (d) 3500 (e) 830 (f) 27   24. 0·75m   25. one hundred times
larger   26. She needs 5cm more.   27. (a) 21 (b) 33   28. practical; 84%

Chapter 1   Problem Solving

Page 19 Exercise 1:2

1. 2 hamburgers, 3 pieces of fish, 4 scoops of chips   2. 24   3. 7   4. 28   5. 1, 2, 4, 5, 8, 11
6. 15   7. Yes   8. 22   9. There are many possible answers. One is 1, 1, 2, 3, 3, 4, 4, 5, 5, 6
Review   If all the darts hit the board: 3, 4, 5, 6, 7, 8, 9, 10, 11, 12, 13, 15. If some darts miss the
board: 0, 1, 2, 3, 4, 5, 6, 7, 8, 10.

Chapter 2   Number

Page 25 Exercise 2:3

1. (a) 9 × 7 (b) 9 × 6 (c) 26 × 3 (d) 12 × 8 (e) 19× 5 (f) 18 × 4   2. (a) 9 (b) 4 (c) 36
(d) 36 (e) 3 (f) 4   3. (a) 3 (b) 6 (c) 5 (d) 9 (e) 6   4. (a) 16 + 8 (b) 8 + 9 (c) 48 + 7
5. 16 × 6 = 96   Review 1 (a) 23 × 4 (b) 29 + 8   Review 2 (a) 8 (b) 9 (c) 11

Page 27 Puzzle 2:5

One possible answer is:
16 ÷ 2 = 8	8 × 3 =24	16 + 2 =18	40 – 8 =32
32 ÷ 4 = 8	2 × 6 =12	18 + 6 =24	32 – 8 =24
24 ÷ 6 = 4	8 × 5 =40	4 + 2 = 6	18 – 6 =12
18 ÷ 3 = 6	2 × 5 =10	6 + 3 = 9	12 – 2 =10

Page 28 Exercise 2:6

1. (a) 2^3 (b) 3^2 (c) 5^4 (d) 3^4 (e) 9^3 (f) 2^5 (g) 7^3 (h) 8^2 2. (a) 16 (b) 27 (c) 64
(d) 16 (e) 125 (f) 32 (g) 8   Review (a) 6^3 (b) $3^2 = 9, 2^7 = 128$

362

Answers

Page 31   **Exercise 2:9**

1. (a)

1^2	2^2	3^2	4^2	5^2	6^2	7^2	8^2
1	4	9	16	25	36	49	64

(b)

1^3	2^3	3^3	4^3	5^3
1	8	27	64	125

(c)

1	2	3	4	5
1	4	9	16	25
1	8	27	64	125

2. (a) 4   (b) 36   (c) 25   (d) 27   (e) 4   (f) 27

3. (a)   10   FOR NUMBER = 1 TO 100
     20   PRINT NUMBER * NUMBER
     30   NEXT NUMBER
     40   END

(b)   10   FOR NUMBER = 1 TO 20
     20   PRINT NUMBER $\wedge$ 3
     30   NEXT NUMBER
     40   END

4. (a) 225   (b) 81   (c) 289   (d) 144   (e) 6·25   (f) 23·04   (g) 1728   (h) 8000   (i) 778·688
(j) 110·592   5. (a) 152   (b) 512   6. The cube of the sum of 1, 2, 3, 4, 5 and 6.
Review 1 (a) 64   (b) 2   (c) 512   (d) 9   Review 2 (a) 169   (b) 2197   (c) 1·69   (d) 2·197
Review 3 The sum of the squares of 5 and 6.

Page 34   **Puzzles 2:11**

1. 64   2. 81   3. 11, 12, 13, 14, 15, 16   4. 1892   5. 4 and 6

Page 37   **Exercise 2:14**

1. (a) 6   (b) 16   (c) 64   (d) 2   (e) 16   2. (a) 9   (b) 10   (c) 7   (d) 1   (e) 2   (f) 5   (g) 1
Review 1 (a) 27   (b) 4   Review 2 (a) 3   (b) 3   (c) 6   (d) 4

Page 37   **Exercise 2:15**

1. 1, 3, 6, 10, 15

2.

3. 35   Review 1, 6, 15, 28

Chapter 3   Whole Numbers

Page 42   **Exercise 3:2**

1. lots of zeros make for easy answers   2. 600   3. 30   Review 1 **(a)** 60000   **(b)** 30   **(c)** 200
Review 2 3200

Page 44   **Exercise 3:3**

1. Estimate first   Review **(a)** 5   **(b)** 2   **(c)** 6   **(d)** 1   **(e)** 7   **(f)** 3   **(g)** 4

Page 47   **Exercise 3:5**

Some of your answers to this exercise may differ slightly from those given.

1. **(a)** C   **(b)** C   **(c)** A   **(d)** B   2. **(a)** 1200   **(b)** 2100   **(c)** 1600   **(d)** 18000   **(e)** 8000
(f) 24000   **(g)** 40000   3. **(a)** 32×17 **(b)** 600   **(c)** 544   4. **(a)** 46×23 **(b)** 1000   **(c)** 1058
5. **(a)** 24×96 **(b)** 2000   **(c)** 2304   6. **(a)** A   **(b)** B   **(c)** B   **(d)** C   7. **(a)** 10   **(b)** 10   **(c)** 30
(d) 20   **(e)** 24   **(f)** 7   **(g)** 10   8. **(a)** $1874 \div 42$ **(b)** 50   **(c)** 44   9. **(a)** $798 \div 38$ **(b)** 20   **(c)** 21
10. **(a)** $834 \div 18$ **(b)** 40   **(c)** 47   Review 1 **(a)** C   **(b)** B   **(c)** A   **(d)** C   Review 2 **(a)** 1800
(b) 2024   Review 3 20

Page 53   **Exercise 3:7**

1.

1.1	2.2	3.9	4.5	8		5.4	6.9	7.3	8.5
9.1	4	4	2		10.1	4	0	8	5
11.2	3	9	4		12.6	8	4	4	1
13.1	9	5	0		14.8	0	4	4	2
	6				3			2	

2. 522   3. 31025   Review £15,698

Page 57   **Exercise 3:10**

1. £69   2. 17   3. 24   4. 18   5. **(a)** 56   **(b)** 8   6. **(a)** Yes; 4   **(b)** 52   7. **(a)** 6   **(b)** 8
Review 1 15   Review 2 **(a)** 16   **(b)** 36

Page 59   **Puzzles 3:11**

1. 64 and 15625   2. 34 or 43

Chapter 4   Decimals.   Order of Operations

Page 62   **Exercise 4:4**

1. (a) 34 (b) 204 (c) 348 (d) 57   2. (a) 0·7 (b) 0·6 (c) 0·31 (d) 0·78 (e) 0·251 (f) 0·025
(g) 0·04 (h) 0·07 (i) 0·009   3. (a) 0·75 (b) 0·48 (c) 0·512 (d) 0·304 (e) 0·101 (f) 0·067
4. (a) 305·4 (b) 25·6 (c) 17·3 (d) 2506·05 (e) 65·23 (f) 7041·042 (g) 0·256 (h) 0·07 (i) 0·008
5. (a) A (b) B (c) B (d) C (e) A   6. (a) 6 (b) 3 (c) 0 (d) 4 (e) 0   7. (a) 100 (b) 10
(c) 10 (d) 10 (e) 100   Review 1 (a) 0·305 (b) 20·07   Review 2 (a) 3 (b) 5 (c) 9 (d) 0
(e) 0   Review 3 C

Page 68   **Exercise 4:8**

1. (a) ÷ (b) × (c) ÷ (d) ×   2. (a) 1000 (b) 10 (c) 10 (d) 100 (e) 10 (f) 100
3. (a) 5·9 (b) 59 (c) 0·059 (d) 0·00059 (e) 590 (f) 0·0059 (g) 123 (h) 1·08 (i) 0·351
(j) 72430 (k) 0·0002 (l) 30·4 (m) 4824 (n) 0·02 (o) 67900 (p) 8·4105   4. 415cm   5. £2·68
6. 0·264mm   7. 260m   Review 1 3   Review 2 (a) £290 (b) 36p

Page 71   **Exercise 4:10**

1. (a) C (b) B (c) C (d) B (e) D (f) D   2. (a) 10 (b) 0·1 (c) 7·1 (d) 3·39 (e) 65·68
(f) 241·38 (g) 0·17 (h) 1·82 (i) 0·16 (j) 6·9 (k) 8·166 (l) 1·34 (m) 31·2 (n) 0·06 (o) 0·05
(p) 0·02   3. (a) all the answers are 4·8 (b) all the answers are 0·32   5. £0·21 6. £0·60   7. 5·8cm
8. £4·36   10. (a) 1·2 (b) 0·24   Review 1 the letter T   Review 2 £192

Page 74   **Exercise 4:11**

1. (a) 5 (b) 10 (c) 8 (d) 11 (e) 5 (f) 23 (g) 11 (h) 14 (i) 10   2. (a) 27 (b) 10 (c) 8
(d) 12 (e) 7 (f) 4   5. Some possible answers are (a) 3 (4 + 6) − 2 = 28 (b) 3 (4 + 6) + 2 = 32
(c) 3 + 4 (6 + 2) = 35 (d) 3 + 4 × 6 + 2 = 29 (e) 3 + 4 × 6 − 2 = 25 (f) 3 × 4 + 6 × 2 = 24
(g) 3 + 4 + 6 + 2 = 15 (h) 3 × 4 − 6 × 2 = 0 (i) 3 + 4 − 6 + 2 = 3 (j) 3 + 4 + 6 − 2 = 11
6. (a) 9·45 (b) 11·88 (c) 9·74 (d) 18·33 (e) 78·79 (f) 25·01 (g) 6·12 (h) 3·12 (i) 7·432
(j) 0·58   7. Possible answers are (a) 1·9 + 3·6 × 0·2 = 2·62 (b) 12·8 − 6·9 ÷ 3 = 10·5
(c) 12·4 ÷ 4 − 1·8 = 1·3 (d) 8·4 × 4 + 1·6 × 2 = 36·8 (e) 4 (11·6 × ·5 − 2·2) = 14·4
(f) 2·4 + 4 (6·8 − 2·7) = 18·8 (g) (6·9 + 2·4 ÷ 3) + 1·8 = 9·5 (h) 3·4 × 2 − 6·6 ÷ 3 = 4·6
(i) (2·7 + 11 ÷ 5) ÷ 7 = 0·7   Review 1 Well done   Review 2 (a) 6·48 (b) 0·54 (c) 2·72

Page 78   **Puzzle 4:14**

Possible answers are 4 + 1 − 2 − 3 = 0; 3 × 2 − 4 − 1 = 1; 4 − 3 + 2 − 1 = 2; 2 × 3 − 4 + 1 = 3;
4 ÷ 2 + 3 − 1 = 4; 1 × 4 ÷ 2 + 3 = 5; 4 + 3 − 2 + 1 = 6; (4 + 3) × (2 − 1) = 7;
4 + 3 + 2 − 1 = 8; 1 × (4 + 3 + 2) = 9; 1 + 2 + 3 + 4 = 10

Answers

Chapter 5   Fractions. Percentages

Page 80   **Exercise 5:2**

1. (a) £3·78 (b) £2·28 (c) 2·4m (d) 5·4m (e) 68cm   2. (a) £1·67 (b) 22p (c) £1·19
3. 4   4. 15   5. 45   6. 3 hours   7. 9 hours   8. 13kg   9. £73·33   10. (a) 28m (b) 3·5m
Review 1 1·2 metres   Review 2 £53·29   Review 3 (a) 420 (b) 280

Page 82   **Puzzle 5:3**

Edwina and Penny are best at science.

Page 83   **Exercise 5:4**

1. Hill   2. 1·12kg   3. £450   4. £16   5. (a) £2·10 (b) 63p (c) £105 (d) 23p (e) 15p
(f) £298·30 (g) 5p   6. £3·50   7. (a) 357 (b) 11   8. 0·39m   9. Yes   10. £80·15
Review 1 13915   Review 2 38·5kg   Review 3 J & C

Chapter 6   Negative Numbers

Page 89   **Exercise 6:2**

1. (a)
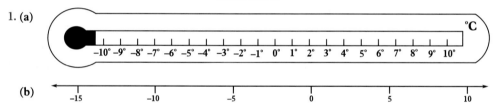

(b)
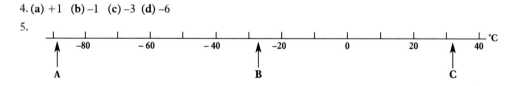

4. (a) +1 (b) –1 (c) –3 (d) –6
5.

Review (a) what is the temperature (b) not too cold and not too hot

Page 92   **Exercise 6:4**

1. (a) 1 (b) 2 (c) 3 (d) 0 (e) –2
(f) –1 (g) –2 (h) –99 (i) –54
(j) 0   2. (a) –7 (b) –50 (c) –4
(d) –0·5 3. (a) –5 (b) –8 (c) –2
(d) –2·6   4. (a) < (b) > (c) <
(d) > (e) < (f) > (g) >
5. 21°, 20°, 15°, 9°, 5°, 4°, 1°, 0°, –1°,
–2°, –3°, –4°, –5°, –6°, –8°, –9°,
–12°, –14°, –16°, –19°
6. There is more than one possible
path. One is shown in red.

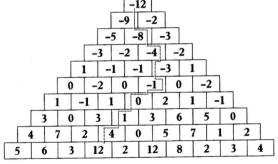

Answers

Review 1 (a) True (b) False (c) False (d) False (e) True (f) True (g) False (h) True (i) True   Review 2 (a) Montreal (b) Jerusalem (c) Moscow (d) Montreal, Calgary, Moscow, New York, Beijing, Kiev (or Warsaw), Warsaw (or Kiev), Jerusalem

Page 94   **Puzzles 6:5**

1. One answer is 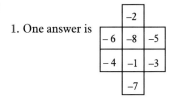   2. –3   3. D, C, E, A, B

Page 95   **Exercise 6:6**

1. (a) 3 metres below normal (b) 1 metre above normal (c) normal level   2. (a) move 3 steps back (b) move 1 step forward (c) stay where you are   3. (a) 4 (b) 6 (c) 8 (d) K.V. (e) M.T. and D.A.   Review (a) 3mm too long (b) right size (c) 2mm too short

Page 96   **Exercise 6:7**

1. (a) +3 (b) –5   2. (a) +2 (b) –1 (c) 0   3. (a) –3 (b)+5

4.

Actual Temperature	18°	21°	22°	19°	20°	18°	22°	19°	20°	20°	21°	18°
Recorded Temperature	–2	+1	+2	–1	0	–2	+2	–1	0	0	+1	–2

Review 1 (a) +12 (b) –8   Review 2 (a) +20 (b) –20 (c) –15 (d) +4 (e) –6

Page 98   **Exercise 6:8**

1. (a) 10° (b) –2° (c) 2° (d) –10° (e) –2° (f) –10°   2. (a) –30 (b) –10   3. (a) –5 (b) +55   4. (a) 7 (b) –3 (c) 1 (d) –1   5. (a) 7 (b) 2 (c) –2   6. (a) 1 (b) –7 (c) – 4 (d) 0 (e) –1   7. (a) 4° (b) 5° (c) 11° (d) 7° (e) 12°   8. (a) 6° (b) 5° (c) 3° (d) 2°   9. (a) 10m (b) 7m (c) 5m (d) 2m   Review 1 (a) 2° (b) –12° (c) –8° (d) –2°   Review 2 (a) 1 (b) 3 (c) 5 (d) 13   Review 3 (a) 6 (b) 4 (c) 10 (d) 2

Page 102   **Exercise 6:10**

1. (a) –2 (b) 8 (c) –8 (d) 2 (e) 2 (f) 8 (g) –8 (h) –2   Review 1 (a) 2 (b) 10 (c) –10 (d) –12 (e) –1

Page 104   **Exercise 6:12**

1. (a) –3 (b) –7 (c) 7 (d) 3 (e) 7 (f) 3 (g) –3 (h) –7 (i) –7 (j) 8 (k) – 6 (l) 1 (m) –10 (n) –12 (o) 4   2. (a) – 6 (b) –3 (c) 12 (d) – 6 (e) –2 (f) –7 (g) 14 (h) –3   3. (a) 6 (b) 4 (c) 10 (d) 2   4. (a) 5°C (b) – 4°C

367

5. **(a)**

+	– 4	5	–2
4	0	9	2
– 6	–10	–1	–8
2	–2	7	0

(b)

+	–2	6	2
–3	–5	3	–1
–2	– 4	4	0
– 8	–10	–2	– 6

(c)

+	–5	4	0
3	–2	7	3
–1	– 6	3	–1
–5	–10	–1	–5

6. **(a)** –2, 1 **(b)** –0·3, –2·3   7. 0·9° below normal   8. **(a)** 60m **(b)** 1300m **(c)** 1805m
9. **(a)** 69 B.C.   **(b)** 56   **(c)** 31 years
10.

18	19	14	9	8	7	6	5	–18
17	16	15	10	9	6	5	4	–17
16	15	14	13	10	5	2	3	–16
14	12	13	12	11	4	–13	–14	–15
–2	–1	0	1	2	3	–10	–11	–14
–3	–2	–1	0	3	–8	–9	–12	–13
–2	–3	– 4	–5	– 6	–7	– 6	–11	–12

11. **(a)** –1·6 **(b)** –9·1 **(c)** –1·8 **(d)** – 4·2 **(e)** 3·4 **(f)** 6·6 **(g)** 2·1
12. There are many possible ways. One way is shown.

+	3	–3	2	–2
–1	2	– 4	1	–3
–7	– 4	–10	–5	–9
6	9	3	8	4
3	6	0	5	–1

Review 1 (a) –8 **(b)** 5 **(c)** –2·5 **(d)** 0·9 **(e)** –11
Review 2 (a) 2a.m. in Santiago, 2p.m. in Peking **(b)** 7p.m. in Brussels, 2p.m. in Santiago, 6 p.m. in Reykjavik.
Review 3 6, 5, 4, 2, 1, –1, –2, –5, –8

Page 107   **Puzzles 6:13**

Possible answers are:

1.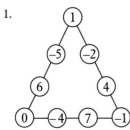

2.

	–3	3	
2	–1	1	–2
	4	– 4	

3. A = 2
   B = 3
   C = –1
   D = 1
   E = –3
   F = –2

4.

– 4	–9	–2
–3	–5	–7
–8	–1	– 6

Chapter 7 Number Review

Page 110

1. Victoria-B, James-C, Thomas-A   2. (a) C   (b) D   (c) B   (d) D   3. (a) a loss of £350
(b) a profit of £500   (c) no loss and no profit   4. £1·45   5. (a) 32×6 (b) $68 + 15$ 6. (a) 100
(b) 10   (c) 100   (d) 1000   (e) 10   (f) 1000   7. One possible answer is 5 1sts, 2 2nds and 1
3rd   8. (a) B   (b) A   (c) B   (d) C   (e) A   9. (a) 2m further down   (b) 3m up

10.

The next two triangular numbers are 15 and 21.
11. (a) -5° (b) -1° (c) -1° 12. The cat in the hat.   13. (a) subtraction   (b) dividing
(c) squaring   14. (a) A possible estimate is $320 \div 20 = 32 \div 2 = 16$.   (b) 19cm
15. 210 B.C.   16. (a) C   (b) C   17. (a) 9   (b) 7   (c) 7   (d) 5   (e) 9   (f) 27   18. all correct
19. (a) A possible estimate is $80 \times 1000 = 80000$.   (b) £81,755
20. 3 is at A, 0 is at B, –2 is at C   21. about 620 grams   22. (a) 5·24   (b) –1·4   (c) 7·08
(d) 7   (e) –6   (f) 15·6   23. about 6 million

24.

25. Yes   26. £28·70

27.

+	–2	3	– 4
3	1	6	–1
–5	–7	–2	–9
– 4	– 6	–1	–8

28. One possible answer is 25·612

ALGEBRA ANSWERS

Algebra from Previous Levels

Revision Exercise

1. **(a)**   21 × 11 = 231   **(b)** 2444444431
          221 × 11 = 2431
        2221 × 11 = 24431
       22221 × 11 = 244431

2. take care with x and y   3. **(a)** 2204 **(b)** 1266, 3378, 4143 **(c)** 2204, 4143

4. **(a)** 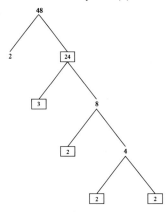   **(b)**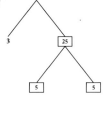

5. **(a)** 16 **(b)** 16 **(c)** 49 **(d)** 21   7. **(a)** 70 minutes **(b)** 60 minutes

8.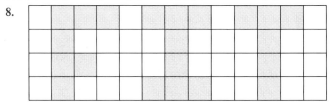

9. The output is 3, 6, 9, 12, 15. The program calculates and prints the first five multiples of 3.

10. 6 and 8

11.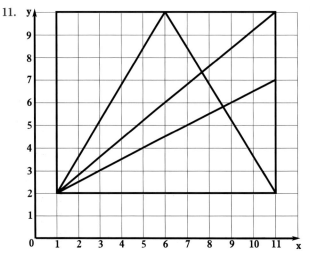

There are 16 triangles in the drawing.

12. Many answers are possible. A possible BASIC program is:
      10   MODE 1
      20   MOVE 100, 400
      30   DRAW 500, 800
      40   DRAW 400, 900
      50   DRAW 100, 400
      60   END

13. The next stable will need 22 matchsticks.

14. (a) 1 does not fit. The rest are prime numbers. (b) 25 does not fit. The rest are multiples of 6. (c) 2 does not fit. The rest are square numbers.

15. 13   16. A possible program is: 10   FOR NUMBER = 1 TO 20
                                     20   PRINT NUMBER * NUMBER
                                     30   NEXT NUMBER
                                     40   END

17. (a) Shape 2 needs 9 dots, shape 3 needs 13 dots, shape 4 needs 17 dots
(b) 21 (c) 41

Chapter 8 Expressions and Formulae

Page 127   Exercise 8:4

1. (a) 40 (b) 100 (c) 200 (d) 20n   2. (a) 20 (b) 100 (c) 10x   3. (a) £24 (b) £60 (c) £12t
4. (a) 17 (b) 22 (c) 12 + c   5. (a) n + 2 (b) n – 5 (c) 4n (d) $\frac{n}{2}$ 6. (a) x + 3 (b) x – 3
(c) 3x (d) x + 4 (e) $\frac{x}{2}$ (f) 2x   7. (a) H = 2h (b) H = 4h (c) H = h + 2 (d) H = h – 3
(e) H = 2h – 3 (f) H = 3h + 2   8. (a) V = 10n (b) V = 20n (c) V = 50n
Review 1 (a) £15 (b) £150 (c) £5t   Review 2 (a) x – 3 (b) x + 5   Review 3 (a) L = 3a
(b) L = a – 2 (c) L = a + 3 (d) L = $\frac{a}{2}$ (e) L = 2a – 1

Page 131   Exercise 8:5

1. (a) £600 (b) £500 (c) £200 (d) £300   2. (a) 48 min (b) 61 min   3. (a) 23cm (b) 33cm
(c) 43cm

4.

a	2	4	6	8	10	12
h	13	12	11	10	9	8

5. (a)

DELIA'S		
Fish	Chips	Price
1	1	£2·35
2	1	£4·10
3	2	£6·45
3	3	£7·05
4	3	£8·80
4	4	£9·40
5	4	£11·15

(b) £19·30

6. £125   7. **(a)** 60 metres   **(b)** 260 metres   8. **(a)** 50 volts   **(b)** 25 volts   **Review 1** £195
Review 2 (a) £3·45   **(b)** £4·65   **(c)** £3·45

Page 133   **Puzzles 8:6**

Possible answers are: 1. **(a)** A - 6, C - 4, E - 3, H - 2, M - 9, N - 7, O - 8, R - 0, S - 1
(b) B - 9, E - 0, F - 1, N - 7, R - 4, S - 6, U - 5, V - 2   **(c)** E - 7, F - 1, I - 2, N - 3, O - 9, R - 0,
U - 8, V - 5   2. **(a)** E - 1, F - 4, I - 5, N - 6, O - 2, R - 0, U - 7, V - 3   **(b)** E - 3, F - 6, H - 7, N - 8,
O - 4, R - 5, S - 2, T - 1, U - 0, V - 9

Page 135   **Exercise 8:8**

1. **(a)** 7   **(b)** 10   **(c)** 6   **(d)** 20   **(e)** 24   2. 11   3. 9   4. 25   5. **(a)** 17   **(b)** 23   6. 41   7. 8
Review 1 9   **Review 2** 8cm

Chapter 9   Simplifying Expressions

Page 139   **Exercise 9:3**

1. **(a)** 6a   **(b)** x^2 **(c)** 3e   **(d)** aw   **(e)** b^2 **(f)** bx   **(g)** 4x   **(h)** 5b   **(i)** 2y   **(j)** xy   **(k)** ay   **(l)** 5ac
(m) 2xy   **(n)** 3ab   **(o)** abc   **(p)** 2bx   **(q)** 3ab   **(r)** 4xy   **(s)** bcxy   **(t)** abcd   **(u)** 4ac   **(v)** $2x^2$
(w) 3ab   **(x)** $7a^2$ 2. beginning algebra   **Review (a)** p^2 **(b)** 4h   **(c)** 9a   **(d)** q^2 **(e)** 7p   **(f)** 3pq
(g) 2ap   **(h)** cdey   **(i)** 5bx   **(j)** $2y^2$

Page 141   **Exercise 9:5**

1. **(a)** 8n   **(b)** 3a   **(c)** 2n   **(d)** 7x   **(e)** 6a   **(f)** 4n   **(g)** 8x   **(h)** 8c   **(i)** 6n   2. **(a)** C   **(b)** A   **(c)** C
(d) B   **(e)** A   **(f)** B   3. carry on doing well   4. **(a)** 5   **(b)** 7   5. **(a)** B   **(b)** A   **(c)** C   **(d)** A
(e) C   **(f)** B   **(g)** A   **Review (a)** 12a   **(b)** 8x   **(c)** 4x   **(d)** 6a + 7x   **(e)** 16a + x   **(f)** 16a − 5x

Page 144   **Exercise 9:6**

1. **(a)** 3x + 6   **(b)** 4a − 20   **(c)** 10p + 15   **(d)** 12 + 8r   **(e)** 4a − 10   **(f)** 18 − 15a   **(g)** 12x + 3
(h) 5 − 10x   **(i)** 2x + 2y   **(j)** 2x + 6a   **(k)** 3a − 6b   **(l)** 6x − 15a   **(m)** 8a + 4x   **(n)** 3x − 9a
(o) 6y − 3x   **(p)** 24a + 20b   2. **(a)** 5x + 14   **(b)** 7a + 18   **(c)** 7x + 18   **(d)** 7a + 17   **(e)** 9a − 10
(f) 19b + 23   **(g)** 9x + 10   **(h)** 9 + 8a   **(i)** 19 + 10x   **(j)** 7a + 6   **(k)** 15y + 1   **(l)** 12a + 7
(m) 4 − 2y   3. P = 2*l* + 2b   **Review 1 (a)** 2a − 14   **(b)** 12x + 3   **(c)** 2a + 6b   **(d)** 15 − 20x
Review 2 (a) 9a + 25   **(b)** 13 + 2x   **(c)** 15x − 17   **(d)** 5x + 6

Chapter 10   Algebra Review

Page 147

1. **(a)** 178 pence   **(b)** 267 pence   **(c)** 89x pence   2. **(a)** 240 kilometres   **(b)** 30 kilometres
3. **(a)** 9   **(b)** 25   4. **(a)** B   **(b)** A   **(c)** C   5. **(a)** £6n   **(b)** C = 6n   6. **(a)** x + 50   **(b)** x − 100
(c) x + 20   **(d)** x − 25   7. 6   8. algebra practice   9. **(a)** 7   **(b)** 13   **(c)** 19   10. **(a)** 10x + 10
(b) 11x + 9   **(c)** 16 − 9a   11. **(a)** x + 13   **(b)** 2x   12. 4

SHAPE, SPACE and MEASURES ANSWERS

Shape, Space and Measures from Previous Levels

Page 158   **Revision Exercise**

1. **(a)** 6 **(b)** 9   2. **(a)** Yes **(b)** Total cost is £57·52 which is a little under £60.

3. **(a)** A and E, B and D **(b)** C and F **(c)** A, B, C, D, E, F   4. **(a)** Team 3, 40·44 sec

(b) 40·94 sec **(c)** Team 4, 42·09 sec   5. **(a)** 2 **(b)** 3   6. **(a)** cuboid (or rectangular box) **(b)** B

(c) 12 **(d)** 8 **(e)** 5   7. **(a)** *l* **(b)** g **(c)** m **(d)** tonne **(e)** mm **(f)** m*l* **(g)** km **(h)** mg

8. **(a)** 57·4°C **(b)** 2·47cm   9. **(a)** 18cm³ **(b)** 24cm³ **(c)** 10cm³   10. **(a)** 0924 **(b)** 0200 **(c)** 1545

(d) 2355   11. **(a)** 4a.m. **(b)** 8·23a.m. **(c)** 2·15p.m. **(d)** 11·40p.m. **(e)** 5p.m.   12. **(a)** 2 **(b)** 0

13. **(a)** W **(b)** S **(c)** SW **(d)** NW   14. **(a)** 8·2cm **(b)** 10·1cm   15. **(a)** 60cm

(b) Justine could have given many answers. One possible answer is 18cm by 12cm.

16. **(a)** AD, BE, GH, FI, CJ **(b)** AB, DE, FG, HI, KJ, BC, DG, EF, HK, IJ **(c)** AC **(d)** GI

17. **(a)**

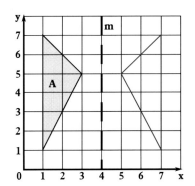
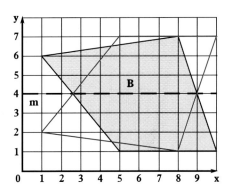

(b) Image of shape A has vertices at (5, 5), (7, 7), (7, 1).

Image of shape B has vertices at (1, 2), (5, 7), (10, 7), (8, 1).

18. **(a)** translation **(b)** reflection **(c)** rotation

19. **(a)** A, B, C, E **(b)** A possible net is:

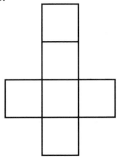

20. 24cm²   21. 7 different triangles can be drawn.   22. **(a)** 10·7cm   25. at B

Chapter 11   Metric Measures

Exercise 11:5

1. (a) C   (b) D   (c) C   (d) B   (e) B   (f) D   2. (a) m   (b) mm   (c) m   (d) km   (e) cm   (f) m
(g) km   3. (a) B   (b) C   (c) A   (d) B   (e) B   (f) C   4. (a) 50kg   (b) 20g   (c) 1kg   (d) 50t
(e) 250g   5. (a) cup   (b) bottle   (c) spoon   (d) bucket   6. (a) B   (b) B   (c) A   (d) B   (e) B
(f) C   (g) C   Review 1 sizing objects   Review 2 (a) g   (b) m   (c) cm   (d) kg   (e) mm   (f) *l*
(g) km   (h) t

Exercise 11:8

2. (a) 13cm   (b) 130mm   3. (a) 4cm   (b) 3cm   (c) 5cm   (d) 6cm   (e) 1cm   4. (a) 40mm
(b) 30mm   (c) 50mm   (d) 60mm   (e) 10mm   5. (a) mm   (b) mm   (c) cm   (d) m   (e) m
(f) cm   (g) km   6. 2000m   7. 40   8. 4km   9. 45mm   10. (a) 10mm   (b) 80mm
(c) 230mm   (d) 87mm   (e) 3mm   11. (a) 100cm   (b) 300cm   (c) 120cm   (d) 30cm   (e) 4cm
(f) 3cm   12. (a) 5000m   (b) 6400m   (c) 2·8m   (d) 0·426m   (e) 0·019m   13. (a) 7km
(b) 5·23km   (c) 0·841km   (d) 0·02km   (e) 0·0708km   14. 10km   15. (a) 30   (b) 2000
(c) 520   (d) 5   (e) 760   (f) 4700   (g) 50   (h) 6·852   (i) 7·52   (j) 52   (k) 48   16. 500cm
17. (a) C   (b) C   (c) D   18. 5   19. 10cm   Review 1 250m   Review 2 (a) 2cm   (b) 552cm
Review 3 (a) 3600   (b) 0·89   (c) 0·157   (d) 2·6   (e) 0·66   (f) 4·8   (g) 0·05   (h) 0·386   (i) 23
(j) 0·472   Review 4 (a) 855mm (85·5cm)   (b) 6·35m (635cm)   (c) 1716mm (1·716m)
Review 5 81cm

Puzzles 11:9

1. 8th   2. 35m   3. £50000   4. 20000km   5. 20m   6. 94mm   7. 80

Exercise 11:12

1. (a) 3000m*l*   (b) 6000m*l*   (c) 4100m*l*   (d) 5800m*l*   (e) 900m*l*   (f) 200m*l*
2. 1200m*l*   3. 0·35 litres   4. (a) 2·175*l* (2175m*l*)   (b) 2·84*l* (2840m*l*)   (c) 1780m*l* (1·78*l*)
(d) 2·853*l* (2853m*l*)   (e) 480m*l* (0·48*l*)   5. (a) B   (b) D   6. No   7. 8   Review 1 250m*l*
Review 2 (a) True   (b) True   (c) True   (d) False   Review 3 40   Review 4 550m*l*

Puzzles 11:13

1. Emply the 5*l* container into the 8*l* container; refill the 5*l* container; pour sufficient from the
5*l* container into the 8*l* container to fill the 8*l* container. 2*l* will remain in the 5*l* container.
2. On the 23rd day.   3. Empty the 5*l* container into the bowl; empty the 4*l* container into the
5*l* container; fill the 5*l* container by pouring 1*l* from the 7*l* container; fill the 4*l* container from
the 5*l* container; pour the 1*l* that remains in the 5*l* container into the bowl.
4. Empty the 3*l* container into the 4*l* container; fill the 3*l* container from the 5*l* container; pour
1*l* from the 3*l* container into the 4*l* container to fill it; fill the 2*l* container from the 4*l*
container.   5. One way is FFFHEEE, FFFHEEE, FHHHHHE: The other way is FFHHHEE,
FFHHHEE, FFFHEEE

Page 184   **Exercise 11:15**

1. (a) g   (b) kg   (c) kg   (d) t   (e) g   (f) kg   (g) g   (h) mg   2. 40g   3. £2·25   4. (a) 3200g
(b) 490g   5. (a) 2000g   (b) 3500g   (c) 800g   (d) 50g   (e) 2534g   6. (a) 3kg   (b) 5·14kg
(c) 0·743kg   (d) 0·038kg   (e) 0·4274kg   7. No   8. 1·25g   9. (a) 8   (b) 7·82   (c) 3100   (d) 0·24
(e) 0·49   (f) 3200   (g) 0·78   (h) 8·924   10. 1·3kg   11. (a) A-True B-True C-False
(b) 56kg–65kg   (c) 63kg–72kg   (d) large   12. (a) B   (b) B   (c) C   13. 2·768kg (2768g)
14. 5·725g (5725mg)   Review 1 (a) 3000g   (b) 7600g   (c) 0·1458kg   (d) 0·82g   (e) 3·415t
(f) 2400kg   Review 2 (a) 1·275t   (b) 2100g   (c) 3·5kg   Review 3 4·25kg (4250g)

Page 188   **Puzzles 11:16**

1. Some solutions are: 5 adults, 25 teenagers, 70 children; 2 adults, 30 teenagers, 68 children;
8 adults, 20 teenagers, 72 children; 11 adults, 15 teenagers, 74 children; 14 adults, 10 teenagers,
76 children; 17 adults, 5 teenagers, 78 children   2. 1kg, 3kg, 9kg
3. Yes. (She puts them into 3 piles of 3 coins. She then puts 2 of these piles on the balance. If they
balance the fake coin is in the pile that she didn't put on; if they don't balance the fake coin is in
the lighter of the 2 piles on the balance. Now she takes 2 coins from the pile that contains the
fake coin and puts these 2 coins on the balance. If they balance, the coin she didn't put on is the
fake coin; if they don't balance, the fake coin is the lighter of the two coins on the balance).
4. Annabel 51·5kg (aged 11), Belinda 45kg (aged 12), Cushla 56·5kg (aged 13).
5. Bert crosses with his rucksack and returns without it; Bert takes Beth and her rucksack across;
Bert returns with his rucksack; Bill crosses with his rucksack; Beth returns with her rucksack;
Bert takes Beth and her rucksack across; Bert returns, collects his rucksack and crosses.

Page 189   **Exercise 11:17**

1.
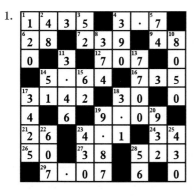

2. 400m   3. 2·56kg   4. 2610ml   5. 1·74m   6. 5·15l   Review 1 2·32t or 2320kg
Review 2 50   Review 3 4

Chapter 12   Imperial Measures. Time Measure

Page 194   **Exercise 12:2**

1. (a) 27″   (b) 61″   (c) 72″   (d) 63″   2. (a) 6′2″   (b) 2′2″   (c) 8′   (d) 3′3″   (e) 9′   3. (a) 16 pints
(b) 64 pints   (c) 13 pints   (d) 41 pints   4. (a) 2 gallons 4 pints   (b) 20 gallons   (c) 6 gallons
2 pints   (d) 112 gallons 4 pints   5. (a) 28 lb   (b) 140 lb   (c) 46 lb   (d) 132 lb   6. (a) 32oz
(b) 160oz   (c) 52oz   7. (a) 7 stone 2 lb

(b) 17 stone 12 lb (c) 8 stone (d) 5 stone 3 lb   8. (a) 1 lb 9oz (b) 5 lb (c) 2 lb 4oz (d) 2 lb 8oz   9. £1648   10. 8 stone 12 lb   11. 40 pints   12. 19′6″   13. £1·20   14. (a) 9′11″ (b) 9′ (c) 9′5″ (d) 3′2″ (e) 8′3″ (f) 5′2″ (g) 1′10″ (h) 3′9″ (i) 3′8″ (j) 6′10″ (k) 11′3″ 15. (a) 7 lb 1oz (b) 1 lb 4oz (c) 12 stone 4 lb (d) 4 lb 13oz (e) 1 stone 9 lb (f) 4 stone 9 lb (g) 14 lb 8oz (h) 4 stone 4 lb (i) 14 stone 5 lb (j) 4oz   16. 440 yards   17. 16 18. 1 stone 7 lb   19. 18 inches   20. 11 lb   21. 18′7″   Review 1 107 stone 2 lb Review 2 220 yards   Review 3 2′5″   Review 4 22 gallons 4 pints   Review 5 £1·02

Exercise 12:4

1. (a) 62 (b) 53 (c) 28 (d) 27   2. (a) 1956, 1968, 1972 (b) 2000, 2116   3. March 8th 4. 2·45a.m. on August 20th   5. Feb 20th 1962   6. 41min 19sec   7. B Review 1 June 19th 1963 at 8·16a.m. (Greenwich time)   Review 2 Jan 1st, 885

Puzzles 12:5

1. 1948   2. June 10th

Exercise 12:6

1. 11·25   2. 2·08p.m.   3. 27min   4. 1hr 45min   5. morning and afternoon times 6. 2hrs 40min   7. (a) 2hrs 40min (b) 7hrs 30min (c) 10hrs 10min   8. 0200 hours on 16th April, 1912   9. (a) 2min 4·28sec for 115, 2min 5·24sec for 85 (b) 89 (c) 24, 59, 27, 378, 13, 128, 307, 85, 63, 31, 149, 138, 235, 115, 89, 234

10.

	Monday	Tuesday	Wednesday	Thursday	Friday
9 – 10	Economics		Economics		
10 – 11	Accounting	Mathematics		Accounting	Mathematics
11 – 12				Biology	
12 – 1					
1 – 2					
2 – 3			Biology Lab		
3 – 4			Biology Lab		
4 – 5		Biology	Biology Lab		
5 – 6			Biology Lab		

11. (a) The earliest train leaves at 0720 (7·20a.m.) and takes 2 hours 10min. The next train takes 10min less. (b) the InterCity leaving London at 5·00p.m. (1700) only stops at Ipswich; the InterCity leaving at 6·00p.m. (1800) does not go further than Stowmarket (c) 1930 (7·30p.m.) Review 1 2hrs 5min   Review 2 No   Review 3 (a) 6hrs 55min (b) 4hrs 55min (c) Clocks at Bahrain do not show GMT. The time at London is 2 hours different from the time at Bahrain.

Puzzle 12:7

1. He began both egg-timers running together; he put the scones in the oven when the 3 minute timer stopped; when the 7 minute timer stopped he started it again; when this timer had stopped

for the second time he took the scones out.   2. If the 3 slices are called P, Q, R then toast side 1 of
P and side 1 of Q; replace P with R and toast side 1 of R and side 2 of Q; replace Q with P and
toast side 2 of R and side 2 of P.   3. 8·21   4. 234

Chapter 13   Metric and Imperial Equivalents

Page 208   Exercise 13:2

1. (a) 10 lb (b) 4 lb (c) 20 lb (d) 3 lb (e) 5 lb   2. (a) 4kg (b) 1kg (c) 2·5kg (d) 125g
(e) 375g   3. 3kg   4. 14 lb   5. 8kg   6. £7·50   Review 1 60p   Review 2 6kg
Review 3 7kg   Review 4 7 lb

Page 210   Exercise 13:3

1. (a) 2 gallons (b) $3\frac{1}{2}$ pints (c) 9 pints (or a little more than 1 gallon) (d) 1 pint
(e) 24 pints (or 3 gallons)   2. (a) 9 litres (b) 270 litres (c) 12 litres (d) 3 litres
3. 360 litres   4. 6 litres   Review 1 18 litres   Review 2 44 gallons

Page 212   Exercise 13:4

1. (a) 25 miles (b) 125 miles (c) 15 miles (d) 61 miles (e) 3 miles   2. (a) 32km (b) 320km
(c) 80km (d) 19km (e) 99km   3. (a) 15cm (b) 5cm (c) 45cm (d) 30cm (e) 150cm
4. (a) 2″ (b) 4″ (c) 12″ (d) 40″ (e) 96″   5. 150′   6. 5 metres   7. 10″ by 7″   8. 20cm
9. (a) 328km, 204 miles (b) 378km (c) 245 miles   Review 1 12′   Review 2 50cm
Review 3 37km   Review 4 15 metres   Review 5 (a) 10km (b) 6 miles

Page 214   Exercise 13:5

1. 28 pints   2. 160km   3. 125 grams   4. 6 litres   5. at least 10 lb   6. (a) 35cm (b) 14″
7. 7 gallons   8. 5 pints   Review 1 2 stone   Review 2 Debbie's car   Review 3 26 miles

Chapter 14   Measurement Accuracy

Page 222   Exercise 14:6

1. (a) to the nearest mm (b) to the nearest gram (c) to the nearest m (d) to the nearest km
(e) to the nearest gram (f) to the nearest mm (g) to the nearest kg (h) to the nearest ml
(i) to the nearest tonne (j) to the nearest l   3. (a) to the nearest km (b) to the nearest tonne
(c) to the nearest m (d) to the nearest ml (e) to the nearest gram (f) to the nearest kg
(g) to the nearest l (h) to the nearest mm (i) to the nearest m (j) to the nearest mm (or cm)
(k) to the nearest km

Chapter 15   Angles

Page 228   Exercise 15:2

1.(a) A (b) BA (or AB) and CA (or AC)   2.(a) F (b) DF (or FD) and EF (or FE)
Review(a) True (b) False

Page 231   Exercise 15:3

1.a = 31°, b = 125°, c = 68°, d = 73°, e = 63°   2.(a) 43° (b) 47°   3.77°, 44°, 59°

Page 234   Exercise 15:5

1.233°, 295°, 257°, 295°

Page 240   Exercise 15:9

1.(a) ∠B (b) ∠P (c) ∠Q (d) ∠Y (e) ∠E   2.(a) ∠ABC (or ∠CBA) (b) ∠APX (or ∠XPA)
(c) ∠AQR (or ∠RQA) (d) ∠QYC (or ∠CYQ) (e) ∠DEF (or ∠FED)
3.SAM HAS ONE PEN AND LES HAS SIX   Review(a) ∠CBD (or ∠DBC) (b) ∠E
(c) ∠HIL (or ∠LIH) and ∠JIK (or ∠KIJ)

Page 242   Puzzle 15:11

The number of ways is 124.

Page 244   Exercise 15:13

1.(a) acute (b) obtuse (c) straight (d) right (e) acute (f) reflex   2.(a) a-obtuse, b-acute,
c-acute, d-reflex (b) a-acute, b-straight, c-obtuse, d-straight, e-right, f-right, g-acute
3.(b) extra terrestrial   Review a-acute, b-obtuse, c-reflex, d-right, e-obtuse, f-acute, g-straight

Page 252   Exercise 15:19

1.(a) E (b) H (c) D (d) A   2.(a) 24km, N 55° E (b) 19km, S 34° E (c) 14km, S 61° W
(d) 22km, N 52° W   3. then N 78° E for 5km, then South for 2km, then S 59° W for 4·9km, then
West for 4km   Review then East for 300m, then N 40° W for 310m, then East for 400m, then
S 45° E for 450m, then West for 420m, then S 70° W for 440m.

Chapter 16   2-D and 3-D Shapes

Page 257   Exercise 16:2

1. (a) 1 axis of symmetry, order 1 of rotational symmetry (b) no axes of symmetry, order 2 of
rotational symmetry (c) no axes of symmetry, order 3 of rotational symmetry (d) 4 axes of
symmetry, order 4 of rotational symmetry (e) 1 axis of symmetry, order 1 of rotational
symmetry (f) 3 axes of symmetry, order 3 of rotational symmetry.

2. A: order 8 of reflective symmetry, order 8 of rotational symmetry, total order of symmetry is 16   B: order 0 of reflective symmetry, order 1 of rotational symmetry, total order of symmetry is 1   C: order 3 of reflective symmetry, order 3 of rotational symmetry, total order of symmetry is 6   D: order 0 of reflective symmetry, order 2 of rotational symmetry, total order of symmetry is 2   E: order 2 of reflective symmetry, order 2 of rotational symmetry, total order of symmetry is 4.
3. (a) (4, 5) (b) 4 (c) 4   4. (a) (4, 3) (b) 4 (c) 4   Review 1 (a) order 1 of rotational symmetry, 1 axis of symmetry (b) order 1 of rotational symmetry, 1 axis of symmetry (c) order 3 of rotational symmetry, 3 axes of symmetry   Review 2 (a) (4, 3) (b) 0 (c) 2

Page 259   **Puzzles 16:4**

1. They all have a vertical axis of symmetry. T fits in this list.   2. They all have a horizontal axis of symmetry. C fits in this list.   3. They all have rotational symmetry of order 2. I and Z fit in this list.

Page 265   **Exercise 16:10**

1. (a) 67° (b) 51° (c) 85°   2. (a) 70° (b) 52° (c) 69° (d) 76° (e) 103°   3. (a) 69mm
(b) 69mm   4. (a) 6·5cm (b) 68mm (c) 7·6cm   5. (a) 51° (b) 56° (c) 67°   Review (a) 65°
(b) 42° (c) 51°

Chapter 17   Shape, Space and Measures Review

Page 273

1. (a) 44° (b) True (c) 128° (d) D   2. (a) 80 (b) 2 (c) 5000 (d) 13000 (e) 6000 (f) 40
3. 60 pints   4. One possible reason is that either Adrian or Beth swapped the last two digits as they wrote them down.   5. (a) 2 (b) (5, 6) (c) 2 (d) 4   6. £7·50   7. 15   8. (a) B (b) D
(c) C (d) B (e) C (f) A (g) B (h) C (i) B   9. 3·40p.m.   11. (a) B (b) D (c) A (d) C

12.

Shape	Number of axes of symmetry	Order of rotational symmetry	Total order of symmetry
A	0	2	2
B	0	3	3
C	0	1	1
D	4	4	8
E	5	5	10
F	2	2	4

13. **(a)** 0·6 **(b)** 300 **(c)** 200 **(d)** 1200 **(e)** 25 **(f)** 160 **(g)** 620 **(h)** 4·84 **(i)** 300 **(j)** 2600 **(k)** 0·62 **(l)** 30 **(m)** 0·48 **(n)** 50   14. **(a)** g **(b)** b, d, e **(c)** a **(d)** c, f   15. **(a)** about 18 litres **(b)** about 100 gallons   16. 21 hours 15 minutes   17. **(a)** G **(b)** Village J is 10km from P in the direction N 60° W   18. 9′9″

19.

1 3	2 2	■	3 1	4 4	5 4
6 5	6	■	7 8	8	0
■	8 1	9 5	0	■	0
10 1	■	11 2	0	12 5	■
13 1	14 3	8	■	15 2	16 9
17 1	6	0	■	18 3	6

21. **(a)** Yes **(b)** about 12 inches **(c)** about 420 miles   22. **(a)** 48° **(b)** 49° **(c)** 70°   23. 976kg 24. 1 stone 5 lb   26. **(a)** the letter K **(b)** Possible instructions are   PU

                                                              FD   100
                                                              PD
                                                              RT   45
                                                              FD   200
                                                              BK   100
                                                              LT   90
                                                              FD   100
                                                              PU
                                                              HOME

27. **(a)** A possible shape is 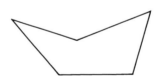 **(b)** No

28.

1 2	.	2 3	3 4	4 5	■	5 2	6 7	■
.	■	7 1	.	0	4	■	8 6	0
9 7	10 4	2	5	3	■	11 4	4	■
■	12 2	.	4	4	13 2	■	■	■
■	■	6	■	14 5	0	.	15 7	■
16 2	.	5	17 9	■	■	■	2	■
.	■	18 4	.	19 2	■	20 2	.	7
21 7	22 6	■	23 5	.	3	■	8	■
24 2	7	3	4	5	■	25 1	3	4

HANDLING DATA ANSWERS

Handling Data from Previous Levels

Page 288 Revision Exercise

1. (a) even chance (b) less than even chance (c) impossible (d) better than even chance
(e) less than even chance (f) impossible (g) certain

2.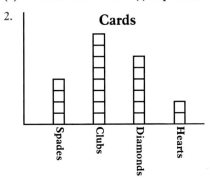

Cards

3. A possible order is B, E, C, D, A
4. (a) 8 knots (b) 14 knots (c) 28 knots at 4p.m.
(d) 15 knots   5. (a) 11 (b) 34   6. (a) 63
7. (a) A-23, B-102 and 103, C has no mode
(b) A-20, B-104, C-12·5   8. (a) 357 (b) 198 (c) 94

9.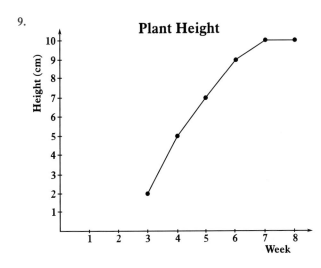

Plant Height

10. (a) 1 (b) 2
11. Possible answers are
(a) very unlikely (b) very
unlikely (c) certain (d) likely
(e) impossible (f) very unlikely
(g) likely 12. (a) 2 (b) 12 (c) A

13.

Number of Goals	Tally	Frequency
0	卌 卌 卌 卌 卌 卌 卌 IIII	34
1	卌 卌 卌 卌 卌 卌 卌	35
2	卌 卌 卌 卌 卌 卌 II	27
3	卌 卌	10
4	II	2
5	II	2

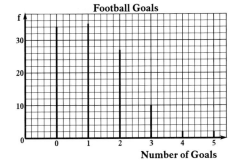

Football Goals

14.

Number of words	Tally	Frequency
1–10	卌 卌 卌 卌	20
11–20	卌 卌 ||	12
21–30	卌 卌	10
31–40	卌 ||	7
41–50		0
51–60		0
61–70		0
71–80		0
81–90			1

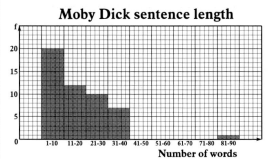

Moby Dick sentence length

15. **(a)** 13 **(b)** Trivial Pursuit **(d)** Some students might play more than one of these games. Some might not play any. 16. No. There are 3 chances in 6 that A will miss a turn but only 1 chance in 6 that B will.

Chapter 18   Sorting Data

Page 296   Exercise 18:2

1. **(a)** Phantom Wolf, The Doomed Mountain, Dark Waters **(b)** Roses Tomorrow £1·90, Summer Holiday £3·45 **(c)** Secret of the Caves, Phantom Wolf, Adventures of Adrian, The Doomed Mountain, Dark Waters, Hills of Gold **(d)** Beyond the Blue, The Noon People
2. **(a)** Marie, Beth, Riffet, Holly, Sarah, Amanda **(b)** Marie, Riffet, Chelsea, Heather **(c)** Holly **(d)** Marie, Riffet, Holly, Chelsea, Sarah, Heather **(e)** Pam   3. **(a)** 125, 127, 131, 133, 139, 141, 145, 147, 149 **(b)** 125, 133, 139, 141, 145, 147, 149 **(c)** 143 **(d)** 127 **(e)** 127, 129, 133, 141 **(f)** 127, 135, 141, 147   **Review (a)** Emma, Tung, Robert, Keith, Scott, Emily **(b)** Claire, Keith, Mark **(c)** Emma, Claire, Keith, Mark, Lin **(d)** Robert, Emily

---

Chapter 19   Mean. Range. Comparing Data

Page 304   Exercise 19:2

1. **(a)** 5 **(b)** 18 **(c)** 9·6 **(d)** 24·2 **(e)** 5 **(f)** 4 **(g)** 3·125 **(h)** 31·25   2. **(a)** 7 **(b)** 34 **(c)** 11 **(d)** 32 **(e)** 9 **(f)** 9 **(g)** 7 **(h)** 70   3. **(a)** 4 **(b)** 1·2   4. **(a)** 44 **(b)** 27   5. **(a)** mean = 11, range = 18 **(b)** mean = 4, range = 7 **(c)** mean = 106, range = 25 **(d)** mean = 7, range = 14 **(e)** mean = 8, range = 14   **Review (a)** 69·6 **(b)** 30

Page 307   Exercise 19:4

1. **(a)** 7 **(b)** 6 **(c)** 6·27 **(d)** 68·25 **(e)** 0·48 **(f)** 1·48 **(g)** 1·44 **(h)** 58·25   2. 1·61 metres **Review** 71·3

Page 310   Exercise 19:10

1. **(a)** mean for A. Mann = 80·6; mean for B. Prebble = 80·5 **(b)** range for A. Mann = 15; range for B. Prebble = 18   2. for Novel A: mean is about 10·6 words, range is 15 words; for Novel B: mean is about 9·8 words, range is 14 words   3. **(a)** Cardiff **(b)** Andover **(c)** Stirling **(d)** Coventry   **Review** Class 1: mean is about 2·9, range = 5, median = 3, mode = 3 Class 2: mean = 2, range = 5, median = 2, mode = 1

Chapter 21 Pie Charts

Exercise 21:2

1. (a) $\frac{1}{2}$ (b) 50 (c) $\frac{1}{4}$ (d) 25 (e) 75 (f) 25%   2. (a) peas and maize (b) oats (c) 67500

(d) 11250 (e) 146250   3. (a) $\frac{4}{8}$ (b) $\frac{1}{8}$ (c) about 126 (d) about 63   Review (a) $\frac{2}{10}$ (b) $\frac{1}{10}$

(c) $\frac{5}{10}$ (d) £50 (e) No (f) 10%

Exercise 21:3

1. (a) 1 hour (b) about 53 min (c) about 27 min (d) 1 hour 40 min   2. (a) 12 (b) 18
(c) No   3. (a) 5 (b) 20   4. (a) about 3·6 million (b) Yes, about 0·08 million more.
Review 1 (a) 36 (b) 22 (c) 150   Review 2 (a) 350 (b) Yes

Chapter 22 Probability

Exercise 22:2

1. certain   2. even chance   3. no chance   4. good chance   5. no chance   6. no chance
7. poor chance   8. poor chance   9. good chance   10. even chance   11. poor chance
Review 1 poor chance   Review 2 good chance   Review 3 certain   Review 4 (a) even chance
(b) no chance

Exercise 22:5

1. H, T   2. 1,4 4,1 2,3 3,2   3. H1, H2, H3, H4, H5, H6, T1, T2, T3, T4, T5, T6   4. H2, H4,
H6   5. HT, TH   6. HT, TH, TT   7. (a) 1,5 2,4 4,2 (b) 4,6 4,7 4,9 5,5 5,6 5,7 5,9 1,9
2,9 3,7 3,9 (c) 1,2 2,2   8. Heart 5, Heart 3 Diamond 5, Heart 3   Review 1 4,6 6,4 5,5
Review 2 (a) 12, 6, 8 (b) 1,8 8,1 3,6 6,3

Chapter 24 Calculating Probability

Exercise 24:2

1. (a) $\frac{1}{2}$ (b) $\frac{1}{6}$ (c) $\frac{3}{6}$ 2. 52   3. (a) $\frac{4}{52}$ (b) $\frac{13}{52}$ (c) $\frac{26}{52}$ (d) $\frac{12}{52}$ (e) $\frac{16}{52}$ 4. $\frac{1}{4}$

5. (a) $\frac{1}{6}$ (b) $\frac{3}{6}$ (c) $\frac{2}{6}$ (d) $\frac{3}{6}$ (e) $\frac{6}{6}$ or 1   6. $\frac{4}{15}$ 7. $\frac{5}{16}$ 8. (a) $\frac{50}{50}$ or 1 (b) $\frac{0}{50}$ or 0

9. 0   10. $\frac{1}{3000}$ 11. (a) $\frac{5}{26}$ (b) $\frac{21}{26}$ (c) $\frac{5}{26}$ (d) $\frac{9}{26}$ (e) $\frac{26}{26}$ (f) $\frac{10}{26}$ 12. (a) $\frac{1}{4}$ (b) $\frac{2}{4}$

(c) $\frac{3}{4}$ 13. (a) 9 (b) $\frac{1}{30}$ (c) $\frac{7}{30}$ 14. (a) $\frac{1}{37}$ (b) $\frac{18}{37}$ (c) $\frac{12}{37}$ 15. $\frac{1}{2}$ 16. (a) $\frac{240}{360}$

(b) $\frac{30}{360}$ 17. $\frac{1}{7}$ Review 1 $\frac{1}{5}$ Review 2 (a) $\frac{5}{30}$ (b) $\frac{9}{30}$ (c) $\frac{16}{30}$ (d) $\frac{21}{30}$

Review 3 (a) $\frac{1}{25}$ (b) $\frac{14}{25}$ (c) $\frac{16}{25}$

Exercise 24:4

1. Yes   2. No   3. Yes   4. Yes   5. Yes   6. No   7. Yes   8. Yes   Review 1 No   Review 2 Yes

Chapter 25   Handling Data Review

Page 351

1. (a) about 15 days (b) 34 days (c) 15 days   2. (a) even chance (b) certain (c) no chance
(d) poor chance   3. (a) $\frac{3}{36}$ (b) 25 (c) 125   4. (a) $\frac{1}{6}$ (b) $\frac{4}{6}$ (c) $\frac{3}{6}$ (d) $\frac{6}{6}$ or 1 (e) $\frac{0}{6}$ or 0
5. (a) Huda, Adam, Linda, Melanie, Charlotte, Kate (b) Linda, Charlotte, Kate (c) Trevor
(d) Huda, Adam, Linda, Trevor, Melanie, Charlotte, Indihar, Kate   6. 3 and 4 or 4 and 3 or
5 and 2 or 2 and 5 or 6 and 1 or 1 and 6   8. (a) $\frac{1}{5}$ (b) $\frac{3}{5}$ (c) $\frac{2}{5}$ 9. No
10. (a) 0 (b) 1 (c) 0 (d) 1 (e) 1 (f) 1   11. a, c, d. For (a) the records would be for the students
in the class, the fields would be the subjects. For (c) the records would be for the students in the
class, the fields would be the magazines. For (d) the records would be for the students in the year
group, the fields would be labelled Aural 1, Aural 2 etc.   12. (a) 100 (b) $\frac{43}{100}$
13. (a) Anna: 13·7 Beatrice: 16 (b) Anna: 9 Beatrice: 11   15. (a) 125 million
(b) 49 million   18. (a) $\frac{1}{3}$ (b) $\frac{1}{24}$